WOMEN AGAINST WAR

WOMEN
AGAINST
WAR

Compiled by
Women's Division of
Soka Gakkai

Translated by Richard L. Gage
Introduction by Richard H. Minear

KODANSHA INTERNATIONAL LTD.
Tokyo, New York, and San Francisco

Note to the Reader

All names of Japanese persons have been transliterated in Western order, surname last, rather than the reverse as in Japanese. The numbers given in parentheses after the names of the authors of the accounts indicate the age of the writer at the time of writing, which was the early years of the 1980s.

Distributed in the United States by Kodansha International/USA Ltd., through Harper & Row Publishers, Inc., 10 East 53rd Street, New York, New York 10022. Published by Kodansha International Ltd., 12-21, Otowa 2-chome, Bunkyo-ku, Tokyo 112 and Kodansha International/USA Ltd., with offices at 10 East 53rd Street, New York, New York 10022 and the Hearst Building, 5 Third Street, Suite 430, San Francisco, California 94103.

CONTENTS

PREFACE

This book consists of selected translations from the twelve-volume series *Heiwa e no negai o komete* (With Hopes for Peace), which is a collection of testimonials about war that has been compiled and published by the Soka Gakkai Women's Division Peace Committee since its creation in 1981. One of our purposes in publishing these books was to make available to younger Japanese people, who were born after World War II and have no direct knowledge of the horrors of war, a true picture of the war as witnessed by women who actually lived through it. In this connection, it should be pointed out that the women of the Peace Committee who collected and compiled these testimonials belong themselves to the younger generation that was untouched by the war. Another purpose was to bring to the attention of peoples everywhere the hardships suffered by individual Japanese women during World War II and its aftermath. In doing this, we hope to go a step beyond merely speaking out against war and make a positive contribution, as women, to its elimination.

Since it is one of women's roles in life to bring children into the world and raise them to maturity, we feel that women possess a particularly deep understanding of the dignity and value of life. This understanding is enhanced for us of the Peace Committee by our study of the Buddhism of Nichiren Daishōnin, which advocates respect for life and fervent devotion to peace. Accordingly, we consider it our duty to do everything in our power to prevent the recurrence of war.

Since the end of World War II, roughly three hundred localized conflicts of various scales and destructiveness have taken place throughout the world. Even today, war continues to cause untold human suffering. And, needless to say, nuclear war remains a constant threat.

To ensure the survival of human life, it is necessary to bring about a state of absolute global nonbelligerence, such as advocated by Daisaku Ikeda, president of Soka Gakkai International. Even though small-scale, localized fighting is carried out only with conventional weapons, there is always the danger that such fighting will escalate into nuclear war. Thus, belligerence everywhere, of whatever kind, must be relentlessly opposed. In the hope of contributing to the creation of a state of international nonbelligerence, we of the Soka Gakkai Women's Division Peace Committee are resolved to continue our antiwar activities.

KAYOKO ASANO
Chairman, Soka Gakkai
Women's Division, Peace Committee

INTRODUCTION
by Richard H. Minear

Well over half the men and women alive today in Japan were born after 1945. They have no personal memories of the Pacific War. Moreover, Japan's rapid economic development since 1960 has made Japan's wartime and postwar hardships seem like ancient history. For Japanese today—as for Americans today—thinking about the 1930s and the 1940s takes special effort. Still, most Japanese readers of the testimonies that comprise this volume bring to their reading a certain knowledge of context: most American readers do not. This introduction offers background in three areas: the Japanese empire, the status of women, and the Soka Gakkai.

THE JAPANESE EMPIRE

War in the Pacific did not begin with the Japanese attack on Pearl Harbor on December 7, 1941. What began that Sunday morning was the shooting war between Japan and the United States. Japan was already at war with China, and had been since 1937. Moreover, its involvement on the continent of Asia dated to the late nineteenth century. While this introduction can scarcely do justice to the complexities of the power politics of East Asia before 1941, consider the following:

As of 1910, Japan had fought two major wars to gain a foothold on the continent (annexing Korea in 1910) and had established itself as a major player in the game of empire.

As of 1920, the following nations had important territorial possessions in Asia: Britain (Hong Kong, India), France (Cambodia, Laos, Vietnam), Japan (Korea), the Netherlands (Indonesia), and the United States (the Philippines).

As of 1930, the following nations had troops stationed in China: Britain, France, Japan, the Soviet Union, and the United States.

Unthinkable as this situation is today with the People's Republic of China united and strong, it was the result of decades of military-political activity based on the premise that strong nations dominated weak nations; it was also the result of weakness on the part of all Asian nations save Japan. This is why many of the testimonials included in this volume begin outside the territory we know today as Japan: in Korea, in Manchuria, in the Philippines.

The important dates between 1930 and 1952 are the following:

1931–33: The Manchurian Incident. The Japanese army stationed (by treaty right) in Manchuria fabricated an incident and used that incident to seize control of all Manchuria. Japan set up a client state, Manchukuo, and when the League of Nations was critical, Japan left the League.

July 1937: An incident near Peking between Japanese and Chinese troops rapidly escalated into wholesale fighting with the Chinese government of Chiang Kai-shek. China's civil war pitted Chiang and his Nationalist forces against Mao Tse-tung and the Eighth Route (Communist) Army; the Japanese eventually fought both.

December 7, 1941: The Japanese attack on Pearl Harbor was accompanied by Japanese advances in Southeast Asia. Hong Kong surrendered on Christmas Day, Singapore in February 1942, the Philippines and the Dutch East Indies in April.

1944–45: Japanese reverses came thick and fast: Saipan (June), the Philippines (October), Iwojima (February 1945), Okinawa (April).

August 1945: On August 6 the United States dropped the first atomic bomb, on Hiroshima; on August 9 it dropped the second atomic bomb, on Nagasaki. In between, on August 8, the Soviet Union—encouraged by the Allies to break the non-aggression treaty still in force between the USSR and Japan—entered the war against Japan, and Russian armies moved south into Manchuria and Sakhalin. Japan surrendered on August 15; the surrender ceremony was held on September 2. Defeated Japan was stripped not simply of its recent conquests but also of its long-term territorial possessions: the Kuriles (USSR), Sakhalin (i.e., Karafuto; USSR), Manchuria (China), Korea (Korea), Taiwan (China), Okinawa (USA, until 1972). Japanese who had been in these overseas areas—3,300,000 troops, 3,200,000 civilians; together, nearly 10 percent of Japan's 1945 population—were repatriated to an economically prostrate homeland.

1945–52: Formally known as the Allied Occupation of Japan, the Occupation was basically an American operation. Japan's sovereignty was restored in 1952 at the cost to Japan of a continuing unequal relation that involved the stationing of American troops in Japan (in 1986 American troops are still there, though by now the relation is much more equal).

Given Japan's prosperity in the 1980s, it is hard to visualize just how total the Japanese collapse was in 1945. Even without the atomic bombs, American firebombing had leveled 50 percent of the area of sixty-six Japanese cities (all the cities of economic significance except Kyoto); in the words of the US Strategic Bombing survey: "By July 1945 Japan's economic system had been shattered." It was this devastation that the authors of these testimonials experienced. Indeed, had it not been for shipments of food to Japan, there might have been widespread starvation in the winter of 1945–46.

THE STATUS OF WOMEN

The women whose testimonials make up this volume range in age from the late twenties to the late seventies, but most were in their fifties and sixties when they wrote. That is, most were born between 1910 and 1930. The status of women in Japan during the prewar years is a critical part of the story behind these testimonials.

Take first education. In prewar Japan higher education was largely if not exclusively something for men. The few women's colleges were finishing schools catering primarily to women of the upper class. Japan's national universities, famous for their high academic standards, were not open to women until after the war. A number of women achieved prominence before the war as writers, poets, painters, activists; but they are the exceptions. In prewar Japan women ruled the home, perhaps, but they played only a restricted role in the world out-side the home. For the most part these testimonials do not specify how much education the authors had received; for the vast majority of them, formal education undoubtedly stopped in their mid-teens.

Few professions were open even to those few women who earned a higher education. Most of the writers of these testimonials were not professionals; they were wives or daughters who followed husbands or fathers to new posts—as settlers, businessmen, minor officials—or waited at home for the men to return. The few women with their own professions were teachers and nurses.

Now take politics. To enjoy the right to vote in prewar Japan, you had to be born male. Indeed, to join a political party legally—not to mention run for office—you had to be a male. And universal male suf-frage was a new thing, dating only to 1925. True universal suffrage came in 1945, a product of the American Occupation. Hence only very few women of the generations that produced this volume had any ac-cess to political action, any experience with political organizing and political argument. This may sound very strange to readers in the late 1980s; but women in the United States did not get the vote until 1928 (the nineteenth amendment). France (1945) and Belgium (1946) are among the countries that granted women the vote at about the time the American Occupation decreed universal suffrage for Japan.

Take ideas about the role of women. One official report of the 1930s included this sentence: "Our female higher education may be said to have the object of forming character in women and of imparting knowledge well-calculated to make good wives and wise mothers, able to contribute to the peace and happiness of the family into which they marry." Sentiments like these reflected the traditional belief that "the only qualities suitable for a woman are gentle obedience, purity, mercy, and quietness." Once again, what was traditional in Japan is not greatly different from what was traditional in other countries.

The authors of these testimonials remember in the 1980s the horrors of the Pacific War, and they write in order to share their antiwar con-cerns with the Japanese public. At the time of the Pacific War, antiwar feelings were hardly an option for most Japanese. Through propa-ganda, censorship, and the activities of thought police, the Japanese government controlled information about the progress of the war and suppressed all "unpatriotic" ideas. (Some Japanese intellectuals had other sources of information; but even so, few gave voice to antiwar feelings.)

The horrors of the Pacific War the writers recount are the horrors they experienced in the defeat and the aftermath of defeat. Only rarely do the writers who were outside Japan proper speak of the sufferings of the Chinese, Koreans, Filipinos among whom they lived. To get the entire picture of the Pacific War as experienced by women, we need the testimony of women of China, Korea, the Philippines, and the other countries involved. This collection makes a start toward that end. Written for Japanese readers, it is particularly valuable in translation, for most of the accounts of the Pacific War available in English present the war from outside, with the Japanese as enemies, and focus on the leaders, not on ordinary people.

THE SOKA GAKKAI

The twelve volumes from which these testimonials are drawn were published in Japanese beginning in 1981 by the Peace Committee of the Women's Division of the Soka Gakkai. What is the Soka Gakkai?

The Soka Gakkai is one of Japan's "new" religious movements, founded in 1930 but rooted in one historic strain of Japanese Buddhism. As do other Nichiren sects, it emphasizes the chanting of the *daimoku*, the practical benefits of religion, and a tight and supportive organization; in its vigorous recruitment, it offers a sense of belonging and purpose that are not always available elsewhere in today's mass society (in Japan or in America). The largest single religious organization in Japan, its membership includes over 10 percent of the population. Increasingly after 1975, when Soka Gakkai International was founded, the Soka Gakkai has emphasized missionary work outside of Japan; the membership of its American branch (Nichiren Shoshu of America) is already over 300,000.

Issues of war and peace have been a major focus of the Soka Gakkai in recent years. Witness this project of the Peace Committee of the Women's Division. In 1979 the Youth Division completed a similar project of fifty-six volumes (two volumes of these testimonials—*Cries for Peace* and *Peace is Our Duty*—are already available in English). The Soka Gakkai has sponsored activities in support of the United Nations "so that it can become a more effective machinery to maintain international peace and security;" in conjunction with the United Nations and the cities of Hiroshima and Nagasaki, it has prepared an exhibition, "Nuclear Arms: Threat to Our World," that has already been seen in over a dozen countries.

These activities of the Soka Gakkai play a significant role in contemporary Japanese thinking about war and peace. Many of the writers of these testimonials comment on how painful their memories are; without the active encouragement of the Soka Gakkai, many of these accounts would not have been written.

Most of the writers of these testimonials—roughly 60 percent of the contributors to the twelve volumes—are members of the Soka Gakkai. None was born into the Soka Gakkai; instead, they are converts, members by choice. The shattering effects of war and defeat are part of the story of their conversion; other factors also enter in. Thus, as Yamada Sadako remembers it in the opening testimonial: "In spite of our poverty and protests that we needed no help, believers in Nichiren Shōshū Buddhism visited us regularly. And in June 1941 our whole family became faithful members. . . ."

In the last analysis, these testimonials speak for themselves. Their writers do not—cannot—speak for all Japanese women, just as no American women can speak for all American women. They speak—eloquently—of their own experience and views, and we benefit from reading what they say. They do not speak for the stereotypical "Japanese woman," because that "Japanese woman" is a figment of our imaginations. Indeed, the range of thought and feeling evident in this set of testimonials should warn us against any easy generalization at all. Instead, let us content ourselves with making the acquaintance of Japanese women who experienced war and defeat and lived to reflect on their experience.

JAPAN

OKHOTSK SEA

HOKKAIDO

○ Sapporo

Hakodate

JAPAN SEA

HONSHU

Misawa
AOMORI

Noshiro
AKITA   IWATE

MIYAGI

YAMAGATA
Sendai

NIIGATA
FUKUSHIMA

Nasu
○ Nikko   Mito
TOCHIGI
GUMMA   IBARAGI
Nagano ○ Sawatari   SAITAMA
TOYAMA NAGANO   Tachikawa
Shimo Suwa Hachiōji   Chiba
ISHIKAWA   YAMANASHI Tokyo
KANAGAWA   CHIBA
FUKUI   GIFU   Yokosuka   Tateyama
Shizuoka   Izu
AICHI   SHIZUOKA
KYOTO L. Biwa   Nagoya
Kyoto SHIGA   Hamamatsu
TOTTORI HYŌGO OSAKA Ōtsu
OKAYAMA Kobe   Nara   MIE
Katsuyama ○   Osaka
SHIMANE   Okayama ○   NARA
Fuchū
HIROSHIMA   WAKAYAMA
Hiroshima ○ KAGAWA
YAMAGUCHI   TOKUSHIMA
Shimonoseki KŌCHI
EHIME
Moji (Kitakyushu)   SHIKOKU
FUKUOKA
Hakata ○Fukuoka   ŌITA
SAGA
○Sasebo
NAGASAKI
Nagasaki   KUMAMOTO
MIYAZAKI
KAGOSHIMA
Kagoshima

PACIFIC OCEAN

OKINAWA
○ Koza
Naha

JAPAN AND OTHER AREAS

SOVIET UNION

Sakhalin
(Karafuto)

MANCHURIA
(MANCHUKUO)

O Qiqihaer

Haerbin O   Linkou O   O Boli

Mudanjiang
Prov.

Changchun O

Shenyang O

Hokkaido

O Sapporo

Hakodate O

Yalu R.   KOREA

Beijing O   O Sinuiju   Aomori

Tianjin O   Dalian   O Pyongyang

O Inchon   38th parallel   Honshu

O Seoul   O Sendai

Pusan   Tokyo O   O Chiba

Hiroshima   Izu

Shimonoseki   Osaka

CHINA   Shikoku

Nagasaki Kyushu

Hubei Prov.

O Hankou Nanjing O O Shanghai

Yangzi R.

Okinawa

Taiwan   Iwojima

Bashi Channel

Luzon   Mariana Islands

O Baguio

Manila O PHILIPPINE
ISLANDS   Guam

Leyte

Mindanao

Davao O

PRELUDE

This account of one woman's recollections of the war has been given precedence over the others because it represents a norm. Mrs. Yamada, having experienced the distress, fear, loss, and misery of war while in Tokyo and then in the countryside, gives an excellent description of the social and political tone of the times from the viewpoint of an average woman. Like most women, she is able to place herself outside politics. Her concern is providing for her loved ones and herself, even when the world around her is being consumed by flames and destruction.

The stories that follow, while sharing much with Mrs. Yamada's, are also different, as each human experience differs from all others. The narrators speak of the horrors of being pursued and of flight in foreign lands, of conflagration and death, of being forced to kill one's own children, of losing all that is dear, and of the struggle to survive in the aftermath of war, whatever the cost in suffering, disappointment, and degradation.

There is, however, one mighty current running through all the testimonials presented here: the adamantine determination to bring an end to that most barbarous of all human undertakings—war—an evil that only human beings can inflict and that only human beings can eliminate.

As I Remember It
Sadako Yamada (59)

I was born into comfortable circumstances in Kōji-machi, Tokyo, on November 8, 1923. In 1931, when I was a third grader in primary school, fighting broke out in Manchuria on the Chinese mainland. In the following year there was the Shanghai Incident, which eventually led to war between China and Japan. At nearby Yasukuni Shrine, which was dedicated to soldiers killed in war, I saw the blood-stained uniforms of Japanese soldiers and captured Chinese swords. That was my first encounter with the reality of war.

In 1937 war broke out with China, and the whole nation turned military. Soldiers crowded the streets, and the movie theaters showed newsreels of our men fighting bravely at the front.

At about that time my older sister came down with tuberculosis, and my father fell seriously ill. For this reason, and also owing to some improper dealings by our hired help, we were forced to leave our Kōji-machi home and move, almost stealthily, to Suginami Ward. There, in spite of our poverty and protests that we needed no help, believers in Nichiren Shōshū Buddhism visited us regularly. And in June 1941 our whole family became faithful members of the Nichiren Shōshū Sōka Kyōiku Gakkai (Value-creating Educational Association, the prewar predecessor of the present Sōka Gakkai). I was then nineteen years old.

Two months later I participated in a summer lecture course at the head temple, Taiseki-ji, where I heard Tsunesaburō Makiguchi, president of the association, speak on religious faith. I was brought to the realization that the spirit of our association is the spirit that Nichiren Daishōnin demonstrated when, triumphing over persecution, he continued remonstrating with the national government concerning its evil approach to religion. I was deeply moved by what I heard. Back at my job as a telephone operator at the Japan Steamship Company, I advised my seniors and friends against worshiping the Sun Goddess, who was held up by the ultranationalists as the divine protectress of Japan, and invited them to attend our meetings. My life was very full.

At the end of that year, however, severe restrictions were imposed on speech, the press, and assembly. And on December 8 (December 7 in the United States), Japanese aircraft attacked Pearl Harbor. The following year the battle of Midway took place, and the entire nation became inflamed by the prospect of victory.

However, in contrast to the optimistic news reports given on the radio, the Japanese were already beginning to retreat from the islands of the South Pacific. The atmosphere at my office became very gloomy. The company's luxury liners, the *Nitta-maru* and *Hikawa-maru*, which had been our pride and joy, were requisitioned and remodeled for military use. This removed all oceangoing ships from operation.

The shadow of war fell on our daily lives too. There were now long lines in front of the bread stores, even in the Marunouchi business district. We were happy to get anything we could. Young boys and girls were mobilized for work in munitions factories. And specially formed groups of ladies could be seen almost daily waving good-bye to soldiers on their way overseas.

Daily necessities were rationed, and more and more food substitutes made their appearance. Metal objects—even the metal fixtures that held up mosquito nets—were confiscated for reuse in the production of munitions. It was also about this time that I was introduced to the man who is now my husband. He too was a member of the Nichiren Shōshū Sōka Kyōiku Gakkai.

Restrictions on religious freedom grew more oppressive. Our organization's newspaper, *Kachi Sōzō* (Value Creation), was closed down, and the police kept a sharp eye on our activities, ordering any meeting disbanded whose agenda they found objectionable. Suddenly, in June 1943, two of our leaders were arrested. Then, in July, President Makiguchi and Jōsei Toda, who became the next president, were thrown into prison. We were all astounded by this turn of events.

Our wedding was only a few days away when my husband received his induction papers. In front of our household Gohonzon (the object of faith for believers in Nichiren Shōshū Buddhism), we held a simple marital exchange of cups of sake in the company of a number of our colleagues. I was dressed in the cotton trousers (*mompe*) that all women wore during the war, and he was wearing civilian national uniform.

With only three days remaining before he had to leave for service, we took an express train that night for his mother's home in Katsuyama,

Okayama Prefecture. No one in the village, a beautiful place where cosmos were in riotous bloom on the hills and through which the Asahikawa river flowed, had ever married a girl from Tokyo.

Everyone examined me with the utmost curiosity. Knowing that my husband would leave the next day, I was filled with apprehension as my mother-in-law took me around to greet the villagers. The farewell party for my husband continued far into the night.

Dawn came quickly. With a number of banners and the Japanese flag leading the procession, my husband marched off, looking very brave with white cords tied around his chest as a sign of his willingness to do his duty. At the entrance to the prefectural park where the men assembled, he saluted the soldier standing guard, and then, without looking back, he departed. We had no idea of his destination. The spirit of the times forbade us to shed tears; everything was being done in the name of "honor."

My mother-in-law, who had lost her husband at the age of thirty-two and raised two sons by herself, had already sent the younger son off to battle. She trembled as she gripped my hand and asked if I, as her elder son's wife, would help her with the farm work. For a long time we wept together, watching the lights flickering in the distance.

I made up my mind to do as my mother-in-law asked. Returning to Tokyo, I informed my parents, who said I was doing the wrong thing and would find the work unbearable. I parted with the chest of drawers and dresser that had been part of my trousseau, and boarded a train back to my husband's family home. Throughout this, my first long journey alone, I could not forget the look on my mother's face as she said goodbye at the ticket window. From the moment I arrived at the lonely country train station, I began my life as a farmer's wife.

Up every morning at four, I would put on my rough working shoes and go to the mountainside behind the house to cut grass for the cows. All the farms in our neighborhood kept three or four cows. They provided manure for fertilizer, and the calves were a source of income. In that part of the country, the women are said to work as hard as the men. We raised rice, kept silk worms, and made charcoal. Sometimes the whole village would go into the mountains—as far as the boundary of the next prefecture—to gather grasses and herbs to dry for food in winter.

I was afraid of our big black cows, who tossed their horns to scare me. Two or three times I dropped their food—leftovers—on their heads, tub and all.

After we had burned wood to make charcoal, my mother-in-law would strap three large bundles on her back and walk lightly across the single-log bridge that spanned the river we had to cross to get home. It was all I could do to carry even one bundle. At home, my soot-covered face drooping after a late supper, I was too exhausted in mind and body to feel grateful for my mother-in-law's words of comfort. Everything was too different from the life I had known. Time and again, I wept aloud in the hayloft, and then struggled on with my work.

In November 1944 B29s began bombing Tokyo. My mother, with my younger brothers and sisters, decided to take refuge in the countryside. Hearing of this, I begged for permission to go and say good-bye. As conditions were, it might be my last chance to see them.

With the war news growing steadily worse, all of Tokyo's train stations had become jammed with people leaving the city for the comparative safety of outlying areas. On the day Mother and my younger brothers and sisters left for Yamanashi Prefecture, Shinjuku Station and its underground passageways were packed to overflowing. Uniformed station attendants waved long sticks at children carrying heavy rucksacks, ordering them to move along as quickly as possible. With pots, pans, and other baggage strapped to her back, her smiling face distorted by emotion, Mother looked back at me many times before she disappeared into the crowd on the platform.

Instead of returning to Okayama, I decided to stay in Tokyo with my father and my older sister, who had been conscripted to work in a factory. Since I had a first-class telephone operator's license, I managed to get a job at the Military Police Headquarters in Kudan. This seemed a good job for the wife of a soldier on active duty.

Ordinary civilians would have been unable to imagine the large amount of food stored at the headquarters. And I could not bear the way young officers shouted at, and at times even struck, men in their fifties for saluting them incorrectly. I sometimes protested against it.

We were all beginning to get a full taste of the wretchedness and futility of war as reports came back of defeats in the Marianas and Leyte (October 1944), the loss of supremacy at sea, and stories of the sailors of the formerly splendid Japan Steamship Company who had gone to the bottom of the sea.

In 1945 offshore bombardment and air raids grew so intense that I was afraid to walk to work. As a precaution, the operations department was relocated in the basement of the building. I was working the night shift on March 10 when two-thirds of Tokyo was burned to the ground. The strong wind that had been blowing all day grew stronger at night. Our fears of a conflagration became reality. Incendiary bombs rained down on the *shitamachi* district, and red flames licked at the windows of our office. All that night high-pitched screeching and other unearthly sounds reached our ears, but luckily our reinforced-concrete building escaped damage.

The hell of that night passed to reveal the hell of the following day. The Chidori-ga-fuchi region, near the imperial palace moat, was packed with refugees from the holocaust. The Sumida River, we were told, was choked with corpses. Military police brought the maimed and wounded on their backs; a parent chewed dried bread to put in a child's swollen mouth; people's hair was plastered to their seared faces. The devastation extended from Kudan to Ichigaya, Yotsuya, and Shinjuku and farther along the Ōme Highway. To get home, I struggled through the ruins, ducking under telephone wires, and once hitched a ride on a horse-drawn cart. I was astonished to find that our house and several others in the vicinity had escaped damage. Many of the houses in that neighborhood belonged to believers of Nichiren Shōshū Buddhism. With complete conviction I attributed our salvation to the power of faith and the Gohonzon. But the air raids continued, and I often had to walk past heaps of charred corpses on my way to work.

About this time an unsigned postcard informed me that my husband was stationed in the Rokkō district of Kobe. Though train tickets were virtually unobtainable, I somehow managed to get one, and found a place to sit in the corner of one of the train lavatories. At Nagoya everyone was forced off the train by an air raid, and when I finally reached Kobe I was much behind schedule. Wandering around Rokkō, a large district, I finally located my husband just three minutes before his unit was to leave. We exchanged one or two words; and then, as his orders were shouted out, he vanished. Fighting back tears, I took a night train home.

A superior at the office, hearing my story, gave me a ticket for the last concert to take place at Hibiya Public Hall for some time. This was in April 1945. The audience wore wartime garb, including military leggings and *mompe* trousers. All of us, the audience as well as the performers on the stage—among them the famous tenor Yoshie Fujiwara and the well-known soprano Tamaki Miura—forgot about the possibility of an air raid. With tears in our eyes, we listened intently, not knowing that some of the performers would shortly take their own lives.

In the summer of 1945 the sea lanes were cut. This, coupled with the strafing of farms, resulted in severe food shortages. In order to provide for ourselves, we office workers and some soldiers planted pumpkin seeds in the garden of a burned-out mansion in the Kōji-machi district. The garden was spacious and indicated the luxurious life its owners had once led. Three memorial plaques had been placed there, making one wonder if the owners had died in the garden's air-raid shelter.

On August 6, 1945, my padded air-raid hat soaked with sweat from dodging strafing attacks, I had just made my way to work when an emergency assembly was called. A mysterious light had burst over Hiroshima, destroying in an instant all living things. We were urged to remain calm. The light, of course, came from the atomic bomb.

The courtyard of the Military Police Headquarters was where the terribly burned bodies of American crew members, who had parachuted from crippled B29s, were brought, to be covered with coarse straw mats till they died. I can still see some of their faces. Other American crew who had been shot down by antiaircraft guns were kept prisoner in the basement. They were usually cheerful and often asked us for water as we walked along the corridor. After a while, some of them even started tap-dancing. The guards always stopped them, but they usually took it up again before long. We are all only human after all, I thought. Even before August 15, the day the emperor announced the end of the war, headquarters knew that surrender was inevitable. At some time or other, all the prisoners were taken away.

Each day, as we gazed into the smoke rising from mountains of burning documents, we wondered what defeat would mean for the Japanese people. The signs were bad. I saw soldiers from headquarters lying in their own blood after cutting a cervical artery; and we heard stories of others—including some women—who had committed suicide in front of the imperial palace. Badges of military rank, once awesome enough to silence crying children at the mere mention of them, now became unwanted burdens. Soldiers were jeered on the streets, and many were rounded up as war criminals.

Then came the American occupation. We were all uncertain about the future. And since the American prisoners who had been kept in the basement could recognize us, we were ordered to leave the city as quickly as possible. In October 1945, on a train with demobilized soldiers, I headed reluctantly back to my husband's home in Okayama.

After I had helped on the farm for about a year, my husband and his younger brother, who had contracted malaria in Singapore, returned. One after another, notifications of death in battle reached the village, which had sent so many men to war. Having sent both of her sons off to fight, my mother-in-law had long since ceased to expect their return. Then suddenly, to her immense surprise and joy, they were both home. At the urging of myself and my husband, his mother and brother became believers in Nichiren Shōshū Buddhism. I was more conscious of being protected than ever before.

WOMEN IN
FLIGHT

Five Victims
Chiharu Kōno (64)

In 1938 my husband and I were sent by the old regimental district branch to a guard post called Boli on the border between Manchuria and the Soviet Union. I went there against the violent objections of my relatives. Manchuria in those days was truly an ideal new land. At sunrise and sunset, the entire sky was dyed the most beautiful crimson. Though evenings' sometimes made me homesick, every day was filled with hope.

But times changed before one knew it. In 1945, in the midst of great commotion, aid and service brigades were dispatched from Boli to various locales. In March of that year my husband was sent as the leader of a detachment of 280 men to an arms depot in a place called Shenyang. Only one or two companies remained behind. Though we were all saddened by the departures, no one complained. All the wives in the official residences did their best to keep things running smoothly.

Early on the morning of August 7, 1945, a camouflaged military truck loaded with soldiers sped furiously down the road in front of our houses. We wondered if some kind of maneuvers were under way. Two days later we were encouraged to see what we took to be a friendly aircraft, white and shining, circling overhead. Shortly after ten that same morning, however, we were all summoned by trumpet to an emergency assembly. With a pained look on his face, the commander took the podium and said, "War has been declared between the Soviet Union and Japan. This battalion will retreat temporarily to southern Manchuria. All of you are to get your things together and be ready to board trucks by tomorrow morning. The day after tomorrow you will be taken to Boli Station, where you will embark on military trains for southern Manchuria."

I thought to myself, "Well, it's happened at last," and silently urged myself to stay calm. Actually, however, with my husband away and with five children to look after—the oldest was a first grader—I was at my wit's end. With the help of five people from the company, I somehow made the necessary preparations. I had a sword my husband had given me before his departure, when he told me that if we were ever attacked by the local Manchurians, I was to kill the children and then commit suicide.

At five o'clock the next morning, intending to return again before long, I left our house and everything we owned just as it was, and climbed with the children onto the truck that we were to ride for two full days and nights in the rain. Conditions got so bad that it became a forced march. By the time we reached Boli Airport, the situation had so deteriorated that we were each assigned military escorts.

We made the last military train and headed south, only to hear that the Soviet army had already invaded Kochochin. Scouts were sent out, and the train moved slowly after them. But it proved impossible to pass through Kochochin Station, and we retreated as fast as possible to Aka.

Near the station someone suddenly shouted for us to get off the train and take refuge in the hills: Soviet tanks were on the way, and the station was going to be blown up. Before the children and I could do anything, the train caught fire. I could hear the ominous crackling of the flames directly behind my back. As we dashed frantically for the hills, the station blew up. It was August 15, 1945, the day the war ended, the day that the six of us began a march of death through trackless mountains.

Since we were surrounded by the enemy, we had to keep clear of open roads. Instead we took narrow paths along sheer precipices. A false step might mean death. There was nothing to eat, and no matter how hard I squeezed my breasts, they produced no milk for my ten-month-old baby. I moistened some of our precious supply of canned bread and gave it to the youngest. The others had to keep themselves alive by gnawing on raw potatoes and corn.

We had no choice but to keep moving, day and night. But the children and I found we could not keep up with the others and fell behind. We slept huddled together out of doors, deep in the mountains, afraid a wolf might attack at any moment. With no hope of any kind, we stared death in the face: if we stayed there, we would die; if we went on, we would die. I made up my mind not to die before the children did, and leave them motherless. That was the only thing that gave me strength.

The children were wonderful, saying things like, "If we can die with you, Mother, we're ready anytime." They were hungry and tired, but they never complained, even though the march was hard enough for a full-grown adult. Silently they kept going. Given the smallest chance to rest, they at once fell sound asleep.

One day I noticed that my second son was limping, and soon discovered that one of his big toes was swollen with an infection. He had never uttered a word of complaint. He put up with more suffering than a child should be expected to. I was so moved that I cried as I held him to me, silently asking his forgiveness.

A soldier we met in the mountains brought his hands reverently together as if in prayer when he saw the six of us, and said that I was radiant with light. "I'm a grown man, and it's all I can do to take care of myself. Here you are, a woman, with five small children to look after. A mother's love is truly a powerful thing!"

What followed was hell on earth. The corpses of human beings and horses and cattle littered the ground everywhere. I saw a baby wrapped in nightwear abandoned by the roadside. A little girl of five or six, dressed in her best clothes, cried out for her mother as she stumbled along, drenched in her own blood and only half alive. She had been sprayed with bullets from chest to abdomen.

We lay down on top of a low hill on the night of August 27, 1945, with not so much as a match to warm us. The air was full of mosquitoes. I had the children sleep face to face as I kept watch, covering them with some of my clothes.

For a long time, Isao, my third son, could not fall asleep and kept asking for water. On the following morning, everyone got up but him. He was dead. We could not bury him or do anything that we would normally do. I spread a pair of my cotton trousers on the ground, laid him on them, and covered him with underclothing. We gathered as many wild flowers as we could and placed them about his body. Then, torn by grief, we continued our march.

There are no words to describe a mother's feelings at having to abandon a child—even a dead child—in those mountains. But I had to steel my heart and continue the death march with my remaining children.

In the evening we came upon a Manchurian village. One woman, though I did not understand the language she spoke, made it clear that she wanted the children and I to come to her house. She gave us food, and with it the first salt we had tasted in a long time. In her house was an old man of about seventy, who told us we could rest there without fear of bandits, for there were none in the vicinity. The old man's kindness brought tears to my eyes. Though we were little short of beggars, he and his family treated us as though we were guests in their home.

After a while, a young married couple from the neighborhood came to visit, explaining in good Japanese how the husband had formerly been with the Mudanjiang army, and how they had recently lost their baby. The wife's breasts were swollen with milk, and she kindly nursed my youngest, Kunio, whom they entreated me to leave with them to raise. I did not know what to do until my oldest son started to cry, saying he did not want to give Kunio away to strangers. I knew that Kunio would last no more than two or three days if we continued the march, but I decided that as long as we remained alive, we should remain together. Thanking them sincerely for their kindness, I declined the couple's offer. The next morning, after receiving some food from our hosts, we set out again.

I think it was two days later when we arrived at a village where some White Russians lived. They told us to go back to our homes, that the war was over. Japan had surrendered unconditionally, and if we continued on, they said, we would be killed by the Soviet Russians who were close by. They offered to put us up for the night, encouraged us, and gave us food to eat. Unable to believe that Japan had lost, we thanked them and continued on.

At the Erdao River Bridge we came under fire from a hill on the opposite bank. The children and I took refuge behind the stone ramparts of the bridge while about ten soldiers and fourteen or fifteen civilians ran for cover. One of the soldiers returned the fire with a machine gun. Before our eyes, two people were shot dead by enemy bullets.

The shooting stopped as evening darkness approached. When I took Kunio from my oldest boy's back, where he had been strapped, I found that he had died during the shooting. Not wanting to leave him in enemy territory, I decided to put him in the river. For a while I could not bring myself to do it, but finally I lowered him into the water. It was some time before the eddying currents pulled him from my side. Though I felt that I might be losing my sanity, I prayed as earnestly as I could for his repose. Then, without a second's rest, the children and I set off again.

On and on we went, for I cannot remember how many days, walking along railroad tracks, until at last we returned to the place from which we had set out. Some of the people there had died. The survivors had existed on nothing but water, raw potatoes, and corn. Exhausted both physically and mentally, our eyes glazed over, we waited for death. Still, I was determined to do my best as long as some of my children remained alive.

At about that time, two or three mounted Japanese soldiers told us that the rumor was true: Japan had surrendered unconditionally. You can imagine our feelings at hearing this news. The soldiers then told us that the Russians were coming to take us prisoner and instructed us to do as the Russians told us.

And so we became prisoners of war. The Russians were kind to us. They said that the Japanese government and military, not ordinary Japanese citizens, were the enemy, and that we weren't to worry.

Crossing the Huangdao River, we moved to the Hailin Prison Camp. At about six on the following morning, as we were preparing to move again to still another camp, I discovered that the long ordeal had ended the short six-year life of Seio, my second son. No sooner had I buried him than we set out for the camp at Lako. I had my fourth son, Takashi, on my back and held my oldest boy, Tadaaki, by the hand. As soon as we arrived at the camp, at about five in the evening, Takashi began crying for water. Other prisoners, having reached the camp ahead of us, gave us water and balls of steamed rice. Takashi drank a little water, and then after barely tasting the rice, he died. Other prisoners pulled him from me and buried him. It was September 13, which I now commemorate as the death date of two of my children.

Only two of us remained. My body had changed horribly. My eyesight was gradually failing. My legs refused to climb even the smallest rising. My skin was scratched and rough and turning a purplish black. Nonetheless, I had to go on as long as Tadaaki lived.

On September 17, at about five in the morning, my last son said to me, "Mother, I'll never see Japan again." I tried to encourage him: "We have to be brave. We'll make it home again. Grandmother and Grandfather are waiting for you." But he smiled and said, "I won't make it back," and then he died. Only the night before he had been strong enough to go to the toilet by himself.

Stricken with an understanding of the fragility of life, I realized then as never before the dignity of human life and the heavy responsibility it puts on us. I made up my mind to try to go on living so I could pray for the repose of my children who had died victims of war.

Finally, on June 8, 1946, at the end of a long period of hardship, I returned to Japan. As time passed, I thought about my children more and more, until at times I thought I would go mad. Sometimes I would get up early and wander along the seashore, thinking that perhaps the bones of my baby Kunio, who I had set adrift on the river, might somehow find their way to Japan. Sometimes I would snatch up large fish bones and clutch them to me. I couldn't help myself. And even today, the misery, sorrow, and pain of having lost five small children to the cruelty of war tears at my heart.

Pioneering that Led to Tragedy
Sakie Maki (60)

The boat passage from Shimonoseki, Japan, to Pusan, Korea, in March 1944 was like a honeymoon for the two of us, a newly married couple. When my husband had been nineteen and filled with dreams for the future, he had left Japan to take part in the development of Manchuria. He had returned to Japan to marry me, and the two of us were now going back together.

Since the establishment of the state of Manchukuo in 1932, interest in Manchuria had risen steadily. The government's policy was to convince people to emigrate and take part in the realization of racial cooperation and the construction of a land of peace and plenty. There was a great deal of enthusiasm for the great Japan-Manchurian empire, with such people as Kanji Katō, formerly principal of the National High School of the village Uchihara in Ibaragi Prefecture, touring far and wide to urge young people to summon up their true Japanese spirit and take part in the development of Manchukuo. Neither a fortune hunter nor a failure at home, my husband was one of those who answered this call out of a sincere belief that it was right and good.

Our destination was an agricultural commune of roughly two hundred households, headed by a man named Kainuma and located six kilometers west of Donghai Station on the Hulin Line, northeast of present-day Changchun. On the commune gate, which was made of thick logs, hung a sign bearing the words *Fourth Hedahe Immigrant Group*. For protection from marauding Communists, so we were told, the headquarters' buildings in the center of the compound were surrounded by clay walls. All the buildings, including the headquarters with a general accounting office and meeting rooms in the center, the post office on the right, the consumers' union on the left, and the rice mill and the veterinary's office in the rear, were of characteristic Manchurian plaster on clay bricks. I learned from my husband that the commune was run in accordance with the Japanese national policy of self-sufficiency in food and contribution to the defense of the homeland.

My first sight of the continent, of its vast spaces and open skies, inspired in me a feeling of supreme fulfillment. The start of each day, with the sound of a braying donkey floating through low-lying mists, meant happiness, activity, and peace of mind.

Water being scant in Manchuria, most crops were grown in dry fields. Soybeans, kaoliang, and millet were the main crops. The soil was so fertile that practically anything thrived. Soybeans grew taller than a human being. Pumpkins were so big that they had to be carried in both arms, and potatoes reached phenomenal sizes. Working happily with my husband in the fields, with a view for miles in all directions, my heart was filled with hopes and dreams for the future.

But a burst of gunfire changed all this happiness to misery. At about noon on August 8, 1945, a Soviet aircraft flew over our settlement and opened fire. My husband had been drafted only a few days earlier—on July 25—and I was too unsettled and frightened to know what to do.

At little after midnight, some local Manchurians told me that we had been ordered to flee, taking with us a week's supply of food. Thinking we would probably return, I piled bedding and food on a horse cart and, wearing a short-sleeved shirt and trousers, left our home as dawn was breaking. Three families traveled together, each with its own horse cart.

As luck would have it, my cart broke down before we reached headquarters, and I had to combine my supplies with those of the Ishiyama family.

At headquarters, with a grim look on his face and a military sword in one hand, Mr. Kainuma was giving orders and directing preparations for departure, crying out repeatedly that no one must break ranks or fall behind. There were tear stains on his cheeks. As we drew away, I waved back to him, not dreaming that we would never meet again.

Mrs. Ishiyama and I walked together, encouraging each other. She frequently stroked her stomach, for her time to deliver was drawing close. Heavy rains turned the roads into quagmires, and the wheels of our wagons sank deep into the mud, making the going very hard for human beings and horses alike.

As we approached Jining we saw that it had been bombed by Soviet aircraft; the sky above the town was a sea of flames. The horses balked at the fire, so we had to get out of the carts and pull and coax the animals until we finally got past the town.

In our initial alarm, we had kept moving without pause, but we finally decided to rest a while and wait for dawn. Before long, word came of pillaging and looting by local people. We were once again strictly cautioned against falling behind or breaking ranks. Those who trailed behind were menaced by the locals with scythes; some were even slaughtered for putting up resistance. Stories of such misery and imminent danger made it impossible for us to know where or how to continue our march.

At the end of our physical and mental resources, we wandered about without any sense of direction or time, listening to a mixture of sounds blown on the wind: the voices of Soviet solders, the shouting of Japanese women, and the sobbing of Japanese children looking for their parents. I thought of many things. I wondered where my husband was and wished he were with me. I thought of my mother at home in Japan, and of our house here that I had left with everything still in place. Tears came to my eyes as I thought that this wet, boggy place might be my final resting place, the place where I ended my twenty-five years of life. Bracing myself against the wind and rain and bitter cold of a Manchurian summer night, I waited for the dawn, unable to sleep.

Trying to conceal our movements as much as possible, we headed in the direction of Linkou, looking up whenever we heard an aircraft in the hope that it might be Japanese forces coming to our rescue.

After a while—I am not certain how long—we met up with about two hundred Japanese soldiers. But our relief was short-lived. They told us to take cover in the hills. In the light of day, they said, we would be excellent targets for Soviet gunfire. Before we reached, not the hills, but a nearby millet field, the firing started. The bullets raised little clouds of dust as they dug into the ground.

Suddenly I heard a moan and turned to see that Mr. Tanaka had been hit in the side, his large intestines spilling from his body. I was helpless to do anything. Finally, however, I managed to take off a strip of white cotton I wore around my waist and, dodging the flying bullets, handed it to him. When she saw that her husband was on the verge of death, his wife began frantically shouting for help. But none of us were in a position to do anything. We couldn't even do anything for ourselves. Very soon, calling out for water, Mr. Tanaka died. From that moment I never saw Mrs. Tanaka or her children again. I guess they were shot as they ran about trying to find help.

Some time passed, and then I heard a man's voice. A Soviet soldier armed with an automatic weapon was standing in front of us. He took a certain Mr. Kamiya, who was carrying a gun, into the millet field. In a moment we heard a shot.

Then we were all lined up on the road, and I thought we were going to be killed. I was resigned to death, but wished I could see my husband once more before the end. When death approaches, Japanese people exchange farewell drinks of water. The only water available was that in the muddy pools on the road. We scooped it up as best we could and carried out what we believed to be our final rite. But no shots came.

We did not understand what the Soviet soldiers were saying, and they did not understand us. Some of our group pleaded with them to kill us quickly. A number of the Russians seemed to be in favor of this idea, and others against it. Finally one soldier picked up our scattered bundles of clothing, tossed them to us, and motioned for us to run away.

We ended up sleeping in the millet field, and on the following morning the last of the three men who had been with us was gone. Maybe he had left in the night; maybe the Soviets had captured him. In any case, our group had come to consist of only thirty women and children, all at their wits' ends.

Sipping dew from the grass and gnawing raw potatoes, we longed for our homes as we watched smoke floating upward from the chimneys of distant houses. We dared not walk near the train tracks; it was too dangerous.

At one point I noticed that the child of our commune director, Mr. Kainuma, didn't have any shoes on. I gave her my own cloth ones and thereafter walked barefooted, too concerned about the danger we faced to bother about cuts or bruises. When, as happened from time to time, I noticed a cut, I rubbed grass juice on it and went on walking.

When the children begged for food, we had nothing to give them. When they asked why we were in such a terrible predicament, we lacked the courage to answer. "Back in Japan, there'll be all kinds of good things to eat," we said to them encouragingly, though we were far from sure we would ever see Japan again.

During the day we crouched in the tall grass of the fields. If we kept walking, we thought, the children might grow tired and peevish and then start crying, giving us away to the enemy. We moved at night, taking the greatest care to avoid Soviet soldiers and the Manchurians. The Japanese Kwantung Army had constructed a military road through the region, but it was now under Soviet control, with tents positioned at strategic spots. We dared not cross it for fear that we would all be killed.

A baby's cry might be enough to bring down on us a rain of bullets. That is why it was decided that a mother would have to kill her small baby. Of course she couldn't do it. In the end, a number of people wrapped their arms around mother and baby so that the baby was suffocated to death. Now, such an act seems inconceivable, but fear had robbed us of the ability to think rationally. Our hands in an attitude of prayer, we left the small corpse at the base of a tree.

Eventually we made our way past the danger points on the road. Then we entered an endless range of mountains. We tied strips of cloth to one another so that no one would get lost as we traveled through the night. All we had to eat were wild chives and grape leaves. With no water at all, we were sometimes reduced to drinking our own urine. Since no one had a watch or map, we sometimes walked for days in circles. And somehow, in all this wandering, I ended up alone, with nothing to eat and only the tattered clothes I had on my back.

My strength had given out. In desperation I stepped out onto an open road. I was prepared to die if only I could have a drink of water. Finally, I even walked up to a Soviet tent. If they were going to kill me, I wanted them to do it quickly and get it over with. My sudden appearance startled a Soviet soldier. He took aim and was about to fire when a Soviet woman officer emerged and, in excellent Japanese, told me not to be afraid. She gave me some canned food and black bread to eat. "Cheer up," she said, "I'll take you to a place where there are lots of other Japanese." Though she was one of the enemy, I was very grateful for her kindness.

Unsure of what was going to happen, I went with her to the First Linkou Concentration Camp, where I learned of Japan's defeat. I think it was late in August. That night, for the first time in a long while, I slept under a roof—that of a spacious brick building that had formerly been the barracks for the Japanese Kwantung Army, but was now a kitchen for the Soviet army.

Somewhat later I was transferred to the Hailin Concentration Camp, where to our mutual delight I met the Ueda family from the commune. But they had very sad news to tell. It turned out that four hundred and sixty women and children from the commune—including the family of Mr. Kainuma, the director—had committed mass suicide. Little children had eagerly eaten the last food prepared for them, calling out for their mothers to eat some too. Then Japanese-manned machine guns were turned against Japanese people. I prayed for their repose. But my prayer was immediately followed by grave doubts about a system that made such sacrifices necessary, that required people to take their own lives rather than return home in what would be considered disgrace.

Before I returned to Japan a year later, I was moved from camp to camp. No matter where we went, Soviet soldiers thrust their guns at us. Finally I boarded a ship that left from an island near Dalian and returned to Japan—I cannot remember the name of the port where I landed.

I was, of course, very worried about my husband. But, after twenty months in a Siberian concentration camp, he returned home safely in June 1947.

Today the Uchihara school, where people were recruited and trained to go to work in Manchuria, has been converted into an ordinary high school; and the old plaza and the buildings that once housed my husband and people like him, who were to become pioneers on the Asian continent, are now a busy training center for people going to live abroad. Merely thinking of the small number of survivors out of the tens of thousands who left Uchihara for northern Manchuria makes me unspeakably angry.

At present, my husband is a member of an organization attempting to locate children who were abandoned in Manchuria and China at the end of the war, and to discover and return to Japan the remains of those who died so many hard winters ago in Manchuria.

Sometimes, when we pause in our farm work and look at the evening sun, my husband and I rededicate ourselves to the fulfillment of our mission, which is to respect the dignity of human life and to do all within our power to prevent the recurrence of war.

Sharks
Setsuko Goseki (56)

My father moved to the city of Sinuiju near the border between northern Korea and Manchuria after the end of the Russo-Japanese War of 1904–5, making a career for himself as a wholesaler of medical equipment and medicine. I was born and bred in this part of Korea; and by the time I was twenty and learned of the end of World War II, Father's store was one of the oldest in the town. But with Japan's defeat we lost everything.

The Soviet army moved in and, perhaps because of the size of our house, made it the residence of the army air commandant. We were given eight hours to vacate. My mother and sister and I packed everything valuable we could into backpacks and put our clothes in a large wicker trunk. With tears in our eyes, we left our old familiar home to live in the local primary school.

Simultaneously with the announcement of defeat, all financial institutions were closed, and the savings of Japanese nationals in Korea were frozen. Consequently, we soon found ourselves in dire straits. Mother went to the Korean and Chinese settlements in town and sold kimonos, watches, and rings to buy rice and other food to keep us alive. Men and women alike were impressed to do heavy labor. Exhausted and ill-fed, people soon began falling ill. Many died with no one to care for them and with no medicine to relieve their suffering. Although we pitied them, there was nothing we could do. We knew that we might be the next to go. Dreaming of Japan, each person fought to stay alive.

We lived for a year this way, through one hot summer sun and a frigid winter (temperatures dropped to as much as thirty degrees centigrade below zero), the characteristic climate for the Asian continent. By this time, there was no telling when we would be sent back to Japan. And the longer we stayed, the more people died. Finally, when the situation had become maddeningly desperate, the chairman of the Japanese Relief Association made plans to smuggle us to places below the thirty-eighth parallel by boat.

Purchasing a small fishing boat from a Korean, the association assembled forty people—the sick, the aged, women, and children—for the first trip. Since I was sickly, I was included in this group. Mother, Father, and my sister were to follow later. When the time came to go, I was so frightened and sad that I could barely see my family's faces through the tears. Still, I waved to them for a long time after the boat had pulled out.

The trip from the Yalu River coast across the thirty-eighth parallel was fraught with danger. We all knew we had to be prepared for death. The Chinese Eighth Route Army swept the sea with searchlights looking for runaways. The knowledge that, if caught, we would all be shot gave everyone a grim look.

As fate would have it, the Eighth Route Army spotted us as soon as we pulled out into the Jinnampo offing. We made for the nearest land and hid in some tall grass. We escaped the Eighth Route Army, but were almost immediately attacked by a local mob that chased us into a junglelike forest. We ran this way and that, trying to lose them, always keeping our voices as low as possible to avoid detection.

When driven to the extremes of fear, human beings lose the ability to think and make decisions in a normal way. In our dashing here and there, some of the children, the sick, and the aged were soon unable to keep up. They would fall to the ground and implore healthier people for help. But they were ignored, left to fend for themselves.

Children were especially pathetic. One small baby began shrieking with hunger pains. Afraid the noise would give away our position, the group leader ordered the mother to strangle the child. At first she tried to quiet the baby by pressing her dry breast against its mouth, but it screamed all the louder. There was murder on the face of the group leader when he shouted, "You damned fool! Choke it!" The mother then pressed her breasts tight against the infant's face until it died of suffocation. None of us tried to stop her.

The instinct to stay alive forced other mothers to throw their children into rivers or abandon them by the roadside, thinking they would be a hindrance or a burden in flight.

Dispirited and exhausted, we could soon think of nothing but a place to lie down and sleep. Somehow we finally escaped from the mob, re-boarded our boat, and headed in the direction of the Inchon offing.

Before long, we ran out of food and drinking water. Our eyes became lifeless and glazed over. My sole belonging, an empty rucksack, was all the bedding I had at night.

Life on the boat was a living hell. With parched throats and no water, we drank our own urine. People who could not urinate fought to drink the urine of others who could. Now it all seems so repellant, but at the time we were too desperate to be either ashamed or disgusted.

After a while the boat began rocking back and forth unexplainably. Then someone cried out that we were in the midst of a school of sharks. The sharks, to our utter horror, were trying to capsize the boat.

The captain of the boat said that we would have to give the sharks something to eat to appease them. But of course we had nothing to give them. The group leader thought about the matter for a while, and then announced that we would start out by throwing the seriously ill into the sea, one at a time. These sick people, though terribly weak, fought back desperately when it came their turn to be thrown overboard.

There was no pity. When it became a question of life or death, even people who till then had sat amiably talking to one another thought ultimately only of themselves. After the deed was done, the four or five people who had finally succeeded in pushing a struggling sick man into the sea collapsed in the boat and prayed.

After a while the sharks came back. Only a person who has actually experienced such wretchedness can really understand it. In that small boat, terrorized by everything happening around me, I wept bitterly and called out to my mother for help. We all prayed, unable to look each other in the face because we dreaded to see who the group leader would choose to be the next victim.

One by one the weakest were thrown into the sea. In the midst of this, a good friend of mine who was frail and tubercular died of shock. She too was throw over the side. By then I had fallen into a daze.

Then the time came to sacrifice the children. The sharks had to be kept from coming close to the boat, and children could be thrown farther out. The sacrifice of a five-year-old was the most pathetic. The child cried in terror, and the mother begged that it be spared, but all to no avail. The child was snapped up by a huge shark before it landed in the water. The mother fell unconscious.

These indescribable horrors were repeated until, ten days after our departure, we were reduced to half our original number. Then, one day someone called out, "Inchon! Inchon!" And we knew we were saved. All of a sudden the tension that had kept us going snapped, and we crumpled in the boat as if only half alive.

The Americans occupying the Inchon Harbor in South Korea immediately gave us rice gruel with kaoliang, a cup of bean-paste soup, and water. To this day I have never forgotten the taste of that food. This nourishment helped us recover a little from the nightmare of the boat trip.

At Inchon we were supposed to have met with the second and third fishing boats from the Yalu shore and then boarded a Japanese ship called the *Kōan-maru* for Japan. But the other boats never showed up. It was maddening to think how all of those people, longing to return to Japan, had probably been killed along the way or fallen victim to the sharks. When it was obvious that they were not coming, we joined other groups of people from different regions and sailed for Hakata, on the southern Japanese island of Kyushu. At last the day we had all dreamed of had arrived.

The moment we arrived at the harbor facilities, we were doused in DDT powder to kill the lice. My tears made two lines through the white powder on my face as I wept uncontrollably.

At the dormitory provided for returnees we were given a blanket and a thousand-yen note by the Relief Association. Then I set to ridding my cotton trousers of lice. On my first night in Japan, I was too excited and happy to sleep. Soon, however, I began to be concerned about Mother, Father, and my sister. I would sometimes go to the beach and call out their names, praying that they were safe.

The mothers who had lost their children went virtually insane. One had terrible dreams, repeatedly shouting out her baby's name in her sleep. During the day she would tear at the tatami matting on the floor and wail horribly. The mother who had suffocated her nursing baby stroked her now swollen breasts and insisted she heard a baby crying. Opening all the windows in the room, she would call for her child from each one of them. In this hellish world, where innocent mothers and children had to endure such horrible suffering, no one congratulated any one else on having managed to escape from death. Instead, people opened the floodgates that had dammed up the sorrow, suffering, and bitterness in their breasts and let it all flow forth in ceaseless tears.

Malnutrition made my bones stand out and puffed up my stomach. I could not walk properly and was soon moved from the dormitory to a hospital, where I underwent treatment for twenty days. During my

Repatriates from Manchuria arrive at Hakata, Kyushu.
Courtesy of Asahi Shinbun Publishing Co.

hospitalization the man who had been our group leader on the boat paid me a call. His face pale and haggard, he said he would never live down what he had done. Then he told me that I had just barely escaped, that if our arrival at Inchon had been delayed any longer, and if the sharks had attacked again, it was to have been my turn. Suddenly I couldn't stand to look at him any more. I pulled the bedcovers over my head and shrieked, "Get out!"

After being discharged from the hospital, I went to stay with a sister in Tokyo. In six months' time, Mother, Father, and my sister made us very happy by at last joining us.

For a long time, however, in my dreams or whenever I saw the brilliant black eyes of hungry war orphans on the streets of Tokyo, I relived the hell of that small fishing boat tossed on the sea off the Korean coast.

The Policy of Madmen
Mitsu Nakaue (67)

In June 1944 Osaka was being bombed heavily. Trailing white clouds behind them, B29s flew at all hours over our house in Totsugawa, Nara Prefecture, leading us to suspect that defeat might not be far off. At about this time I received orders from above to join a group of thirty-four girl students, who had been recruited from the sewing departments of various local high schools, and accompany them to Manchuria as part of a five-year agricultural development plan in what was called Patriotic Farming. A group of twenty-nine boys was also being sent, and three of us teachers were to be in charge of them.

For three nights I could not sleep for worrying about the trip. Finally, my father said, "It's for the sake of the homeland. It makes no matter where you die. So make up your mind, and go." Now that I have children of my own, I cannot imagine how he could have permitted me to go to Manchuria. Though he said it was all right since it was in the name of the homeland, I suspect he must have agonized over it. The parents of the children we were taking no doubt suffered much more. I now deeply regret my part in the whole matter.

We assembled at an inn in Nara on a gloomy day of the kind typical of the Japanese rainy season, but an air raid delayed our departure. Indeed, we encountered air raids everywhere along our land route and the danger of torpedo attacks on the sea. And it was a miracle that we ever reached Pusan, Korea. From there we traveled for four or five days to reach Manchuria. It was late June when we finally arrived at what was called the Totsugawa Pioneer Group in Zhalandong.

We immediately started work at the Patriotic Farm. Because I was physically weak, I had received a letter from our village headman saying that my work was to be confined to supervising the children. But five or six of the girls had come down with typhus fever on the way, reducing the number of our working force and making it necessary for me to take part in the planting. Working with the help of five or six horses in fields stretching as far as the eye could see, we enjoyed ourselves in planting potatoes and corn, and forgot all about the war. In our free time we went on excursions to a Shinto shrine and other places to look at the beautiful flowers that bloom in Manchuria.

But this peaceful way of life lasted only a short time. After about two months Russian aircraft were seen flying in Manchurian skies, a good indication that the Soviet Union was now in the war against Japan. Then one day, the group leader, another teacher, and I were summoned to the regional office and informed of Japan's defeat.

Evacuation orders were given, and preparations began immediately. The pioneering group killed their beloved horses, set fire to their homes, and abandoned the village they had labored so hard to develop. A group of more than three hundred and seventy, we set off silently for Zhalandong Station. As we walked, I couldn't help crying as anger and frustration welled up within me at this miserable turn of events.

Who would have dreamed that, only two months after we left home, we would meet such a fate? Sending a band of school children on an overseas service mission when defeat was practically a certainty seemed like the policy of madmen. Who was responsible for this war . . . ? But being angry and resentful was of no help at all in our present situation. My gloom was deepened by the sense of responsibility I felt for the twenty thousand yen I had been given when we left the camp, money that was to be used to care for the children until we returned to Japan.

Sighting Zhalandong Station in the distance, we felt a tremendous sense of relief. But this feeling was soon betrayed as we heard the whistle of the last evacuation train, which was leaving without us. Not knowing what to do, we lost our way and wandered here and there at the mercy of bandits and mounted thieves. One by one, people fell from enemy bullets. And finally we were convinced it was all over with us when we encountered a front-line Russian tank.

For a while we felt we would all probably die on foreign ground. But our group leader negotiated with the Russians, who said they would spare our lives if we abandoned our weapons and surrendered. We agreed and, raising our hands over our heads, gave ourselves up.

Each morning at the Zhalandong Concentration Camp, we left the camp for work before dawn. Guards nudged with rifles anyone who stopped working to rest, shouting, "*Davai*, get back to work!"

We were responsible for a group of young girls who were just coming of age; and the nights were the most frightening because each evening the Russians came demanding women. After long deliberation our top leader ordered the girls to shave their head and put on mens clothes. "To protect themselves, women of the past burnt their faces with hot iron chopsticks. Cutting off your hair is nothing," he said. "It'll grow back."

After some hesitation we teachers took the lead, and the girls followed suit. But even with our heads shaved, we did our best to hide at night in places where the Russians could not find us.

One night, however, we heard talking outside, and suddenly a rifle butt crashed through the glass panes of the door. A group of four Russians forced their way in. Most of us leapt up screaming and huddled in one corner of the room. But for some reason one girl didn't wake up, despite all the noise. The Russians grabbed her and quickly took her away. She wept and called out for help, but there was nothing we could do. The other teacher and I held each other and cried.

Two hours later the girl appeared in the doorway with an indescribable look on her face. We knew no way to console her. Before long this unfortunate girl died of cold and hunger. Back in Japan, when I returned her few possessions to her parents, I was at a loss for words and could only cry.

After two months of living in mortal dread, we were at last ordered

THE POLICY OF MADMEN

to move south to Qiqihaer, where cold and hunger combined with typhus to claim still more of our girls. With no medicine and no way of caring for them, we could only look on and try to make their last moments as comfortable as possible.

Four months after the defeat, orders came for us to move still farther south to Haerbin and Shenyang. Two other teachers went ahead with the strong girls, but I remained in Qiqihaer to look after the sick and weak. Though I did not suspect it then, my farewells with some of that group were to be our last words, for a number of them died of cold and hunger in Haerbin.

After a while I came down with typhus myself and ran a very high temperature for about two weeks. Apparently I was delirious the whole while. Out of pity for me and the students, some kind people looked after me. I was extremely grateful. But later many of them caught typhus and died.

Struggling everyday with cold and hunger, we nonetheless kept our spirits up by vowing to stay alive until we could see the cherry blossoms in Japan just one more time.

The people who had been official inhabitants of the pioneering camp in Manchuria had possessions they could sell to buy food. But we were only members of a service group with nothing to barter. Since several of us were sick, it was difficult to find the work we needed to survive. Just when I had become desperate enough to entertain the idea of mass suicide, a kind old man recommended that we make and sell cigarettes, and advanced us the capital for materials. I felt like a soul in hell who has unexpectedly been helped by a compassionate Buddha.

We immediately set to work making cigarettes with great enthusiasm. We invented names like *New Wealth* and *South Wind* for our products, which at first were irregular in size and not especially known for their flavor. Gradually, however, we became more skillful; and Manchurians began not only buying but also praising our work.

Just as our cigarette business was running smoothly and we had a little money, orders came for us to be sent home. Before making preparations, we went to the Japanese cemetery, where some of our girls were buried, to say good-bye. Of all the things I had done in that year, the hardest was to part with these students, who bravely left Japan to do their part for the homeland and ended their short lives on foreign soil. I bowed at each grave with a prayer for their peaceful repose, leaving them to sleep in the cold ground.

Reluctantly we returned to our concentration camp and began getting ready. Although only six of my group of girls were still alive and in good health, we were all happy to be going home again in two weeks time. As mementoes we took with us twenty packs of our cigarettes— ten each of *New Wealth* and *South Wind*.

But things didn't go according to plan, and bandits attacked our freight train at each station. When we reached Haru Island, I had another attack of typhus fever. I told the girls to go ahead, but they decided to stay with me. After several weeks I was strong enough for us to board a hospital ship for home.

Arriving in Japan, we embraced each other and wept when we saw a grove of golden persimmons framed by the deep-blue November sky.

Philippine Death Diary

Sueno Ōkita (65)

It was in January 1938 that I went to the island of Mindanao in the Philippines to join my husband, who was a young businessman. Not long thereafter diplomatic relations between the Philippines and Japan began to deteriorate, and attacks on Japanese by Philippine locals grew more frequent. No doubt, the people around us also sensed the growing tension between Japan and the United States.

Following the directions of the Association of Japanese Citizens, I prepared emergency packages of clothes and food. But we were all convinced that, even should war break out, the Japanese army would land on the islands at once to establish a base of operations. We might have two or three bad weeks to put up with, but there was no doubt in our minds about Japanese victory.

The situation we had feared came all too soon on December 8 (December 7 in the United States), 1941. It was about three in the afternoon that day when Mr. Abe of the Magoppo Branch of the Ōta Company rushed into our house, bringing news of the attack on Pearl Harbor and the declaration of war against the United States and England. Before leaving, he told me to prepare for evacuation, that he would return for me in an hour. All Japanese were to assemble at the Ōta Company and to coordinate their activities. At once I sent word of the crisis to my husband and the people working for us who were out on the plantation.

When Mr. Abe came back, my husband was paying the wages of our hired Philippine help. He told them to use all the food and fuel on the place but not to do anything wrong. The Japanese army was certain to land on the islands, and it would go hard for anyone discovered misbehaving. Finally he told them that we ourselves would be back in a week or two. All of our servants wept and entreated us to come back soon. With a change of clothes and a little food, my husband, two sons, and I set out on foot for the designated meeting place.

On the way, however, we were stopped by a government truck carrying a man who was apparently an official and some soldiers in civilian clothes. Though my husband explained in Filipino where we were going and why, the soldiers swung their bolo knives over their heads and told us to shut up and get on the truck.

Driving through the dark with no idea of our destination, we were resigned to die if we could all die together. After fifty or sixty kilometers the truck stopped, and we were ordered off at the gate to a primary school. Philippine soldiers searched us thoroughly. From me they took a valuable ring, but they missed the money my husband had concealed in the sole of one of his shoes. Finally, together with many other Japanese in the same predicament, we bedded down on the school sports field, completely exhausted, and slept throughout the dewy night.

On the following day the men were separated from the women and children and taken away. Where, we did not know. We women and children were taken to a Japanese primary school at Davao. Every morning and evening we were given two or three tablespoons of food, usually soybeans. Shut up in the heat of a small room and hungry most of the time, the children soon grew weak. Some of them eventually died, and their bodies were thrown into the sea. There was enough room for the children to lie down, but the small space was so crowded that adults could only sit, day and night.

At about two o'clock on the morning of December 20, we heard a strange sound from Davao Gulf. It was a Japanese aircraft carrier entering the bay. At dawn, when I went out into the playground to wash my child's diapers, I saw a formation of planes overhead. On their wings was the red circle of the Japanese flag. I was so happy that I waved the diapers I was carrying. But almost immediately I heard the shrill notes of a whistle. We were ordered inside, and guards were set to watch us. Windows and doors were shut, and we were not allowed out of the room even to get a drink of water or go to the toilet. Hungry and suffering from the heat, the children cried and wailed. And the stench from the urine and excrement on the floor made breathing difficult. When we could stand it no longer, we opened a window, only to find Philippine guards standing outside with their rifles trained on us. We quickly shut the window again. This was repeated several times.

We could hear the sound of an air battle raging overhead and the shelling of the shore in preparation for a Japanese landing. As we were listening to these sounds, machine-gun bullets burst through the walls of the room and sent us scrambling in the filth covering the floor. Some of us thought the end had come and bitterly felt the irony of the situation, Japanese citizens being fired on by the Japanese military.

Finally, no longer able to stand the suffocating stench, we opened a window, ignoring the fact we might be shot, and found to our amazement and delight that our armed Philippine guards were no longer there. We dashed out and drank our fill of the fresh air and the water from a nearby tank. We had eaten nothing since the night before, but the air and water restored our spirits.

In the evening, a fire in a nearby town that had been started by the Japanese began to move in our direction. Listening to its fearsome crackling, we were at a loss what to do until four or five of our men came for us.

We set off down the road toward our own settlement. The men cautioned us to keep together because a long drawn-out line would provide easy targets for the Philippine soldiers still in the area. Although we did as instructed, a number of people were wounded anyway. Finally, however, we reached our settlement, entered the primary school building there, and fell exhausted on the wooden floors.

At first relieved at reaching safety, we were suddenly called back to reality by an air battle being fought in the night sky directly above us. Aircraft from our side and from theirs burst into flames and plummeted to earth in balls of fire.

One by one, husbands came for their wives and children. Because my husband did not appear that night, I was unable to sleep. He finally came the next morning, however, telling the story of how he had escaped being bombed by Japanese planes when he held up an improvised Japanese flag made of pieces of white and red cloth.

We managed to stay alive on rations of thin gruel, but my nineteen-month-old son, Katsuji, who had been strong enough to walk and run when only ten months old, grew steadily weaker. Now unable to walk at all, he wasn't even strong enough to hold his head up straight.

Because of the many years my husband had lived in the Philippines and his extensive knowledge of the terrain, he was recruited by the military to help round up straggling Philippine soldiers, and so was constantly being sent to the front lines. Often, as he set out on a patrol, he would laughingly say to me, "The next time you see me I may be a corpse."

The brilliant Japanese victories at Bataan and Corregidor in March 1942 had demanded immense sacrifices, as had the capture of Mindanao. When we returned to Magoppo, we found our factory burned to the ground. The corn we had planted had grown about thirty centimeters, but Filipinos had occupied our house. Since our position was far from secure, we Japanese lived together as a group. My husband was sent about sixteen kilometers inland from Magoppo as part of a military patrol. His being in constant danger kept me worried and anxious.

In July 1944 the Americans began shelling and raiding Davao in order to recapture Mindanao. Black smoke poured into the sky for hours after the Americans struck the Japanese airfield at Sasa. Realizing that our retreat might be cut off by American shelling, and also that Philippine army stragglers were becoming more numerous as American power increased, my husband and I decided to move closer to the city of Davao. Four people from our house—my husband, our sons Katsuji and Shigenobu, and our maid Kimiko—joined a group of other people.

On the way we had to be particularly vigilant about airplanes, for they would often come down to strafe us. On one occasion we were forced to take refuge in a field of wild roses, whose thorns left our hands and legs covered with blood. Once we got a ride in a Japanese military truck, and ended up crawling under it when we were attacked by an American plane.

Near the Japanese airfield at Sasa the American aircraft dominated the skies; not a single Japanese plane was to be seen. We made it safely to military headquarters, but the army would do nothing for us. We were further disappointed to find that the food shortage prevented one of my husband's friends—the man we had counted on—from helping us. Finally, we took refuge with the family of a man named Nagao, who worked in the military pharmacy, and somehow managed to survive on a few sweet potatoes from his garden.

Then, in May 1945, the long-dreaded American offshore shelling began, forcing us to flee into the mountains. In the foothills we came under fire from Philippine soldiers, and many Japanese were wounded. Drenched by occasional tropical squalls and always hungry, we were forced to drink water from muddy streams and were overjoyed to discover a single eggplant. By the time we reached the base of some nearby mountains, we were totally exhausted.

After we had slept on the ground, my husband managed to find about ten raw potatoes. We brushed off the dirt with our hands and immediately began gnawing on them. It turned out that when the local people had descended from the mountains after the Japanese army had arrived, they had left behind some potatoes and a few other things to eat. That night I boiled some of the sweet potatoes, and we had our first cooked food for a long time.

By the time we began climbing the mountains, our number had fallen to about half. At one of our camps a certain Mr. Shimabukuro, from Okinawa, started digging a bomb shelter, which he said we could all use together. Then, unexpectedly, some planes attacked us that very night. When it was over, my husband called out in the dark to see if everyone was all right. Mr. Shimabukuro didn't answer. It was forbidden to use a light at night, but this was an emergency, so someone lit a candle. Mr. Shimabukuro lay dead at the entrance to the bomb shelter.

Deciding that this area of the mountains was still too dangerous, we climbed up to the eleven-kilometer point. There we made a shelter by stretching a blanket over some sticks and spreading a grass mat on the ground. When squalls soaked the blanket, we had only our body heat to dry it out.

Though my husband suffered from malaria and was extremely weak, we had to go on. During our march we often came across dead Japanese soldiers, their bodies covered with maggots and giving off a terrible stench in the tropical heat.

Not long afterward about twenty Japanese soldiers climbed to where we were and upbraided us for not being further inland. The American front line had already advanced to the eight-kilometer position, they said, and then they started on their way. At the sight of soldiers abandoning noncombatants like us, I replied with a good deal of sarcasm: "Oh, you soldiers have no one to look after but yourselves, so you can go where you please. People like us with children and sick people can't move as freely as you can. But go ahead and leave us. We have a hand grenade and can always take our own lives!"

That night I told my husband that I did not want to die away from all the other Japanese on the island and suggested we try to find some of our countrymen. But he said that since there was no hope for him anyway, Kimiko and I should take our sons and continue on. He would remain where he was and die alone. Of course, I could do no such thing, even though I knew he wouldn't last much longer.

A couple of days after that, I went in search of salt at a place where fighting had been heavy, near the American front lines. Weeping all the while and praying that what I did would enable us to stay alive a bit longer, I took things from the bodies of the four or five Japanese soldiers I found lying there. From the shoes of one I found an obviously treasured handful of uncooked rice. In the pocket of another, wrapped in a piece of newspaper, I found some salt. Knowing I could be shot at any moment, and aware of the folly of being killed without taking back to my children and husband the salt for which I was risking my life, I started hurrying back.

But I had gone only a short way when I came upon two Japanese soldiers in white orderly uniforms lying abandoned on stretchers. One of them called out to me. I approached and saw that he was an officer too wounded to walk. The other one was an enlisted man whose entire body was so swollen that his eyes were mere slits. The officer handed me a canteen and asked me to get him some water, which he and his wounded comrade would drink in the ceremonial farewell toast Japanese exchange at moments of hopelessness or mortal peril. Although I was worried about my own family and did not want to lose the time it would take to find water in the mountains, I could not refuse. It was difficult, but finally I found a little water trickling from some rocks and collected enough to cover the bottom of the canteen. I asked the officer his name as I handed him the water, but he was ashamed to tell me, saying only that he had been assigned to the Shirai Engineers. Then, after asking my name, he said that he and the other soldier would soon drink the water and die, but that they both prayed that I, who had done so much for them, would live to see Japan again. As I walked away, I remembered having been invited to the completion ceremonies of a new bridge constructed by the Shirai Engineers.

Before I had gone far, another seriously wounded soldier stopped me. He had a rope in his hand and asked me to find a water buffalo that had strayed off. I tried to refuse on the grounds that I had never handled water buffaloes before and was afraid of them. But, once again, the soldier pleaded, so I agreed to do what he asked. Not far away, in grass taller than my own height, I found the buffalo. Once I had tied the rope around its horns, it followed me docilely.

The soldier climbed on the water buffalo's back, handed me the rope, and told me to lead. Still apprehensive about my husband and children, I nonetheless did as he asked. But after we had gone only about a hundred meters, the soldier climbed down from the water buffalo and said that he would give it to me. He walked off in the opposite direction, dragging his feet. Wondering what I should do with such a large animal, I led it back to the place where my family waited.

That night American planes discovered the bamboo thicket where a number of starving Japanese soldiers and we civilians had gathered to eat the new bamboo shoots. The thicket was strafed and set afire, and small gravellike objects flew through the air to hit us painfully in the face. The roar of the burning thicket was so awful that my whole body began to tremble.

The next morning I pleaded with my husband once again to continue on to the fourteen-kilometer mark, but he refused. I then told Kimiko, our maid, who was with us and whose mother had been a Filipina, to go and turn herself over to the Americans; they would certainly help her. We would remain and see things through to the end, and if the worse came to worst, we had a hand grenade and were ready to commit suicide. But Kimiko said she preferred to stay and die with us. Kimiko's father, a native of Toyama Prefecture, was a victim of the war. After his uncle's suicide, he became neurotic. His Filipina wife and the mother of his three children died before the war started. Kimiko's father died without ever seeing Japan again. Upon his death, my husband and I took custody of Kimiko, who lived with us as a maid.

It seemed that our final hour had come. My husband was about to remove the safety pin from the hand grenade when, suddenly remembering my mother's face, I shouted out for him to stop. "Women are cowards!" he said weakly. "No," I said. "It's not cowardice. Mother told us to come home alive. As long as we have the hand grenade, we can commit suicide any time we like. But there's still hope now." I wrested the grenade from his hand and told him to get on the water buffalo. We would go as far as we could. Though he objected, I got him on the animal's back, and we started up the mountain path.

On the way, we passed a place where enemy attacks had been particularly heavy. From a heap of wood chips a badly burned, completely naked little girl—only her voice made it clear she was a girl—cried out weakly for us to take her along with us. She said her mother and father, their luggage, and their water buffalo had been burned. I could see the charred remains not far away. I felt very sorry for her, but in her condition, and with my weak husband and small sons to care for, it was an impossible situation. It grieved me to do it, but I deliberately lied and said I would come back for her later.

Enemy reconnaissance planes continued to buzz overhead. Completely exhausted, I finally lowered my husband from the back of the water buffalo and gathered the children around me in the dark. I dozed till dawn, when I found myself sitting on what appeared to be a handmade gravestone in a cemetery.

There was smoke from a campfire rising nearby, and I discovered there two or three soldiers cooking a meager mixture of rice, water, and grasses in their mess kits. After they told me where to find the grass, I gathered some and made a soup for everyone with some of the salt I had left over. Locating edible plants in the sunless jungle was so difficult that it was obvious that both civilians and soldiers would soon starve if the war continued much longer.

Once again, with my husband riding the water buffalo, we started out for the fourteen-kilometer point. But we had gone only about a hundred meters when the animal bogged down in some mire. The more it tried to extricate itself, the deeper it sank, until it could no longer move. This was all the more disheartening since our next destination was not far away. Helping my husband dismount, I supported him as we started haltingly on our way. We had gone only a few meters when we came upon about twenty soldiers who asked me to give them the water buffalo. They wanted to kill it for meat. Although I felt obliged to the animal that had carried my husband so far, I consented on the condition that they would give us some of the meat.

We walked on to the fourteen-kilometer point and found there a log-floored, grass-thatched hut apparently built by soldiers. It provided adequate protection from the rain, and the water of the nearby valley stream was clean. Once the family was settled there, I hurried back to find that the soldiers had already slaughtered the water buffalo. Greedily I demanded as much as I could carry on my back. I shared the meat with some of the other people back at the hut and bartered other pieces for corn. Once again the water buffalo had come to our rescue.

Two or three days later all of the people who had been there when we arrived, except the Nakamura family, had either moved farther on or had died of malnutrition.

Four days after our arrival, on July 15, 1945, my husband breathed his last. He had commented on how good the water tasted that our five-year-old boy, Shigenobu, had given to him in a spoon. Just five minutes before his death, he asked for some more water. Shigenobu and I both gave him some. Already by that time his eyesight had failed. Perhaps it was because he had grown so terribly weak that he gave no sign of pain when he died. He had a quiet look on his face.

He lost both his life and everything he had laboriously built up in the years since he arrived in the Philippines in 1927. About a year before the war broke out, he had decided to sell our land and return to live quietly in Japan. But what with the deterioration of relations between Japan and the United States at the time, a buyer was difficult to find. Dead at the early age of forty-one, he had failed to fulfill his dream of being a success in the Philippines and then returning to Japan.

With Mrs. Nakamura's help, I wrapped my husband's body in a blanket and placed him between two boulders on the banks of the stream. Covering him with branches and leaves, I asked his forgiveness for not doing more, but added that this was better than being abandoned to maggots by the roadside. I then resolved to stay by his side for a week.

On the fourth day, my oldest boy, Mrs. Nakamura, and I were sitting together when an enemy shell bounced off a tree and exploded as it hit a boulder not far away. I immediately grabbed the children and rushed inside the hut, expecting Mrs. Nakamura to follow. But apparently fragments from the explosion had gone past me and hit her where she sat behind me. When Mrs. Nakamura called my name, I shouted that she must hurry indoors: the next shell might come at any moment. When she didn't come, I went out and found her lying on her back, paralyzed. Undressing her, I saw that a triangular piece of shrapnel had stuck in her back. Though I pulled it out easily, she remained paralyzed. I dragged her indoors, only to discover that my younger son, Katsuji, had been hit in the right knee by shrapnel. I gave him the best first aid I could, but in the jungle there was little to be done.

Before long, Mrs. Nakamura was unable to speak and merely lay there, not saying a word, her eyes closed. Her two children never moved from her side and ate nothing until, three days later, their mother died.

The next day I returned from gathering papaya roots to hear Katsuji ask Kimiko for some water. Rushing to his side, I found him looking up with a smile on his face. He swallowed a little water and then, still smiling, died. It was almost as if he had been waiting for my return. Perhaps his father had called to him from the world beyond. In less than ten days, I had lost my husband and a son. Wrapping Katsuji in our last blanket, I carried him to the boulders beside the stream and laid him at his father's side.

The following day, one of five or six soldiers who had climbed to our position along the river bank refused to accompany his companions any further. He said he could not take another step. After the other soldiers had left, he suddenly shouted out that I should move at least ten meters away, and then he pulled out a grenade. My son, Shigenobu, grabbed me by the hand and screamed that we had to run, that the soldier was going to commit suicide. When we had gotten about ten meters away, the grenade exploded. I went back to find the soldier's intestines floating in the stream.

I made up my mind that we couldn't stay there any longer and decided to move on to the seventeen-kilometer point. At first there were three of us—Shigenobu, Kimiko, and I—but before long Kimiko had dropped behind. We never saw her again. All the way we heard the roar of exploding artillery shells. And once the noise was so great that, convinced this was our final moment, I pulled Shigenobu under me, covered my ears, shut my eyes, and waited for an explosion that, surprisingly, never came. Opening my eyes and looking around, I saw that the shell had landed on a heap of leaves and vines, and was simply smoking and hissing like sparkler fireworks. Once again we had been saved.

Though Shigenobu was only a small child, at the fourteen-kilometer point he witnessed something so terrible that he couldn't forget it. During the night of our arrival there, we heard something that sounded like the explosion of a hand grenade. Supposing it to be another soldier's suicide, the next morning we went in the direction of the sound and found something quite different. A group of people had banded together, amassing a fair store of food. But Japanese soldiers in search of something to eat demanded that the food be handed over to them. "What right have you to all that when there's not enough even to feed wounded soldiers?" they asked. When the civilians were reluctant to comply, the soldiers tossed a hand grenade among them, killing one and wounding two, then stole the food. Nothing could better illustrate what war does to people.

When we reached the seventeen-kilometer point, a sunny spot by a wide stream, Shigenobu sat down for a while on the bank to play with some stones. Suddenly, however, he went pale and rushed to me with the warning that a Japanese soldier was coming and that he would take away our salt. He had remembered what had happened to the Japanese civilians who refused to give up their food.

On August 13, as I was out searching for grasses to eat, an American reconnaissance plane spotted me and dived. "At last, the time has come," I thought. But the plane flew away without doing anything.

The next day we found leaflets dropped by the Americans. Written in large letters in Japanese, they said it was only a matter of time before Japan would surrender unconditionally to the Allies. On the fifteenth we found some other leaflets, this time addressed to the Japanese army and bearing a photograph of a Japanese soldier, with his eyes blacked over to conceal his identity, eating what seemed to be curry and rice. The text, in Japanese, said the Empire of Japan had surrendered unconditionally to the Allies and urged soldiers to give themselves up instead of battling with malaria germs in the jungles. The leaflets promised good food and clean quarters. Still other leaflets were addressed to civilians: "You are noncombatants. Come out of the hills, and we will protect you. The war is over!"

At first I doubted what I read. But then, considering the situation, I realized that the shelling had stopped and the airplanes had disappeared. More than any emotion related to defeat, I was simply relieved not to have to hide from the shelling anymore. If we stayed in the mountains, however, we would starve. So I made up my mind to go down. But the Americans had bombed the bridge across the river to prevent Japanese soldiers from fleeing inland. This meant we would have to cross a dangerous stream flooded by recent squalls. I sought out the shallowest place I could find. Then, with Shigenobu on my shoulders and a stick to measure the depth as best I could, I took our lives in my hands and started across.

We made it safely, and at the eight-kilometer point I found a quiet stream where I could wash my clothes, hiding my nakedness with a towel. When my outer garments dried, I washed my underclothes. These few pieces of clothing were all I owned. I had long ago thrown away my shoes, since they were only a nuisance in the jungle. Finally, I threw away a few long-cherished photographs.

As I was doing all this, some American soldiers found me. Frightened at first, I put my hands over my head in a gesture of surrender, and the Americans came to where we were. One of them smiled as he picked up Shigenobu, and that made me feel much better.

They took us to the American lines at the eight-kilometer point, where we had our first real food in a long time. After we had eaten bread and milk and had been given malaria injections, we were put on a truck and taken to the prisoner-of-war camp on the Talomobang shore. On the way Philippine children threw stones at us. A camp for civilians had been prepared next to the prisoner-of-war camp. When we arrived there, I learned that a number of people had given themselves up before the war ended. Perhaps we would have come out of the mountains sooner if the Japanese soldiers had not told us to flee farther into the forest.

The Americans were kind to us. After a physical examination showed I needed treatment, I was taken to another camp and given two bottles of intravenous glucose a day. I was allowed to keep Shigenobu with me.

At about that time, an acquaintance entered the camp and congratulated me on having made it through safely. When I told her I had lost my husband and one son, she said almost hysterically: "You're lucky; yours died. I had to kill two of mine." She, her very weak husband, and their four children were coming down from the mountains when they reached a swollen river. She didn't think they could all ford it safely, so she decided to help her husband and two older children and to kill the two youngest, a boy and girl who were twins and just three years old—the age at which children are most charming.

Lining up the two and making them promise to obey her, she cooked the little rice they had left and gave it to the children, who ate it gladly.

First she threw the little boy into the river. When she was about to throw the girl in, the child cried out, "Mama, I promise to be good and do what you tell me. But please don't throw me in. Please don't." But the woman closed her eyes, and threw the girl in too. Calls for help rose from the river as the child, floating face up, was swept away.

"I'll be tormented by those words the rest of my life," the mother said. "And I only tell people the story to try, in some small way, to make up for what I've done." But there was not the slightest hint of consolation in her eyes.

War had driven her mad. Still I could to some extent understand a mother who was willing to sacrifice two of her children to save the rest of the family. I had seen many parentless children abandoned and wandering aimlessly in the mountains.

We got rice gruel every morning and evening in the camp, and the children were happy to have mid-afternoon snacks of raisins and dried apricots. I was so thin that lying on my back made my tailbone sore and kept me awake, but I was mentally alert.

Later it was rumored that the American troops who landed in October would take us back to Japan. I had very mixed feelings at the news. Of course, I was happy, but I was ashamed too. Even if the war was to blame, I was unhappy to have to return with nothing but what I had on my back. At the same time, I didn't expect they would let me stay in the Philippines for very long. To tell the truth, I had never thought I would see Japan again. Of the nine Japanese who had lived in our house on Mindanao, only Shigenobu and I were still alive.

We were scheduled to be repatriated on a Japanese coastal-defense ship on October 20. It was so stifling hot on the ship that, during the fourteen-day voyage, many of the physically weakened children on board died. But my son and I arrived safely at Kajiki Bay in Kagoshima Prefecture, Kyushu, on November 3.

Peace after Wandering

Anonymous (52)

During most of the first half of my life of wandering from place to place, it would never have occurred to me that I might someday have the leisure to sit down after cleaning up the dishes and drink a cup of coffee while I wrote down some of my memories, as I am doing now.

I was born in 1930 in a fishing village on Hokkaido. My father, who was an enterprising man, operated seven different lodgings for construction workers and made it possible for me to have a happy childhood. In 1941, in connection with father's work, we moved to the Kitanayoshi coal mines on the west coast of Karafuto (Sakhalin), where we lived comfortably until World War II started.

Before long all the miners were drafted or called away to do military-related work in places like Fukushima and Yamagata prefectures. Father too was taken. In fact, practically no one but the elderly and children remained. At fifteen, I worked in the mine offices, handling the telephone and other routine work and helping with designs. Everyone in the family pitched in to do the work, and our mother, a strong and reliable woman, provided the leadership.

But Mother, who suffered from high blood pressure, died suddenly in July 1945, while Father was away. We got in touch with him, but it was impossible for him to get a boat at the time. He did not return until ten days after Mother's death.

At about this time, the Soviet Union declared war on Japan and began bombing Karafuto. Every night we went to bed fully dressed and wearing our air-raid headgear. The walls of our office were riddled with holes from practicing with the bamboo spears that were to be used in case the Soviet army landed. Everyone was in a constant state of gloom and uneasiness.

As the bombing grew more intense, we had word that the Soviet army had landed. Taking some blankets and what little food we could, we fled into the mountains about eight kilometers away. There were no men with us.

No words can describe what we went through in our flight. We knew we would all be killed if caught. Mothers who had to care for nursing babies could not keep up with the group, and gradually began throwing them into valleys or abandoning them by the roadside so that they could save the older, more independent children. This kind of thing occurred again and again in a kind of chain reaction. The actions of these cruel and pitiless women vividly show how extremes of danger can rob human beings of rational thought and allow the ego to run wild.

As protection against being molested, young women wore men's clothes and rubbed soot on their faces. We dug up tree roots to eat and drank river water. After about twenty days of this, we heard one day of Japan's unconditional surrender, which aroused in us complex feelings of sorrow at defeat and relief that the fighting was over.

I can still see the grief and horror on the faces of those women who had abandoned their nursing babies a few days earlier. Having coldly thought of nothing but escape, they were now suddenly driven nearly mad with remorse and tried to return and find their children. But, in spite of their frantic searching, not a single baby was found alive.

The Soviet troops were now in the mountains where we had fled. At first sight of them, I shuddered with fear, a reaction that turned out to be an omen of the course that much of the rest of my life would take. About thirty of them, armed with rifles and speaking a language we could not understand, stood on either side of the road as we passed along. My body shook from head to foot.

Back at home, the first thing I did was to lock the door, and then I called the local barber. I asked him to cut my hair and the hair of the other girls with me in a masculine style. Thereafter, we all wore men's clothes, but still were unable to conceal our gender.

At the office we Japanese worked under two or three Russians stationed in each department. When the fall harvest and the spring planting times came, we all took part. Once I stayed in the country for a week to help with the reaping.

It was then that a Soviet soldier raped me. I was sixteen at the time and shall never forget it. I was too terrified to cry out. Not long after I realized that I was pregnant.

My kind mother, to whom I might have turned, was dead. And I couldn't tell my father and sisters what had happened. My life became a living hell. I tried strenuous exercise to no effect. I had heard that drinking a lot of soy sauce would cause a miscarriage, but it only gave me a fever and made breathing difficult. I tried cold baths, but that didn't work either. My days of solitary agony dragged on.

Thinking I would make amends to Father and my sisters, I sometimes contemplated suicide. Nonetheless, in the fall of 1947, at the age of seventeen, I gave birth to a red-haired son. People looked askance at me and talked behind my back, but Father worked as hard as he could for me and his grandson. Our situation wasn't too bad as long as the boy was just a baby. When he began to toddle around, however, people turned very chilly toward us.

In 1948 the time came for us to leave Karafuto for good. In those days, old-fashioned, feudalistic ideas were still prevalent in Japan. How could I take a child of mixed blood there? My son and I had no choice but to suffer what was heaped on us, but I did not want to be a source of humiliation to Father and my sisters. I made up my mind to part from the rest of the family and remain on Karafuto. But Father persuaded me to give up the idea. He impressed on me the strong bond between parent and child, saying he would take the two of us with him to Japan even if he had to tie a rope around our necks and drag us there. I am still grateful to him for his love.

Some of the passengers on the boat were too ill to travel, but they made a supreme effort so as not to be left behind and perhaps never see Japan again. A number of them died with the shores of Hokkaido before their eyes.

My bitter history began when we settled down with relatives in a coal-mining town on Hokkaido. We stayed with my uncle, who was generally a taciturn man. But perhaps because he could not tolerate the criticism heaped on him for harboring a woman who had brought home a child of mixed blood, he sometimes got drunk and abused us, doing such things as tearing up the tatami mats in the room where we slept.

The upshot of all this was that we could no longer stay with our relatives. Father took my younger sister and went to work in a village some distance away. My older sister found work in a place that would board her. Deciding to live alone with my son, I started a life of wandering.

I found all kinds of jobs—in construction camps and fishing villages, at a livestock broker's, in noodle shops, and so on—and always did the best I could, though I was only a seventeen-year-old girl with a half-breed baby living among rough men. I was so busy that I had no time to feel sorry for myself.

Like a gypsy, I went where I heard work was available. Once I cooked in a remote construction camp where there was not a house for miles around. I remember a kind old woman there who encouraged me.

I was young and, as is to be expected, men approached me. Some even proposed marriage, but no matter how hard a worker I was, they changed their minds when they saw that I was what was commonly considered a tainted woman with a half-breed for a child.

After seven years, during which I changed jobs ten times, a man came along who said he didn't object to my son. He introduced me to his parents and younger sister, and we were married. At last I was able to enjoy some ordinary human happiness. By the time my son was in primary school, I had already born my husband two daughters. A short-tempered, rough man, he let the girls have whatever they wanted but was unduly severe with my son.

In his third and fourth years of primary school, the boy was at the age when children most love to play. But if he came home from school even a little late, his step-father refused to let him eat supper. Sometimes, after a scolding, the boy would run away. I secretly told him to hide in the storehouse and not to go where people might tease and make fun of him. In my heart I completely sympathized with him.

In those days in Japan, sweets were relatively rare. Once, when my husband was deliberately eating some cakes in front of the boy but offering him none, my son said, "When I grow up, I'm going to buy all the cakes I want and eat my fill of them." I could barely hold back the tears. This scene remains vivid in my mind's eye even today. Filled with sorrow and anger, there was nothing I could do but think how different things would have been if the war had not taken place.

Not long after my second daughter was born, my husband took up with another women, left us, and stopped sending money. We were reduced to eating little more than soup made of the leaves of the *daikon* radish. My son must have felt guilty because he once asked me if he were the reason why I could marry only a man like his step-father. I tried to console him by saying that the cause of the trouble between my husband and me had been, not him, my son, but my own stubborn independence. I got a divorce not long afterward.

I made up my mind not to part with the children, no matter how hard things got. The struggle to survive taught me the hard art of economizing. For instance, at the construction camp kitchen, scorched rice often remained in the bottoms of the pots, and I would scrape the grains out, dry them, and make gruel of them at home.

Throughout all my suffering, my red-haired, mixed-blood son, who suffered with me, was my salvation. He grew straight in body and mind. Getting up at three in the morning, he delivered milk and newspapers to buy mufflers for his sisters. But the warmth with which he enveloped all of us was more heartening than any gift he could give. I am deeply grateful to him.

At the age of thirty-six I met the kind man who is now my husband and who has loved and cared for all my children just as tenderly as he has for the children I have born him.

My son, who is now thirty-six himself, is a considerate, generous young man on whom his new step-father and his step-sisters all rely. He manages his own business in Tokyo and employs a large number of people. Now, thirty-nine years after the end of the war, I know peace of mind at last.

My red-haired son made it possible for me to triumph over the cruel fate that war thrust on me. Now, looking with affection on my children and grandchildren, I realize all the more poignantly the preciousness of daily life in a peaceful world and the need to prevent war and the misery it causes.

A child repatriated from Korea receives a dose of DDT. Courtesy of Mainichi Newspapers.

PEACE AFTER WANDERING

WOMEN WHO
STRIVE TO
HEAL

Nursing, Fleeing, Hiding

Tsuruko Matsuda (61)

I was born in Kitami Mombetsu, Hokkaido, the seventh daughter in a family of ten children. It was a beautiful place, deep in the mountains. When the snows thawed in spring, first the brilliant yellow flowers called pheasant's eyes burst into bloom, then one by one the white *kobushi*, wild azaleas, and the cherry blossoms. The song of the cuckoo echoed throughout the hills. The fish called *yamabe* swam in the streams, and trout and salmon came up the rivers to spawn.

When I graduated from high school in 1941, I was assigned, with the help of my older brother who was in Manchuria, to the Xian Prefectural Nurses' Training School. My spirits were high as I took my first train ride on the initial leg of my journey to Manchuria. Without having been seasick even during the storm that struck as we crossed the Genkai Sea, off the shores of Kyushu, I arrived at my destination nine days after leaving Hokkaido.

For the first three years I devoted myself wholeheartedly to my nursing studies and to learning the Manchurian language. Then, in 1943, I was assigned to the internal medical department of the Kaiyuan Prefectural Hospital.

The next two years or so were spent working happily, but then, as the war grew more intense, my own situation began to change. On March 2, 1945, I suddenly received a telegram from Hokkaido reporting the death of my father. Next I received word that my older brother, who had been transferred to North China, had died in battle. He had been killed by the Eighth Route Army on the same day that Father had died.

Told to report to my dead brother's duty station at once, I set out for North China, but marauders at the Manchurian border forced me to turn back. Finally in early June of that same year, I traveled to Shenyang Station accompanied by two soldiers, and there I was given an urn containing my brother's ashes.

In the meanwhile the war continued to escalate. One day a Manchurian surgeon told me of the "honorable defeat" that had occurred on an island called Attu. When I said I didn't know the meaning of "honorable defeat," he explained that all the Japanese soldiers on the island had been killed to the last man. He went to say that the Japanese news media told nothing but lies, and that since Japan was certain to be defeated, I ought to return to Hokkaido as quickly as I could. He finished by advising me to listen to the night Beijing-Chinese newscasts. But I only got angry and refused to believe what he said, and thereafter avoided him whenever I could.

At the time, none of us considered the possibility of defeat. But we soon began thinking differently when B29s raided the Anshan Steel Works, and then when the Japanese army unit stationed behind the hospital was ordered to move south.

In early August the order for us to evacuate was given. The luggage of staff families was prepared for transporting, but the doctors and nurses were ordered to stay behind and defend the hospital to the last.

By then all male Japanese except doctors had been drafted. The mood at the hospital was uneasy. The Manchurians, who till then had quietly followed orders, suddenly turned recalcitrant. They refused to do as they were asked, whispered among themselves in groups, and stole medicine from the dispensary. Nonetheless, the hospital had so many patients that we were kept busy every day.

On August 9, 1945, the Soviet Union entered the war, and Manchuria was transformed into a world of pillage, violence, and slaughter. Japanese women and children, in tattered clothes and completely exhausted, came flooding in, trying to escape from the advancing Soviet army. One pregnant woman, with a nursing baby strapped to her back, staggered into the hospital and immediately gave birth.

A few days later the Soviet army attacked the hospital. Taking some of the patients with me, I ran into the field of kaoliang behind our building. The field stretched practically as far as the eye could see. Soon a line of Soviet tanks began cutting across it, rolling over small Manchurian huts that happened to be in their way, raking the field with random machine-gun fire. One after another, people were struck and fell. The man next to me was hit by a bullet that entered his back and passed through his body, spraying his intestines out as it went. Afraid of giving us all away, he suffered in silence for about ten minutes before dying. Though we wanted to help, there was nothing we could do but watch him die. No words can describe the horror of that moment.

On August 15, the day the war ended, all of the Japanese hospital staff were ordered to move into the doctors' official residences. Since this meant we would have to part from the Manchurian, Korean, and other non-Japanese nurses, we planned a farewell dinner. As we were making preparations, a group of Japanese soldiers burst into the room. Japanese soldiers had been ordered to disarm, but these men were unwilling to part with their swords—a warrior's soul, as they said—and asked us to hide the weapons. They lifted up the tatami mats and were about to put the swords under the floor boarding when there was a loud clattering noise from the neighboring room. Looking around, I saw two Russian soldiers training automatic rifles on us. For a second I felt as though I couldn't breathe. Then, with a cry of "Russkies," I turned off the lights and fled along the winding corridor to the main dining hall behind the hospital.

At that time about two hundred Japanese soldiers were eating emergency rations there. I squatted down and hid myself among them. The next thing I knew, I was totally alone. All the soldiers had run away, taking two trucks parked outside. I was too terrified to move. But an old Manchurian man, to whom I had been kind, beckoned me to follow him. He took me to the basement, where he lived with his family, and hid me there. What few personal belongings I had had were looted, and I was left with nothing but the clothes on my back.

Disorders of various kinds occurred one after the other. One day there was a riot at the Korean school in front of the hospital. A crowd of about a thousand people, swarming like ants over a piece of sugar, attacked the building and literally tore it down, including the floor boards. Some Japanese were killed. Russian soldiers mounted on mules opened fire on the crowd, killing a number of Manchurians.

Russian soldiers often broke into the houses where we were staying. At first we hid safely in the *fusuma* closets, whose sliding doors the Russians didn't know how to open. But this stratagem failed to work for very long. Later, when we began hiding above the ceiling, the Russians figured this out too and began thrusting their bayonets through the thin boards. Once, blood poured from the hole the Russian bayonet had made in the ceiling, though not a cry was uttered.

The Soviet soldiers in the first line of invasion raped all the women prisoners they took. It was a living hell. One young mother was violated in front of her children—one a three-year-old and the other a small baby. Then she was killed, and her crying children were left clinging to her body.

The kindly Manchurian man in the hospital arranged for us to hide in an old temple called the Miaofa-si, where fifteen of us lived together with four ex-soldiers, who had risked their lives in slipping away from Soviet trucks headed for Siberia. The head nurse decided to conceal them because if they were found by the Soviets, they would be taken prisoner again, and if they were found by the Chinese Eighth Route Army, which was eager to swell its own ranks, they would be drafted. A good number of Japanese soldiers actually served in the Eighth Route Army.

Nor was it only soldiers the Chinese wanted. One day soldiers from the Eighth Route Army came to the temple and insisted that they wanted to buy me for a thousand yen. I screamed and cried until they finally went away, vowing to return the next day and complete the purchase. To avoid being sold, I hid myself for about a week in the houses of several of my former patients.

Early one morning the Japanese head surgeon at the hospital arrived at the temple with three Russian soldiers. They were threatening to take his wife away and he was trying to dissuade them by revealing the whereabouts of plenty of younger women. Things looked very bad when, using sign language, we asked the soldiers to bring someone who understood Japanese. That person arrived, and we explained how the head surgeon, who should have been protecting us, was trying to sell us simply to save his own family. I do not know whether the Russian soldiers understood, but they soon took the head surgeon away.

Even the temple was not entirely safe. Bandits raided us under cover of night, depriving us of any place where we could sleep in peace. From time to time we were compelled to take shelter under the temple floor boards.

The war had ended in summer, and summer clothes, which were all we had, were insufficient protection against the severe cold of winter. People began dying like flies.

Many of us found ourselves indebted to a group of people to whom we never thought we would owe anything. The large number of Japanese geisha and other women of the demimonde identified themselves and their professions and, by selling themselves, protected the rest of us. It was due to their efforts that ordinary women felt safe enough to go into town to sell dumplings or rice cake or do whatever they could to eke out a living. We were eternally grateful to those women.

Under these miserable circumstances, pregnancies occurred in large numbers. I often accompanied the head nurse, who was a midwife, on her missions at any time of day or night. No matter what the hour or the danger, when a woman was about to give birth, we hurried to her side. At night, street guards shot anyone who didn't know the password, which we never knew. It is still a miracle to me that we escaped being shot.

The new mothers and the midwives were both risking their lives. In spite of such horrible conditions and the fact we couldn't use hot water, all the babies were healthy. This work impressed me tremendously with the force of life. It was only after public order had been reestablished somewhat that strict protection was extended to anyone wearing a Red Cross patch.

At about the end of November, the Russians left, and war began between the Eighth Route Army and the Nationalists. The doctors and we nurses were compelled to work in field hospitals of one side or the other. Mine was with the Nationalists. I was taken away at night, without being told my destination, and found myself in a Manchurian house converted into a field hospital. Wounded soldiers lay on rush mats waiting to be treated. I wanted to cover my eyes at the sight of men whose veins had been severed with shrapnel and who had bled so much that nothing could help them, men whose limbs had been blown off, whose eyes had been shot from their heads, or whose intestines spilled from their bodies. My heart was torn with pity as I heard these men—like the Japanese soldiers I had heard—call for their mothers as they died.

Since we lacked proper medicine, one death was soon followed by another. Tetanus broke out, and respiratory difficulties killed men in no time. I do not know how many of them died in front of me without my being able to do anything for them.

Guerrilla fighting at night forced us to move from place to place, never remaining anywhere two days in a row. Unless we Japanese kept a close

NURSING, FLEEING, HIDING

eye on the Manchurian doctor to detect any hint of preparations for departure, we might be ignored and left behind when the time came to flee. That is why, at night, each of us had one hand attached by a cord to the hand of someone else, and took turns keeping watch, sleeping only lightly. At the order to flee, we all woke and dashed through the dark for our lives, making as little noise as possible and clinging to the clothes of the person in front. If one person stumbled, all the others were liable to fall. We had no idea where we were going, and were terrified of being separated from the others. Looking back, I am amazed at some of the things I was able to do. I shall never know, for instance, how I scaled walls that were taller than I was. But I did it.

Before the end of the war, I had never seen a scorpion. But as our situation grew more confused, these insects seemed to thrive. The frightening, disgusting things would drop on our bedding at night and then rustle about, nearly driving us mad. One day I suddenly felt an excruciating pain in my arm and lifted the blanket to discover a large scorpion. My arm swelled and stiffened so that I could hardly move it. Since I was incapable of work, I requested permission to return to the temple until my arm healed. This was at last granted.

Although talks began about repatriation at about that time, single people, technicians, nurses, and doctors were ordered to remain. After discussing the matter with the head nurse, I decided to marry one of the four ex-soldiers who had been with us and with whom I was on good terms.

After my arm recovered, I returned to the field hospital. When time came for the last repatriation train, we were thrown into a prison with barred windows and told that, because of the fighting between the Eighth Route Army and the Nationalists, we would have to stay and work. The situation seemed hopeless. If we ran away, we would probably be shot.

But the Manchurian doctor unlocked the cell door and said that those who wanted to escape should do so. My friends and I decided that if we had to die anyway, we may as well try to escape.

At the nearby station soldiers with rifles were hunting for fugitives, but we managed to elude them. We all breathed sighs of relief as our freight car pulled out and passed through neighboring Tieling. At last, it seemed that our dream of returning to Japan might be realized.

But, as it turned out, our suffering wasn't over. With our light clothing, we found the sharp drop in temperature that takes place at night on the continent difficult to endure. Food was scarce, and drinking water cost one hundred yen a bottle at a time when a man earned about a hundred yen a month. I had no change of clothes nor the thousand yen that Japanese were allowed when they were repatriated. Once again Manchurians to whom I had been kind in the hospital came to my rescue by giving me boiled soybeans. After surgery in our hospital, Japanese patients were given steamed white rice to eat whereas Manchurians got only kaoliang. Some of us nurses gave the Manchurians our own rice rations, and the patients helped us now when we were in a bad way.

Next, the train we were on was attacked by marauders. I recall lying on our bellies, scarcely breathing, on two occasions. Fortunately, however, no one was injured.

Children and old people, however, fell ill because of the cold nights and the scarcity of food. We jumped from car to car on the moving train trying to take care of them. There was one young mother, I remember, who refused to part with her dead baby. In the heat of the day the body soon became infested with maggots and the stench was intolerable. We finally convinced her to allow us to throw the body from the train, but there was nothing we could do to console her.

At last, when we arrived in Jin Prefecture, we were given food, water, and a place to sleep, and allowed to live like human beings for five days.

It is impossible for me to express the joy I felt at seeing the Japanese crimson sun painted on the ship we boarded at Koro Island. Though only a freighter, the ship was heaven. I slept for days, free of the fear of being pursued or shot. As might have been expected under the circumstances, food was poor—one rice ball and one bowl of bean-paste soup a day. But the peace of mind was wonderful.

Rumors were rife: some horrendous bomb had been dropped on Japan, destroying everything and leaving us no place to return to; no women were left alive in the nation; and so on. Even though we had come through so much, we didn't know what lay ahead. Some people, who had endured indescribable hardship to get aboard the ship, now died with the Japanese islands before their eyes. Even now I sometimes hear the sound of their coffins plunging into the sea.

About a month after we left the continent, old and young climbed on deck to see the Japanese islands, rising in the morning mist before us. Tears filled our eyes. I shall never forget the beauty of that sight.

But contagious diseases on the ship prevented our docking at Sasebo as scheduled. A few days later, however, we finally landed at Hakata, where, doused from head to foot in DDT powder, we bade farewell to our lice. My head shaved and dressed in rags, I saw a woman sporting a permanent wave and a red skirt, who had come to greet a relative. The sight of her so astounded me that I literally could not move.

We boarded a hideously packed train and went to my husband's family home in Hyōgo Prefecture. I was delighted to see the whole village turn out to greet us. It was just the time of year when rice seedlings are transplanted to the paddy fields. And I thought how beautiful Japan is, how wonderful peace is. As the accumulated tension subsided, profound fatigue set in.

After a while I returned to Hokkaido. Though my old familiar mountains and rivers remained as they had been, the family had changed. Father was gone. Waiting for me were Mother, whose back was now bent, my younger brother and sister, and a cousin in the first year of primary school. Only one of all our many horses remained. Mother wept and stroked my body as she told me how happy she was to have me home.

One after Another They Died

Hiroko Kanazawa (65)

By June 1937 the war with China had already begun, and the scale of fighting was gradually expanding. Everyday we heard shouts of *Banzai!* as people saw soldiers off to war. In August of that same year, owing to a shortage of medics in both the army and the navy, for the first time ever a group of doctors and nurses from the Japanese Red Cross received pink induction notices. (There was a regulation that, in an emergency, Japanese Red Cross nurses could be drafted at any time.)

Having graduated from a girls' school in March 1934, I had immediately enrolled in the Shizuoka Red Cross Nurses Training School, from which I graduated in March 1937 at the age of nineteen. When the conscription notices arrived, one of my seniors in this first group, who had a nursing baby, was so feverish with inflammation of the nipples that she could not possibly serve. Since entering the Red Cross had been my most cherished dream, I was delighted when her conscription notice was passed on to me.

We assembled in Osaka and then went to what is now called Hiroshima Bay to be shipped out. As we waited, we saw Japanese soldiers from all parts of the country arrive and set sail for the battlefield. I was assigned to the beautiful hospital ship *Kasagi-maru*, which had a broad green stripe about a meter wide along its sides and flew the Red Cross flag. Though a woman, I was proud to be going to war in the place of my older brother, who was very unhappy about being rejected for service.

When the war with China started, Japan had only four hospital ships, all of them remodeled freighters. Though later in the war hospital ships were as big as ten thousand tons, ours was only three hundred tons. Indeed it was so small that, in a storm, wounded soldiers and nursing staff alike were tossed about like autumn leaves in a high wind. On this little ship we made more than thirty round trips between various places in Japan and Tanggu, the port for Tianjin, in North China, as well as Shanghai and Nanjing (Nanking).

The staff was divided into two groups. In each there were three head nurses and twenty-seven ordinary nurses, for a total of sixty. In addition, there was one military doctor, two Red Cross doctors, one pharmacist, and one noncommissioned officer, but no military medics. We carried about one hundred and fifty wounded soldiers on each trip.

I first experienced the cruelty of war when I made my initial trip to Nanjing shortly after the Japanese attack on the city. As we sailed up the Yangzi we could see large numbers of prisoners being lined up on the shore and shot, their bodies falling into the river.

As long as your side is winning, the horror of war seems far removed. Radio news broadcasts of one Japanese victory after another made our patients forget their suffering and some of them even said they wanted to get well as quickly as possible so they could return to the battlefield. Of course, there was no danger to our ship at the time since Japan held complete control of the sea and air.

As the fighting grew fiercer, our once beautiful white ship was painted

ONE AFTER ANOTHER THEY DIED

jet black. On the way out from Japan we carried soldiers and military supplies. On the way home, once again flying the Red Cross flag, we had wounded on board. After eighteen months on the ship, where I never felt very close to the fighting, my term of duty expired.

Before war was declared on the United States in 1941, I had continued to serve by caring for war casualties in the First Army Hospital in Tokyo and then in the Navy Hospital at Izu. In 1941, however, I was drafted again and this time sent to Hankou, Hubei Province, in central China. During the 1911 revolution in China, significant uprisings took place in the three most prominent cities in this region: Hankou, Hanyang, and Wuchang, a provisional government being set up in Hankou.

The buildings of Wuhan University were converted into a central military hospital. Under it were station hospitals, evacuation hospitals, and field hospitals at the front lines. I was assigned to the evacuation hospital at Hankou, very close to the front lines. There were only medics and no nurses at all at the front-line field hospitals.

Unlike the stationary central and station hospitals, our unit moved each time the front advanced. It took part in the action connected with the famous battle of Changsha, a city of major importance in Hubei Province. We followed the troops as they battled night and day for over a month. When we had to, we flew by plane to field hospitals that had fallen behind the front-line troops. Evacuation hospitals were then set up in the houses of Chinese or in hastily thrown up barracks or tents.

The fighting was continuous and violent. From both near and far the roar of small-arms fire and field artillery battered our ears. Soldiers who had waved good-bye to us in the morning would return on stretchers a few hours later, gravely wounded. Sometimes they had bullets lodged in their bellies, which swelled up as big as drums. The pain was such that they screamed for us to kill them. They were usually beyond surgery; and in many cases they died only a few hours after reaching us, often calling for their mothers with their last gasp.

People tend to think that hospitals near the front lines deal only with the seriously wounded requiring surgery, but actually such patients comprised only half of our cases. We handled all kinds of other sicknesses the men were susceptible to because of fatigue after heavy fighting and continued advances carrying heavy backpacks. We did our best for these men, but frequently injections did them no good. They had no appetite and were so completely dispirited that they died.

The summer heat was so severe—thirty-five and thirty-six degrees centigrade for days on end—that we had to sleep out of doors. (In such weather, the story went, sparrows that lit on the electric-power lines were burned to death.) But the fighting continued unabated, and the number of wounded became unmanageable. In the blood and heat of the barracks, flies were everywhere, sometimes completely covering the patients' bandages. In many instances, when the bandages were removed from a wound, as they were everyday, we found a mass of maggots, some of which dropped to the floor.

Some men arrived from the front lines with tourniquets on arms or legs, but they had taken so long in reaching us that rot had set in and we had to amputate. Others had been shot in the head and a line gouged across the face, blasting out both eyes. We saw all this and much more that is indescribable. And one after another, with the names of loved ones on their lips—most often the word *mother*—these men ended their lives. So it was that, covered with blood, we followed the men from one front to another.

Looking around us, we saw that the land of the Chinese lay in ruins. While artillery and rifles could be heard, nothing was to be seen of the local people. But when the firing ceased, they appeared as if from nowhere to see what had happened to their homes. The Japanese military took many of them for coolie labor, forcing them to do extremely heavy work and whipping them like cart horses. In broken Japanese, they told of how they had been separated from their families and had virtually nothing to eat. Though they had the swollen faces and scrawny bodies of people suffering from malnutrition, they nonetheless had to obey the orders of the occupying Japanese forces.

I had never felt that way while assigned to the hospital ship, but at the front lines I came to hate the cruelty and misery of war. Determined to do all I could to save even one more precious life from this horror of repeated military campaigns, I struggled among the suffering and wretchedness of an evacuation hospital for more than two years before our unit was at last replaced. In June of 1944 I returned to Japan, where I went to work at the Army Hospital at Hamamatsu.

ONE AFTER ANOTHER THEY DIED

I was surprised by conditions at home. All the young men had been drafted. The only people left were the elderly, women, and children. All children of middle-school age were compelled to join labor brigades and help in factory work. Women were being trained to use spears made of bamboo poles.

It is puzzling now to think why anyone should have considered using bamboo spears to defend the homeland in an age of nuclear weapons. But, even then, Japanese believed what they had been so diligently taught: that Japan, as a divine nation, simply could not lose the war.

Before long, as we learned from radio broadcasts, B29s began bombing the major cities on the Japanese islands themselves. Hamamatsu, too, underwent air raids day and night since air-force, artillery, and infantry units were stationed there and several large factories turned out military supplies. Fighter planes dove and strafed anyone at all, even if it were only one person. And the bombs dropped by B29s on all the strategic areas in Hamamatsu made the ground rumble the way Mount Asama—a volcano near where I now live—does when it erupts.

As soon as the enemy planes had gone, the wounded—civilian as well as military—were carried into our hospital. I remember one charming child of five or six who screamed for help before dying of a massive hemorrhage. Many people were killed before they had a chance to run for cover. Once, having gone to help remove bodies after an attack, I saw a mother who had tried to protect her child with her own body. Both had been shot dead.

Every other day, and sometimes daily, we began to hear the song associated with the so-called special attack forces, which was composed of young boys who had left middle school at the age of seventeen or eighteen and volunteered to pilot a single-seat aircraft and sacrifice their young lives by crashing into enemy ships. They were just children, but that didn't prevent them, dressed in white, from flying off in their training planes. Each time I heard the song that accompanied their departure, I thought that, once again, young lives were about to be given for the protection of the nation, and wondered anew what the purpose of the war could be.

As the war situation grew steadily worse, we heard hourly radio reports of transport ships with hundreds of people on board that were torpedoed, and of military ships attacked and sent to the bottom, taking with them who knows how many precious lives. Then, too, we heard about the so-called honorable defeats on islands in the north and south Pacific; *honorable defeat* meant that there were no survivors at all.

Before long, enemy aircraft had assumed complete control of the sky. There were no Japanese planes left. Material was exhausted, almost all the factories lay in ruins, and it was no longer possible to manufacture weapons. But the long period of misery came to an end on August 15, 1945, when, after the horrendous atomic bombings of Hiroshima and Nagasaki, the emperor announced that Japan had unconditionally surrendered to the Allied powers.

When we heard this report, for an instant everyone went pale. Not a word was spoken. What had been the purpose of this war in which the entire Japanese people had sacrificed everything for the sake of victory? We nurses, who had been entrusted with so many irreplaceable lives and had witnessed so many scenes of horror, suffering, and death, were filled with loathing for war. An entire people, until now forbidden by strict regulations from criticizing the war, cursed the Japanese state with the force of water raging through a broken dam.

We nurses continued our work of caring for human lives in the confusion of the immediate postwar years, when soldiers with enormous backpacks tried to make their way back to their families, when people rushed about in search of something to eat, when those who had taken refuge in the country returned to packed and jammed city railway stations, when people were willing to break coach windows in order to get on overcrowded trains, and when homeless adults and familyless children slept everywhere in underground passageways. Still today I can clearly hear the shrieks of agony of men dying in the field hospitals of China and the cries for help of children killed in Japan.

What It Can Mean to Lose a War

Yoshiko Kumada (60)

From October 1940 until March 1947 I worked as a nurse at military hospitals in various parts of China and Korea. In mid December 1941, when Japan had captured Shanghai and was scoring victory after victory, I was transferred from the Shanghai-Nantong Central Hospital to the island of Chongmingdao. I learned what it can mean to be on the losing side in a war from the way the Japanese soldiers abused the Chinese there. From my own experiences it was easy to visualize the terror of an incident related to me by a generous, studious young Chinese man who worked at our hospital and studied German with one of our doctors. This youth told me how, when the Japanese had first landed on Chongmingdao, they had locked up the Chinese residents in their houses, which had thick clay walls and no windows, and then set fire to the buildings. In their agony some of the Chinese had managed to break holes in the thick walls just large enough to put their heads through, only to die that way.

I had first seen with my own eyes how the Chinese were treated when I went with Japanese soldiers on boats sent upstream to clean up after a battle. In our boat were Chinese prisoners with loops of wire wrapped around their necks. Their arms were attached to the wire in such a way that the slightest movement strangled them. At the port of Chongmingdao a woman of about forty was waiting to board our boat. She was carrying a basket of eggs, which she no doubt intended to sell. Perhaps at the time it was forbidden to take eggs to Shanghai, but at any rate, when she boarded, the Japanese soldiers in the boat struck the basket and broke all the woman's eggs. As I watched the weeping woman staggering on bound feet as she boarded the ship, I felt as if I were observing the defeat of China. None of us ever dreamed then that Japan, too, would face defeat.

In 1942 I was transferred from Nantong to a hospital attached to Pyongyang Medical University in Korea, where I had friends and knew many of the doctors. At about that time, however, doctors and other members of the medical staff were being drafted into the military, and I felt sure that my turn was not far off. And before long, just as I had thought, I was ordered to serve as a nurse in the Southern Pyongyang Army Hospital. The part of Pyongyang where we were stationed was covered in red dust in summer and subject to frigid temperatures of minus thirty degrees centigrade in winter. All around, as far as the eye could see, there was nothing but military facilities and barrenness.

The fighting was growing more and more violent in 1944 when I was put in charge of a training program for nurses. My first class consisted of fifty Japanese girl students from such places as Pyongyang and Seoul. Ignoring the fact that graduation was only a few months away, they had taken severe nationwide tests and volunteered to become nurses for the sake of the homeland. In this, the first military-nurses' educational course ever instituted, the girls had to undergo the same kind of training as military orderlies. When I took them in hand, I was stricken with sadness that Japan should find it necessary to treat pure-minded, sincere girls of about nineteen as soldiers. Yet I had to shake off such feelings if I was to guide them through a stiff course of training.

We arose at six and jogged in morning air so cold that our breath froze and turned white on our eyebrows. Eager to do anything they could for the sake of victory, the girls called out to one another in voices that reverberated among the sleeping houses.

Since the course was the first of its kind, we had no hospital uniforms. On rainy days the girls wore baggy coats and huge soldiers' overshoes; almost real soldiers themselves, they went on with their training. For these girls, who had never known want at home, everything they experienced in this new world must have been startling. Nonetheless, determined not to give in, they fulfilled all the requirements, graduated in June 1945, and then left us to work in various military hospitals. Three months after I received my second class of one hundred girls, the war was over.

August 15, 1945, is a day I shall never forget. It marked the end of my youth, the end of a period when I lived like a soldier in a foreign land, to which I had gone, overriding the objections of my family, as a volunteer nurse. After having given everything for a nation that I firmly believed would emerge triumphant, I dreaded that we Japanese might have to suffer the same kind of treatment I had seen meted out to the Chinese.

With the defeat, everything was seized by the Soviet army. Our naive hopes that hospitals and medical supplies would be spared were brutally betrayed. The occupying Soviet soldiers, who had arrived looking poor enough, were soon sporting wristwatches—sometimes several on one arm—that they had apparently taken from Japanese soldiers. I remember seeing a Soviet woman carrying three straw mattresses on her back at

TO LOSE A WAR

one time. (One would have been the most a Japanese woman could have managed.) As we watched these people, we were filled with mortification at Japan's defeat.

One day, believing the word of a Soviet officer that they were going to be sent back to Japan, a number of nursing students packed up and got ready to leave. In fact, however, they were taken to a place called Yanji in northeastern China, from which they did not return for seven years.

The Soviets took over the buildings we had used and packed us off to the rearmost wing. In the middle of the night, we nurses had to clean the Soviet soldiers' quarters. Since none of us understood any Russian, we were constantly afraid that one of the sleeping soldiers would wake and attack us while we scrubbed the floors.

After a while, it was decided that we were to be sent inland to a military maneuver point called Sanheli, about an hour's truck ride away. During the war, it had been a munitions depot, but after the fighting had become a receiving station for the wounded. We had to take our patients from the Pyongyang hospital with us.

Upon arrival we immediately saw that the hospital wards existed in name only. Some boards had been spread on an earthen floor, and each patient had only one blanket. The only medical supplies we had were what the Soviets shared with us from time to time. Soon soldiers began dying from malnutrition and contagious diseases.

One day a Soviet officer came and said "Yaponskie, home!" We had heard these words over and over again, but had never given up hope of returning to Japan. We immediately set about making preparations. Unexpectedly, however, more than a thousand wounded Japanese soldiers arrived by truck. In more wretched condition than beggars, these men had been taken from Manchuria to Siberia where they had been kept in Soviet prison camps. Many of them suffered from advanced malnutrition, and a number of them lay in crumpled heaps in the trucks, already dead. This was not the time for us to leave for home. Once again we began caring for the ill and wounded.

The condition of these men was horrible. Some of them couldn't get down from the trucks unaided, some died shortly after their feet touched ground, some were no more than skin and bones and huge rolling eyes.

All seemed on the brink of death. We saw clearly how cruel life in Siberia had been and realized once more the bitterness of defeat.

The soldiers said they were so glad to have come this far and see fellow Japanese once again that they could how die in peace. They wept as they ate their gruel—their first white rice in years. The condition of many suddenly worsened, however, apparently because the relief was too great to bear. Our hearts ached for them.

As if it were not enough that these men suffered from dysentery and intestinal typhus, before long cholera broke out among them. It is said that some Korean pickles a soldier purchased in a nearby town were the source of the infection. The weakened men fell victim to the sickness in great numbers, as many as ten or twenty in a single day. We were supposed to put identification tags on the patients the minute they entered the hospital, but sometimes this proved impossible. The men were so sick that they died without telling anyone so much as their names. It is said that death from cholera is lightning fast. And it certainly was in these instances. Men whose bowel movements were nothing but water died in no time at all.

One morning, stopping at the morgue to see how many patients had died during the night, I noticed something white on the eyes and noses of the corpses. A closer looked showed the white things to be maggots. Chills ran down my spine, and I covered my eyes. Had it not been for the war, these men would have been healthy and at home.

We had, of course, the problem of disposing of the corpses. At first we dug individual graves, but as the number of men strong enough for this work dwindled, we were forced to bury, first two, then more, in mass graves. In this hell on earth, clothing shortages forced us to remove the hospital robes from the dead to put on the living.

All kinds of horrid things took place. One soldier stretched an emaciated arm toward me and said that he was from Nagano Prefecture, which was my home too, and asked me to tell his family what had happened to him when I returned to Japan. At the time I was giving another soldier an injection of Ringer solution and suddenly noticed that the level was dropping at an abnormally fast rate. Lifting the blanket that covered the man's face, I saw that he had removed the needle from the tube and was drinking the solution.

Though nurses in name, we were forced to do all kinds of other work, for instance, laundering patients' lice-infested clothes in a dribble of water that came from the faucets. We had no choice but to get on with our work. At the end of a day of watching many soldiers die, I would be attacked by the fear that I would soon be following them. Miraculously, however, I never fell prey to anything contagious.

Once again a Soviet officer cried out "Yaponskie! Tokyo, *davai!*" At first no one believed him. But when a move to Hungnam was announced, we began to hope that perhaps this time, at last, we would see Japan. Longings for home welled up in all of us. Reluctant to leave behind all the soldiers who slept in graves there, we and the patients made vows to come to Sanheli again in peace time.

None of us knew where the trucks carrying us were headed; but after a while we arrived at a spot somewhere between Sanheli and Pyongyang. There we found a large group of other men on their way back from Siberia. Some of them had lost limbs to frostbite. I wondered what kind of life awaited them back in Japan. But by this time I myself was very weak. The time had come for me to think of my own physical well-being.

While at this location, we were subjected to thorough Communist indoctrination. We had to write pamphlets advocating the overthrow of the emperor and sing Communist songs. We were all eager to do as ordered for fear that, if we refused, we would not be allowed to board the home-bound ships. Once left behind, we might never see home again.

On December 31, 1946, we were ordered to move out. Once again, the Soviet officer shouted "Tokyo"; but none of us was sure that we were not being sent to Siberia. At Pyongyang Station we and our patients were loaded on railroad cars used to transport pigs. After riding for a long time—I think for two days and nights—we finally arrived at the company houses of a nitrogen plant in Hungnam. Having come this far, we all relaxed, feeling relatively sure that we actually were on the way home. And, indeed, after about three and a half months, the day to board our ship finally came. The passengers included patients, nurses, and other staff members from several hospitals. On March 19, 1947, we landed in Sasebo, our dreams realized. After years of suffering and anxiety, it was hard to believe that we were on Japanese soil. We cried, we wept, and ultimately—nurses, students, and soldiers—we parted ways.

Though only a few years had passed, my sojourn away from home seemed like decades, unforgettable decades. In Nagano I found my mother and father considerably aged. My eldest brother had been wounded in the war in China; my younger brother had died of sickness; and for a long time my whereabouts had been unknown. The people at home had also suffered. But Mother told me she knew I would come back some day. At times, however, she would be too anxious to sleep at night and would have to walk around to calm herself. Hearing her say this made me vow to take the best possible care of her. And this sense of mission has enabled me to live to the present, though when I arrived in Japan, my condition had been so bad that I was told I would probably last no more than six months.

No Longer Angels in White
Sachiko Umezaki (66)

At the back of my chest of drawers is an old diary I kept while serving as a nurse in the Philippines during World War II. Each August 15, the day on which the war in the Pacific ended, I take it out and reread it. As one person who has witnessed firsthand the misery of war, I have written this account, based on the diary, in the hope that it will help inspire greater respect for life among all peoples, especially in this day and age when people tend to undervalue life.

In August 1943 I was inducted into the Fukuoka Branch of the Japanese Red Cross Nursing Corps to serve with the Army Medical Corps in the Pacific. The twenty members in our group, including a head nurse, were assigned to the Twelfth Army Hospital in South Manila. With hope in our hearts and the desire to do our part for the country, we set out for the Philippines, little imagining that we were taking the first steps in what would become a flight from death.

Our hospital ship set sail from what is now Hiroshima Bay, went from Moji to Jilong on Taiwan, and then along the east coast of Taiwan toward Manila. When we reached the Bashi Channel (at the north of the Philippine Islands), one of the crew warned us that we were now in dangerous waters. In spite of all our mental preparations for anything that might

NO LONGER ANGELS IN WHITE

lie in wait for us, we shuddered at these words. That night an alarm sounded to tell us that a Japanese transport flotilla had been torpedoed. From the deck we saw the whole horizon in flames. It was all I could do to suppress my frustrated anger as we sailed on, unable to do anything for the Japanese soldiers who had been thrown into the burning sea and were calling out for help. Uncertain when our ship too might be attacked, we spent several sleepless nights wearing our life vests and were greatly relieved when we finally sailed into Manila Bay.

After some preliminary formalities, we went at once to our duty stations in the surgery wing of the Twelfth Army Hospital. In Japan, where supplies had been short, we had been forced to make sparing use of such things as gauze and even to wash and reuse bandages when possible. We were therefore surprised at the abundance of supplies at the hospital, which had formerly been operated by the Americans. Nonetheless, the work load was heavy. Most of our patients were gravely sick or injured; there was a great deal of surgery and no one to relieve us at night.

In the early autumn of 1944, the worsening war situation began to have a direct influence on our lives. Air-raid alarms sounded for several days in a row in Manila. Hospital air-raid shelters were put in readiness. We practiced emergency evacuation procedures and went through night-time musters.

Then, on September 21, Manila was attacked from the air for the first time. We had just finished our morning rounds in the wards when, at about noon, an unusually long and violent squall struck. We stood watching the rain and commenting on the length of the storm. Just as it had finally passed, we heard the roar of antiaircraft fire. The fighting had started. Enemy planes, the sound of whose approach had been drowned out by the squall, boomed across the sky. We thought it might be a practice run until we saw a man descending to earth in a parachute. In this, our first experience with actual fighting, we soon had to begin caring for increasing numbers of shrapnel patients.

Thereafter the raids occurred daily. Fortunately, few of the hospital staff were wounded, but patients increased so rapidly that the wards quickly overflowed and wounded patients were left on stretchers in the corridors. Rubber tubes for Ringer's-solution injections hung in a virtual forest. As soon as we finished with the last of a group of patients, we would have to return once again to the first man in the group. And we kept making the rounds over and over, changing catheters, making injections, and redressing wounds. Once having entered the ward, we never left it, even for a minute, till the following morning.

Tropical mosquitoes attacked constantly. Each bed had its own mosquito net, through which we peered to check the patient's condition. Sometimes, a wasted, weakened patient who had replied weakly to our questions a short while earlier would be silent in death the next time we came round.

In spite of the Red Cross emblem on the roof and on the hospital flag, enemy aircraft invariably strafed our building on their way back from attacking nearby Clark Air Force Base, then occupied by the Japanese army. At about this time, the enemy began attacking hospital ships too, because they knew that many of the vessels disguised with white paint and red crosses actually carried soldiers and military supplies.

Japanese cargo ships were frequently sunk in nearby waters, from which soldiers escaped to the Philippines. These men accounted for the growing number of burn patients who became our responsibility. Their bodies were covered with oil and so badly burned that it was impossible to tell where their eyes and noses were. Their eyebrows were usually burned away. The stench of blood and death hung over the whole hospital. We did our utmost to help men whose limbs dangled useless, from whose abdomens intestines had burst forth. But there was too little we could do; and many of them died holding our hands and calling for their mothers. I never heard one die with a *Banzai* for the emperor on his lips. I tried to encourage them as much as possible, but I was weak from lack of sleep, and suffered from headaches and nausea. My mind was losing its grip, and for days on end I had to force myself to go on.

By December Manila had become so unsafe that it was decided to move the hospital to Baguio, which was considered a natural fortress and had such a pleasant climate that the rich went there in peace time to escape the Manila heat. Packing clothing and miscellaneous supplies and putting our patients on buses, we started out on what was to become a nightmare.

Not having been out of the hospital for months, we were diverted by the scenery we saw on the way. On both sides of the road were houses with red tin roofs. In the fields there was billowing rice in green and yellow, though it was already winter in Japan. Because it's warm the year round, two rice crops are possible there. From time to time we saw flowers familiar in Japan blooming by the wayside, and were deluded into thinking this was a Japanese country road. But we were sadly awakened from this dream each time we saw a ruined Japanese military automobile abandoned by the road. Tears came to my eyes as I thought of home and wondered how my parents, brothers, and sisters were. As I daydreamed, the bus passed over a bridge. Some time later, I heard that the Americans had blown up that bridge, and a chill ran through my body.

As we neared Clark, there was a special-attack plane hidden in some trees, unable to fly. The thought occurred to me that we might never see Manila again. A feeling of unease swiftly spread throughout my body.

After bouncing and rattling over roads pitted by air raids, we finally reached Rosario that evening, where we nurses were put up separately in native houses. Nothing could have made us happier than satisfying our hunger with rice fried in palm oil as we did that night.

The following morning we boarded different trucks and continued on our way to Baguio. Whenever we heard the roar of explosions or saw a formation of planes, we hid under the trees. At night, guerrillas dropped flares near our truck to reveal our position to the enemy; we slept in the jungle with no more protection than the clothes we wore. At last, after having been intimidated by low-flying aircraft as we traveled through riverbeds and valleys, we arrived at Baguio.

The hospital was located on the highest point in the city, some 1,700 meters above sea level. Although we were told we would be safe there for three years, in less than a month after our arrival a large formation of fighter-bombers attacked, cutting off both electricity and running water. The water had to be hauled from a valley river several hundred meters below, a job that left us dizzy and gasping for breath. It was more and more obvious that we suffered from malnutrition.

As the fighting grew fiercer, the hospital became a target for attack. Because our white uniforms were too conspicuous, we dyed them and the patients' clothes with grasses and other plants. Next we began digging air-raid shelters for the bedridden patients, but violent squalls soon washed away the loose red soil, making all our efforts futile.

From early in the morning on January 23, 1945, I felt a certain foreboding. Soon a large formation of fighter-bombers and bombers appeared in the sky. Shortly afterward, I heard an earth-shaking roar and thought, "They've struck some place nearby." Then I turned to see Baguio transformed into a sea of flame. The raid lasted for about three hours, and the lovely resort town was completely destroyed.

Our military doctor was so severely wounded in the raid that he lost both legs; and our head nurse, who had been wearing a steel helmet while caring for seriously wounded patients, was shot through the head with machine-gun fire and died instantly. We all wept; hers was the first death among the nurses.

Casualties increased, but the hospital had very little to feed them. Everyone was hungry. Sometimes patients would fight over a single ball of cooked rice. I remember scolding a soldier who tried to take another's food. Dressed in rags, his hair long and unkempt, sunken eyes glowing, he fell to the ground, looking up longingly at the food. As I watched him, my heart overflowed with a mixture of pity and horror.

But things got worse. After a while there was no longer enough rice to makè rice balls, and we fed the patients thin rice gruel—and only a little of that.

Whenever we went outside, we automatically walked with our heads ducked because of the shells from offshore artillery that whistled overhead. Once as I was going toward a shelter to have a look at the patients there, I heard an explosion and looked up to see a formation of about twenty aircraft. I sensed that they were going to attack the hospital. Riveted to the spot, I heard weird metallic sounds, the whistling of falling bombs, and the rattle of strafing. I covered my ears and shut my eyes, my body quivering, until I heard a badly burned soldier calling from a shelter where there were some dysentery patients. They had only one bedpan. Unable to pour it out, the men had merely passed it from one to another till it was completely full.

Things of this kind happened again and again. Then, on March 1, the main hospital came under direct attack. Gaping holes were opened in the building, and some patients lost their lives. While we felt sorry for them, we ourselves were hungry, suffering from lack of sleep, and drained of strength.

Enemy planes raided regularly in the morning and evening; and each time more men died. We buried them in great bowl-shaped bomb craters. Emaciated, weak silent porters of corpses on stretchers, we were no longer angels in white but the emissaries of hell.

On March 10 we were notified by the military medical authorities that, as of that day, Nursing Corps 302 (from Osaka, Nagasaki, Ōita, and Fukuoka) was assigned to Field Hospital 129, for the damage to the Twelfth Army Hospital had been so great that it could no longer function as a hospital or even serve as living quarters.

We set out for our new destination, having only one meager meal a day as usual, but we were unable to reach our goal by nightfall, of course. After days of dragging our weary legs and resting in air-raid shelters on the way, we finally reached the 129th field hospital, which was a hospital in name only: it had no food and insufficient medical supplies. In the effort to stay alive somehow, we formed groups to go into the forest to search for edible grasses and bracken, which we treated with ashes to remove the bitterness.

After a while, we of the Fukuoka group were assigned to surgery, but, in fact, the daily enemy raids made us so jumpy that practically no one was able to function properly. Every day men in the shelters and wards died. It was our job to carry them out on stretchers. But after going only two or three meters we were stumbling and panting heavily. It was as if we were carrying, not human corpses, but stones.

Soldiers strong enough to dig graves grew fewer and fewer. Still trucks from the front brought more wounded every day. The hospital had no beds and no blankets, and the men were put on the floor in their bloody clothes. There wasn't enough material and medicine to give daily treatment, and finally the doctors told us to leave the maggots in the patients' wounds since they did the work of antiseptics. There is no way to describe the hellish scenes we witnessed. At about this time, we started wearing trousers and shirts made of dark denim. Sarcastic soldiers, perhaps referring to our inability to be of any real help to them, hurt us deeply by calling us angels in black.

On April 10—I think that was the date—we picked up some leaflets dropped by an American aircraft. They asked us to think of the future of Japan, told us Japan had already lost the war, and advised us to give ourselves up. By this time, our daily rations consisted of one-third of a canteen of gruel that was practically all water and whatever edible grasses we could find.

On April 22, we were suddenly ordered aboard trucks. The hospital was to be moved. We had no idea where. With our handmade combat hats and backpacks, we gathered up our few belongings and moved out. On the way, we saw many soldiers who had dropped out, lying by the roadside and staring at us maliciously. Even in cases of high malarial fever, dropping out was forbidden; their units simply left them behind.

At the eight-kilometer point, the truck could go no further. We had to walk and threw away everything we could to lighten our load. Some people even discarded soap as being too heavy.

At the thirty-one kilometer point, we met a large number of nurses and soldiers who had converged from two other directions. We cooked enough food that one night to last us the next day, but some people were vicious enough to steal others' shares. It is difficult to express the ugliness of such acts, especially when we were all alike in that we were starving. Still, under the circumstances, nothing could be done.

While we were still on the run, news arrived that the enemy had occupied Baguio about three days earlier. Orderlies there had administered lethal injections to patients too ill to move and then had set fire to the hospital. At the very thought of what they had had to go through, those who escaped and those left behind, none of us could help crying.

How long was this going to last? We were blocked by the enemy to the north and the south. It seemed we were expected to go on indefinitely on the three bags of dried bread and two cans of food we had been given when we left Baguio. Our march had degenerated into a search for something to eat.

On May 5, the 129th station hospital was set up. But it was only a formality. All we had was an awning over the road. The soldiers lay on the ground, and we nurses went from one to the other giving injections of Vitamin B_1. All the while, in small groups, others who had fled joined us. Our reunions were often tearful.

May 18 got off to an ominous start with Lockheeds circling overhead from early in the morning. Then the roaring and crashing of the shelling began. One of my seniors was killed by a bomb. All our precious foodstuff was burned. Smoke filled the air. Four of my colleagues were victims of this attack. The headquarters was completely destroyed. The attack was still raging when I noticed a soldier lying by the road. An ignited fragment had lodged itself in the raincoat he was wearing, and he lacked the strength to brush it away. In spite of his calls for help, I was too terrified of the bursting shells to go to him.

The enemy continued dropping leaflets. But on the night of the twenty-ninth we were ordered to rejoin the Twelfth Army. Our captain said in parting that he was grieved to say good-bye to us after three months of shared hardships, and urged us to keep our spirits up and to continue to be, as he said, "the flowers of Japan." My feelings on this occasion were extremely complicated.

As the fighting grew worse, we once again took our patients and fled into the jungle. When we reached Callao, a captain addressed us. "You are no longer required to attend to the patients. From here on we enter trackless mountains, where the rivers are swift. If worst comes to worst, remember to die with honor." Saying this, he gave each of us two hand grenades.

After August 15, few aircraft flew overhead. We had no idea whether Japan had won or lost the war. At night, hearing the explosion of a hand grenade, we knew that someone had committed suicide. But we resolved not to die until we had seen Japanese soil. When one of the soldiers heard over the wireless of the destruction of Hiroshima and Nagasaki by something called the atom bomb and the perilous condition Japan was in, we refused to believe it.

It was not until two months later that we learned of the unconditional surrender. Sorrowful, resentful, impotent, and exhausted, we lay in an air-raid shelter waiting for the rain to stop. My own condition was serious. Both of my legs were so swollen that I couldn't walk, much less carry a backpack. I was suffering from malnutrition and malaria. Convinced I could go no farther, I made my final farewell with a close friend. As she tried to console me, I trembled with fever and thought how short my life had been. I envisioned the faces of my father, sisters, and dead friends, and experienced a kaleidoscope of happy and sad memories. My friend and I cried for a while, and then quietly fell asleep.

When the orders to march were given the next morning, I stood and, to my surprise, found that the swelling in my legs had gone down. At this heaven-sent salvation, my friend embraced me.

We became prisoners of the Americans and came down from the mountains to a camp where the Stars and Stripes flew beside a white flag signifying Japanese surrender. The swords of officers and noncommissioned officers were confiscated. As we rode along in packed trucks, the native populace threw stones at us, calling us all kinds of names. I was nearly bursting with vexation and resentment.

Packed into a truck and driven a night and a day without being allowed to go to the toilet, we finally arrived at the Caramba prison camp. Though we were unable to satisfy our hunger, we managed to survive by sleeping all day. Then we were doused with DDT to kill the lice in our hair and clothes.

In early December it was at last our turn to go home to Japan. *Tsukushimaru*, the hospital ship on which we had come out, arrived to meet us. It was a treat to see the sailors with whom we had traveled before.

Finally at home, I stood in front of the bombed site where our house had been, frantic with worry about my father and sisters. I had just decided to go to the Fukuoka office of the Red Cross when, miraculously, I saw my father. He had been watching me. Running toward each other and calling each other's name, we embraced, little caring who might be watching.

Not long afterward, we moved into a shack built on the land where our house had been, and started anew in a war-torn and hungry homeland.

WOMEN WHO
STRIVE TO
TEACH

Learning What Education Really Is

Kimiyo Kobayashi (66)

In April 1944 I joined the faculty of the Hachiōji Metropolitan Higher Girls School, where I was put in charge of the third-year students. In July of the same year my students were mobilized to weed dry-rice fields in Moto Hachiōji, about an hour's walk from school. In those days, pure white rice, with no admixtures of any kind, was a great rarity. The children were therefore overjoyed to be able to eat balls of white rice for lunch on these workdays. Sometimes they were given their fill of steamed potatoes. This too was a treat at a time when they were practically never able to eat their fill of anything. After the students had gone home in high spirits, the fields were left cleanly weeded. Unfortunately, according to some accounts, the fields were too clean because some of the children didn't know the difference between rice plants and weeds.

When I was taking teacher-training courses, Japan was already engaged in what was called the Greater East Asia War (that is, the Pacific War). In addition to the specialized education courses, the curriculum stressed the inculcation of ideas that would contribute to the nation's overall strategy. Sucked into the onrush of the war, we were all called upon to work to our fullest by the exigencies of the times.

Starting in September, our third-year students were ordered to go to work in munitions plants. Wearing trousers and padded protective hoods and with first-aid kits hanging from their shoulders, the girls assembled at their place of work, a small temporary building in Tachikawa where they were to make wire coils for communications equipment. The building was just large enough to hold the one hundred students from two grades. Each month the children received forty yen for the work they did, which they treasured as the fruit of their sweat and labor.

Toward the end of 1944, American aircraft began appearing in the skies over Japan, bombing airfields and aircraft-manufacturing plants. When the large aircraft plant in Tachikawa was bombed, I heard that many mobilized student-workers who had taken refuge in air-raid shelters there were killed or wounded.

As the air raids intensified in 1945, the school auditorium was converted into a workshop. The floor was ripped out and replaced with

WHAT EDUCATION REALLY IS

concrete. Lathes, drills, and grinders were brought from Tachikawa, installed, and operated around the clock. They were manned by fifth-year students working three eight-hour shifts.

Appointed leader of the students about to enter the fourth year in April 1945, I was mobilized to work in a fighter-aircraft plant in Tachikawa. There we assembled fuselages by filing steel, riveting with electric riveters, and polishing cocks with emery. Since we were doing the work of male machinists, guidance was needed every step of the way. It was difficult, strenuous work. And I couldn't help wondering how useful the bent rivets put in by these inexperienced girls could be. Would the planes actually be able to get safely into the air?

Once a month, the faculty assembled at school to eat a simple meal and hear reports from various work sites, receive guidance from the principal, and discuss all-important steps to ensure student safety.

At the plant to which I was sent, we worked from eight in the morning till four in the afternoon with an hour off at noon, during which many students picked grasses and weeds to take home as supplements to the meager family meal.

At the sound of the air-raid alarm, all the students and we three leaders assembled at once and then ran for the shelter in a nearby forest. The Chūō Line of the National Railways ran through our area, and the big factories north of it were heavily bombed and suffered a great deal of damage. We were located south of the railway line, where air raids were less destructive. Our students felt less threatened than some of the others, and often sat in the shelter munching parched soybeans brought from home.

In June and July supplies to our plant began dropping off, and we frequently heard the managerial staff muttering among themselves. Rumor had it that the war had taken a bad turn for our side. With much less work to do than before, students spent a great deal of their time in the factory yard.

I observed some of the students crying as they waved to the small aircraft that took off from nearby Chōfu airfield. They told me they were so-called special-attack (or kamikaze) planes. Students who lived near the field had caught glimpses of the handsome young pilots of these planes, dressed in white, preparing to take off on missions from which they would never return. These young men had been taught that dying for the homeland was the highest goal in life.

One day American planes dropped leaflets warning of an imminent air raid on Hachiōji. At dawn on August 2 the raid took place, reducing most of the city to ashes. The alert had sounded before eight, and so the students remained at home, as they were told to do in such cases. With no one at the Tachikawa factory, I caught a ride in one of the factory cars and went to Hachiōji to see how things were at the school. Smoke was still rising from the city when I arrived. The machines that had been installed in the auditorium stood out starkly among the ruins. At the time of the bombing, the fifth-year students on night shift had put on their padded hoods and, under the leadership of their teacher, dashed through a rain of incendiary bombs to take shelter in the Asakawa riverbed. Miraculously, none of them was hurt, though they were all frightened out of their wits.

Some students, those whose homes in Hachiōji had been destroyed in the raid, went to live with relatives in the country. Other students, because of the daily air raids, were ordered to remain at home. Only the faculty reported for duty and, after building a small shack on the school grounds, started cleaning up the rubble.

The incendiary bombs that devastated Japanese cities were said to come down like rain.

WHAT EDUCATION REALLY IS

After the atomic bombings of Hiroshima and Nagasaki the war took on an entirely different tone. Without our really understanding what was happening, it was suddenly August 15, 1945. We were ordered to assemble in front of one of the few houses still standing in the city to listen to the emperor's radio broadcast proclaiming the end of the war.

In September we were able to use part of the Komiya Primary School building, about thirty minutes away in the mountains, and started morning and afternoon shifts of instruction. Of course, educational materials were practically nonexistent. I recall that, for sewing class, girls had to do smocking on small bits of cloth. The skimpy nature of our school work at the time was brought home to me recently when one of my former students said to me in passing, "We really didn't do much studying then, did we?"

By 1946 we had managed to build a temporary shack on the school grounds and, somehow or other, to start normal instruction. But in the textbooks for geography and history, the Occupation General Headquarters ordered us to black out passages they found offensive.

One day, before morning assembly, a group of Americans, talking so loudly it seemed as if they were shouting, appeared at the school doors. They were an inspection team from GHQ. In the past, we had always had the students stand in orderly formation for morning assembly. When the meeting ended, the student in charge mounted the rostrum and, in a loud, clear voice, gave the order to march into the classrooms. The students would then step briskly forward, swinging their arms in unison as they went. When the head of the American team saw this, he suddenly shouted out, "Militarism!" and startled us all.

The students went into the building and were instructed to stay there. Teachers were told to remain with their classes. We all wondered what the inspection team intended to do. Over an hour later, their heavy military shoes resounding down the corridor, they came into my classroom. The students were ordered to stand along the walls after putting all their textbooks on their desks. One member of the American team spoke and read Japanese, and he proceeded to check each book to make certain the deletions ordered by GHQ had been made.

From the following day, morning assembly changed. The loud and clear militarylike order to march forward was replaced by a quiet request. And instead of stepping off briskly, the children ambled into the building. Blacked-out passages in textbooks increased in number.

As the old educational system crumbled, groups formed here and there to study democratic education. I too went from place to place attending conferences and taking part in the movement. I studied hard and made a great effort, but was somehow dissatisfied with the new ways.

I experienced an awakening, however, when I became a believer in Nichiren Shōshū Buddhism and a member of Soka Gakkai in 1951. Studying in their Educational Division, I came to see that the crux of education is respect for life. Though a teacher since about 1944, I had done little teaching because the war limited my duties to shepherding the students between factories and air-raid shelters. After the war I had thought of teaching as nothing but the transmission of knowledge. But my work in the Educational Division taught me that true education must be the care and cultivation of each individual child. At last, I was able to approach the students as an enlightened educator.

Remember How Precious Your Own Life Is

Tae Nakatsuka (70)

From the spring of 1930, a time of economic depression and agrarian movements, until March 1947, I was a teacher in Noshiro, Akita Prefecture. From our vantage point in the far northern part of the island of Honshū, we looked on the beginnings of the war in China as something only indirectly related to us, and were convinced that Japan was strong, was winning, and would win in the end. We were a very complacent lot.

When the fighting broke out in earnest, we had students write encouraging letters to soldiers and send them in handmade envelopes. The children were delighted when they got answers. The prevailing philosophy of the time was that dying for the homeland was the supreme virtue in life, and that all Japanese boys wanted nothing so much as to become soldiers when they grew up. When the Pacific War began in 1941, the children were taught that Japan had acted only after putting up with as much as could be tolerated, and that dying for the emperor, and consequently becoming a "god," was the highest thing a human being could hope for. The entire school made pilgrimages to Shinto shrines to pray for what was believed to be inevitable Japanese victory. When a Japanese victory was announced, the mood was like that of a festival. Of course, we knew Japanese soldiers were often victims of war. But no matter how much they suffered, survivors always maintained the surface attitude that death in battle was honorable and therefore a cause for joy.

As the Japanese army moved from Shanghai to take over many of Britain's former colonies, some of us amateurs came to suspect that the time was right for negotiations to bring the war to a close.

A number of our middle-school boys were shipped overseas as soldiers before their graduation. One holiday, two of them, Murata, a teacher's son, and Yamashita, a merchant's son, came to visit me. From beginning to end, Murata said nothing. But Yamashita expressed himself openly: "We are like pigs, being fattened up for slaughter. But I don't want to die."

Though moved to the point of tears, I could say nothing but "I'm sure negotiations for peace will start soon. Whatever you do, remember how precious your own life is."

Shortly thereafter, we received word of Yamashita's honorable death in battle. But his death can only be considered cruel in light of the things he might have achieved had he lived. After the war, Murata came to visit, but he said nothing about Yamashita's death.

By 1944, when I was in charge of the sixth grade, the food shortage began to affect even rural areas like ours. The school provided for the children of poorer families, taking pains to keep the other students from finding out.

At about this time, neighborhood groups and higher-grade students were instructed to dig up pine roots from which to extract oil for use in planes and battleships. This all seemed futile considering that no matter how many roots were dug up and no matter how much pine oil was produced, Japan had no chance of winning the war.

Perhaps reflecting the unease of the teachers themselves, the students began to misbehave badly. I hoped to calm them down during the music hour by singing with them. The principal, however, objected that music would not win the war. "Use the time you'd spend on music and calisthenics to dig up pine roots," he said.

I then recalled the success I had had with music when I was in charge of lower-grade classes just after becoming a teacher. Some of the children were acting up in class and stole money at home, and their parents discussed the matter with me. Since scolding did no good, I decided to try music. For about an hour after classes were over, we would listen to records and talk about the songs. Soon parents began telling me that on music days their children kept out of mischief at home. Before long, their classroom behavior improved too.

I insisted that, in times of upheaval like the present, children should still have an emotionally satisfying education. My belief was reinforced later when fighting broke out and students were injured in the principal's classes. Some of the other teachers agreed that since the war couldn't continue forever, we were obliged to do our duty as teachers to overcome the problems imposed by the war.

When the war ended on August 15, 1945, the adults wept and felt a profound unease, but the children rejoiced.

General MacArthur ordered the removal of all militaristic material and references from the education system. This meant going through encyclopedias, textbooks, and other works and blacking out passages considered offensive. We were on pins and needles the day an Occupation General Headquarters team came to see how we had complied with orders. It turned out that an airplane model used in teaching was still on top of a telephone booth in the faculty office. A tall American spotted it at once. The principal took responsibility and was fined a year's salary.

WOMEN WHO
KNOW WANT

Black Market Days
Kiyoko Kagi (54)

Some of us stood stock still, and others, both men and women, had tears in their eyes. But we all felt relief as, on August 15, 1945, we heard the quavering voice of the emperor over the radio announcing Japan's unconditional surrender. At eighteen, I felt resentment, futility, and impotence. Remembering the hellish sights I had witnessed during the air raids, I sobbed till my shoulders shook.

The war was over, but there was new suffering in store for the survivors. The most serious was the shortage of food. Most housewives organized foraging parties in both the cities and the country.

At that time, my mother and father were separated. We six children lived with Mother, who was constantly on the move from morning to night trying to get enough food to keep us alive. Waiting for her to come home, we prepared our supper by making dumplings from corn meal or brownish flour, and concocted a rice soup seasoned with the leaves of peanut plants or the *daikon* radish. Not infrequently she was very late coming home. Thinking that something might have happened to her, we would go out into the dark and wait at the street corner. Sometimes I was so worried that I would stay up all night crying, but doing it quietly so as not to wake my little brothers and sisters. On not a few occasions Mother wouldn't return until the evening of the following day. When this happened, she would usually show us proudly whatever prize articles of food she had managed to get by bartering. But then she would trade these precious things for something else, and they didn't reach our mouths after all. Nonetheless, I was unspeakably grateful to Mother for hurrying about frantically day and night, thinking not of herself but only of us children.

Such food-hunting forays were undertaken by practically every family, sometimes with tragic results. For instance, I remember the story of one housewife who took her small baby with her on one such trip. She strapped the child to her back, as is customary in Japan, and set out to find some food, taking trains that were, literally, murderously crowded. When she returned home and unstrapped the baby, she discovered to her horror that it had been smothered in the packed train.

Some of the transactions engaged in by such people as my mother were illegal, and the police kept a sharp eye out for offenders. But the people in question were not without their devices. Some put false linings in their coats and filled the resulting pouches with their goods. Others disguised parcels as babies, putting shawls or baby wraps on them and strapping the parcels on their backs.

One day, on a station platform, I saw a group of these food hunters in the process of being taken away by the police, who had confiscated their precious purchases and were giving them a scolding. Some of these people pleaded with the police, saying they had only bought enough food for their families. Others, seizing whatever chance presented itself, ducked under the platform and made their escape. Still others sat down and refused to budge. Realizing that these people continually faced the danger of being caught, I began to understand why they went to such lengths to conceal their merchandise.

If the police had merely checked their packages, returned them, and then let the people go free, the matter wouldn't have been so serious. But in some instances these people were put in jail for two or three days. Their children, not knowing what had happened, would go out in search of their parents, whom, I have heard, they sometimes never saw again. Although I felt very sorry for such people and thought the police might be a little more lenient, I understood the need for some kind of control.

At the time an increasing number of people were using the food shortage and food forays as a means to get rich. The police, who after all are only human, could sometimes be cajoled into passing on to these profiteers the goods they had confiscated from other people. This is how the black markets started.

Black marketeers were glib talkers and stopped short of nothing to make a profit, without the slightest compunction for the hardships they caused. Soon their numbers were growing rapidly. Wearing expensive clothes and accessories, in first one town then another, they opened roadside stalls that soon became black-market districts. You could find practically anything at the black markets: clothes, furniture, bicycles, pots and pans, and, most of all, food, including meat, fish, and alcoholic beverages.

These places held an indescribable appeal for young and old alike, whether men or women. In the morning people would make outings to certain black markets and, if they had the money, have a splendid time. The penniless were compelled to look on enviously. It was like a festival, some people bargaining furiously, others buying as much as they could carry.

Before long such rarities as chocolate, cookies, cigarettes, and balls of white rice (it was called silver rice because it was in such short supply) appeared in the stalls. Children would elbow their way through the crowd, grab up as many rice balls as they could, and run for dear life. Some old people tried their hand at stealing but were so slow afoot that they were always caught. Even then they would stand their ground and beg the black marketeer for just one rice ball. Whenever I saw this happen, I wished I were able to buy a rice ball for the old person.

Some children became black marketeers in their own right. After the war many orphans roamed the city streets. They had no money, of course; but their business required no capital. They would steal things to sell on the black market. Steal and sell, steal and sell. This was the only way they had of staying alive. They stole what they found out in front of private homes, even making off with the clothes of people who were

War orphans hang out at Osaka Station. Courtesy of Asahi Shinbun Publishing Co.

taking baths. They never sold their goods for very long in the same place, and were careful to attract the least possible attention. The police patrolled the black markets to prevent illegal transactions, but the black marketeers always seemed to have the upper hand.

The years of my early youth are marked by the indelible nightmare of the war. Nonetheless, I emerged without a single scratch on my body. It was my good fortune to have come through all the many air raids. For the sake of all my fellow countrymen, I feel it my duty to make use of my good health and speak out loud and strong to help see that the fires of war never ravage our land again.

Kimonos and Potatoes
Kimi Tatebayashi (53)

During the less than five years that the war in the Pacific lasted, the Japanese nation was virtually destroyed, and the hearts of the people were deeply scarred. In the immediate postwar period, merely surviving was the primary concern; there was no room for helping others.

Food was so scarce that people picked all the edible weeds and grasses down to the very roots, leaving roadsides and embankments bare. At our home in a rural district in the northeast area of Honshū, we also experienced hungry times, but since we at least had some small fields to cultivate, we were far better off than city people.

Our village was one of the places where large numbers of people fled from the cities to escape the air raids. I recall one day seeing a strange woman, pale and thin with disheveled hair but wearing costly city clothes, asking my grandmother if she knew anyone who would be willing to sell her some food. Grandmother poured her a cup of green tea and said, "We have no food to sell, but at least drink this." The woman courteously bowed her head and accepted the offer. Holding the cup in her hands, she said pleadingly, "I would very much like to buy five measures of rice. But anything will do. Are you quite sure you know no one who could oblige me?"

In those days, money was practically worthless. And as she spoke, the woman removed from her bag a *haori* coat to be worn with a kimono.

It was decorated in gold dust and bore her family crest. Holding it very carefully, she showed it to Grandmother and said, "I was hoping to trade this."

At about this time my father came home from the fields. Nodding to the strange woman, he sat on the floor next to the hearth and packed his small *kiseru* with tobacco. Puffing on the pipe, he listened to the women talking for a while and then said, "Nowadays, you have to be careful about things like this. People who sell and people who buy are liable to be arrested, you know." I recall that father tapped the ash from his *kiseru* as he said this.

Of the five children in our family, I was the only girl. The other four were growing boys with big appetites who came first as far as clothing was concerned. All I ever got was made-over hand-me-downs from my mother or grandmother. At the age of seventeen or eighteen I was said to dress like a twenty-five or twenty-six year old. Though I was my father's favorite, he couldn't afford to buy me any of the things that all young girls crave to have.

When he mentioned to the woman that we had a few potatoes on hand, I wanted to stop him. What would happen if we ran out of food? Before this, any number of people had come to our house asking for food, and Father had never said anything like that. I couldn't imagine what had gotten into him.

Even in the country, unadulterated white rice was called silver rice in those days and considered a great luxury. People reported neighbors who were seen eating rice unmixed with any of the grasses, husks, or root vegetables that were used to make the rice last longer. The police might dash into the house in question—sometimes with their shoes on, the epitome of rudeness in Japan—and demand to know where the rice had come from. Had the family bought it on the black market? Had they lied about the quota of rice that they were obliged to turn over to the local authorities? Then the house would be searched from the attic down to the ground.

I remember coming home from work one evening to see on the table bowls of what—if a little watery—looked like pure white rice. Afraid of what would happen if the police found out, I dashed barefooted into the garden to shut the gate. My mother laughed and told me to try the

KIMONOS AND POTATOES

rice. I picked up the bowl and, to my relief and disappointment, found that the rice was mixed with slivers of *daikon* radish, which I had not noticed at first since it is white too.

We used to wonder when we would be able to eat pure white rice once again. The situation was all the more frustrating since we raised rice ourselves but couldn't do with it as we pleased. Both during and after the war, local officials would come around to estimate crop production and decide how much was to be handed over to the government. No matter whether crops were good or bad, the farmer had a certain quota to meet. The amount that a farmer could keep was determined on the basis of the number and age of family members. As it turns out, the amount we were allowed to keep was about half as much as people to-day consume in a year. That is why we had to stretch out the rice by adding leaves, stalks, potatoes, radishes, and anything else we could find. We even used the leftover bran from milling wheat. This was usually horse fodder, but even the horses turned up their noses at it unless something else was mixed in. Nonetheless, we human beings had to eat it.

Under these circumstances, not knowing what was going on in my father's mind, I was firmly opposed to his selling our potatoes to a stranger. However, when the woman said, "I'm not asking for something special—anything at all would be fine," Father rose and went to the air-raid shelter where we stored our food. He returned with a basket of precious potatoes. "This is all I can let you have," he said. "Will it do?"

"I'm immensely grateful to you. And I promise this won't cause you any trouble," replied the woman. Putting the potatoes into her bag, she bowed repeatedly before leaving.

"A very fine lady," said Father, and then turned to me with a huge smile on his face and exclaimed, "Look what I've bought you. Try it on." I was both happy and sad at the same time. Though still a child, I understood something of what I saw in Father's face. In those days, a garment like that was worn by brides. For a while I was speechless, feel-ing myself on the verge of tears.

Cradling a cup of tea in her hands, Grandmother, who may have been recalling the past or simply grumbling, remarked, "What people were in the past means nothing now. Today poor and rich are alike. It's hav-ing something to eat that matters."

Detestable War

Masako Kadono (48)

As World War II drew to an end, my father, who operated a construction company in Kyoto, took a number of workers with him to Maizuru, where they were to build army barracks. They lived on the site, worked in the snow, and ate soybeans mixed with a tiny bit of rice. My father had a weak stomach to start with, and before long this regime broke his health. When he returned to us in the spring of 1945, he was very weak and often stayed home from work.

At about that time most of the cities in the Kansai region in western Honshū, except for Kyoto, were being bombed. To prevent all our clothing from being burned in an air raid, my family decided to evacuate some of it to Takatsuki in Shiga Prefecture, where my youngest brother, a fourth grader in primary school, had already been sent to live with relatives. My father and next oldest sister packed a rear-car with wicker trunks of family belongings and, with Father on the bicycle pulling the cart and Sister pushing from behind, they set out on a journey of some 150 kilometers.

Though only in the sixth year of primary school myself, I realized how difficult it was to get train tickets or ship parcels and luggage. Still, as I saw them off before sunrise, I was somehow disturbed by what seemed to me to be reckless behavior on my father's part.

According to what my sister told me later, by the time they had crossed Mount Hōsaka and gone along the eastern side of Lake Biwa beyond Ōtsu to reach Yonehara, it had already grown dark and snow was falling. They did what they could to blunt their hunger by buying from a farmer some *daikon* radishes that grew in a roadside field; they ate them raw. Father was in a hurry to reach my uncle's house on the following day because my cousin, of whom Father was especially fond, was to leave for the military. Father wanted to be on time to see him off. He and Sister finally reached my uncle's house late that night; but owing to the strain of the journey, Father was unable to get out of bed the next morning.

At about this time, the rationing of rubber shoes was terminated and we had to wear either straw sandals or wooden clogs. When Father was

■ 108

DETESTABLE WAR

feeling up to it, he made clogs for the family. One day he left a pair half done because he was tired, saying he would finish them the following day. But he never did. Those unfinished clogs later proved to be a dear memento.

After Father had fallen ill, we tried everything in our power to discover the cause, but it was all in vain. His condition gradually grew more serious until, immediately after the defeat on August 15, 1945, he was hospitalized in the Kyoto Municipal Hospital. The hospital was then in a very poor state. The X-ray equipment had all been removed to the country for safety. There was no food, so we had to carry a small charcoal brazier from home and cook rice gruel for Father ourselves. There was no ice for packs when he ran a fever, so we bought some from an ice dealer at a black market near our house and took it to the hospital by bicycle. Unable to receive the prompt attention he needed, Father died a week after he was hospitalized, at the age of forty-six.

Mother, who had just turned forty herself, was left with five children— three girls and two boys, the oldest nineteen and the youngest three— and had to make her way through the confusion of the postwar period as best she could. Though Father had left us some money, it was soon eaten up by spiraling inflation. Life became difficult for mother and children alike. Now that I think back on it, I can appreciate just how hard things were for Mother. But of all my memories, perhaps the most vivid is of the time my older sister and I went into the country to barter for food.

The food situation had grown steadily worse since the end of the war. On this particular occasion, during a holiday on November 3, Mother, my older sister, and I stood in line all night at Kyoto Station to buy train tickets for a food-searching trip. Mother was going to her younger sister's home in Okayama, and my sister and I were headed for Shiga Prefecture, where, as I have already said, we had relatives. The reason that my sister, who was fifteen years old, and I, twelve, were allowed to make the trip by ourselves was probably that all we had to do was pick up some rice that had already been bought with such things as my sisters' kimonos, and was waiting for us at our uncle's home.

Around noon the next day we walked four kilometers from Takatsuki Station to my uncle's house. After eating better food than we had tasted in months, we walked back to the station and waited all night to buy tickets back to Kyoto. Bracing ourselves against the chill of that November night in the countryside, we sat patiently on rucksacks filled with rice. Lack of sleep and the cold soon made us throw up all the good food we had eaten.

When the long miserable night finally ended, we were disappointed to learn that the person ahead of us had bought the last ticket through to Kyoto, and that we could get only as far as Nagahama. Too unhappy even to cry, we had no recourse but to travel to Nagahama, get off, and wait in line again for tickets to Kyoto. Rice was a regulated item at the time, and ordinary civilians were forbidden to buy or sell it. The police were always on the lookout for violators. That day, as we waited for the train at Nagahama, a policeman was examining the luggage of all the people on the platform. It was pretty obvious from the looks of my sister's rucksack and my two cloth-wrapped bundles—one in each hand—that we were carrying rice. If the policeman searched our things, we would be caught for certain. My sister told me to stop staring, to look straight ahead and act nonchalant, but that didn't keep my knees from knocking together.

The policeman stopped at the man in front of us and, as was bound to happen sooner or later, discovered he was carrying rice. As the policeman pulled the bundle from the old man, it split and rice spilled out on the platform. I can still see the misery on the old man's face.

Just then the train pulled in; and, to our great relief, the policeman dismissed us as children not worth bothering about. We dashed on board.

But even this train only went as far as Yonehara, where we had to get off and wait some more. Finally the Tōkaidō main-line train arrived. It was so crowded that people were hanging from the decks. There seemed no hope of our getting on. Yet if we didn't, there was no telling when we would get home.

My sister, who was carrying only a rucksack and therefore had her hands free, managed somehow to get on, but she left me, with my hands full, crying loudly on the platform. And it was she who had the tickets. All of a sudden, someone said, "The poor little thing. Help her get aboard." And I was dragged and pulled until I managed to clamber up and find a place. The little lunch our aunt had packed for us—rice balls wrapped in bamboo husks—was as crumpled and crushed as we were. But we shared it, and late that night finally arrived home.

The food situation continued to get worse. Sometimes we went for months with nothing but meal dumplings and sweet potatoes, but not a grain of rice. Being constantly hungry was a dreadful experience for us children, who were at the age when appetites are biggest. We would never have been forced to live that way, and our father might still be alive today, if it had not been for that detestable war.

Worse than the Deprivation
Kikuko Ueda (57)

Though there was really no end to them, I have nevertheless tried to describe in the following pages some of the hardships and inconveniences we Japanese women suffered in providing for our families during and immediately after World War II.

As the fighting began in earnest in 1941, laws were passed against what was considered luxurious living. Instead of long sleeves, we had to wear short sleeves on our kimonos. Kimonos themselves were then replaced by baggy trousers called *mompe*. Clothing and cloth were rationed on a point system, which meant that families with daughters had to skimp so that the girls could have nicer things to wear. Silk disappeared to be replaced by rayon, and flannel was woven with a mixture of rayon. Supplies of staples like bleached cotton were unreliable. Both fabrics and dyes were so inferior that, once washed, the original shapes and colors were lost.

We lived in the country and were especially troubled by not having enough working clothes. Since thread was in short supply, we planted cotton for spinning and weaving. But before long the government put a stop to this and called for the planting of sweet potatoes, from which alcohol for fuel could be made. My grandmother tried to get around this by spinning thread from the cotton stuffing of our bedding. Mother wove the thread into cloth.

In one respect, we were better off than people in the city. We raised

silkworms and thread for weaving, sending the thread to Kyoto for dyeing. Unfortunately, after the war, when our food rations were often late,
most of this silk disappeared into pawn shops. Mother used her spare
moments to pull threads from waste cocoons. This thread was then dyed
and woven into striped or checked patterns for everyday clothing or bedding covers. Mother also collected the waste threads produced in weaving. During the lulls in the field work, she would sit on the embankments
tying hundreds and thousands of them together to be woven into cloth.
All of this was necessary to keep a large family of ten in clothes.

My mother, whom we joked about because of her poor-woman's ways
of making use of discarded material, tore waste muslin and red silk and
used them for the woof in weaving striped and patterned sashes. We
also redyed used cloth as best we could and made Western-style clothes
out of old cotton *yukata* kimonos.

One of the most distressing shortages was that of antiseptic absorbent
cotton used during menstruation. This was a hygienic necessity if we
were to become the healthy mothers and grandmothers of future generations. Perhaps the government overlooked this particular need. Perhaps
it was a regional distribution problem. At any rate, we were forced to
do something. A doctor told us that we could make absorbent cotton
by boiling the cotton stuffing in bedding with caustic soda. But there
was a limit to stuffing, and I preferred to boil and sterilize fibers from
cotton plants whenever I could get them.

After the war, certain government stocks were made available cheap
to the public. For instance, military clothing that had been secretly stored
in nearby mountains came to us as rations. It was possible to make an
overcoat from an old army blanket and then a sleeveless jacket out of
the leftovers. It was fashionable to make handbags from what was apparently felt soundproofing and decorate them with embroidered patterns of rayon thread. Woolen army socks could be unraveled and reknit-
ted into baby clothes.

Diapers were a serious problem. There was never enough silk or rayon
to go around. We had to rely on whatever old cotton fabrics we could
find. Some of them were so rough that they chafed the babies' skin nearly
raw.

Even in this time of shortages, a relative gave me a splendid black overcoat of the type worn by navy officers. I had long dreamed of having a new dress, and now, with wartime restrictions ended, I was free to make one for myself from this coat. It took some time, but I was pleased with the results. For a belt I twisted short strips of tanned pigskin into a kind of rope. I still have a photograph of myself in that dress.

Old people, with the wisdom that comes from experience, advised us to use unbleached cotton for our bedcovers since it lasted longer. Of course, it was necessary to repair and patch the covers as they wore out. And, on fair days, when wives followed the Japanese custom of airing such things out in the sun, the mattresses and quilts looked like so much patchwork.

Informality in everyday dress was still the rule at this time. Even as late as the 1950s, it was not unusual to see women moving about in front of their gates in slips or for men to go shopping in long johns. At weddings, an arm band was the needed item for the groom to be considered formally attired, and most brides wore *mompe* trousers. In my case, however, my husband's father, who had lived abroad for many years, wanted the bride to wear a proper Japanese kimono. Of course, this was still during the war, which ruled out the colorful, elaborate kimonos usually worn at weddings during peace time. What I did was wear a black mourning kimono that I decorated with white basting along the front, and then arranged some small flowers in my hair, which was cut in a Western fashion.

Before I married and moved to Osaka in 1944, I had, as I mentioned before, lived in the country, where food was relatively abundant. In addition to what we grew ourselves, the nearby ocean provided us with fresh seafood. And there were seasonal fruits and berries in the fields and forests throughout the year. Edible grasses grew along the levees between paddy fields. But even in the country the strict enforcement of rationing meant we had to mix our rice with plenty of wheat and other things.

In Osaka, however, at a time when the war situation was worsening, even the government distribution system tended to break down. There were really no fresh vegetables or fish, and yams and pumpkins replaced rice as our staple food.

At one juncture I became so emaciated that we sent an SOS to the country. My father, in spite of the difficulties of shipping things at the time, contrived to send me a straw sack filled with vegetables such as onions and yams and a wooden box of rice, which he had saved up from the ration his family received. He arranged the vegetables around the rice so as to conceal it and took care to compensate for differences in weight. The vegetables, which would not keep long, I shared with our neighbors. And I bartered some of the rice to get the tobacco my husband so loved; the rest we used to make the thinnest rice gruel. The going rate was 1 *shō* (1.8 liters) of rice for one package of tobacco, which came loose and had to be rolled at home. Cigarettes were rolled thin to make the supply of tobacco last longer. It makes me sad to think that some of the rice my father had gone to such pains to send us had to be used in this way.

After the war, we at last managed to get food fit for human beings in the form of soybean pulp, sugar, palm flour, cornmeal, and diced and dried yams. But the confusion reigning throughout the country at the time made supplies from home impossible.

The least little patch of ground was planted and then fertilized with night soil from our own toilet. From Osaka's streams and ponds, which were clean enough then for wild parsley to grow in, we caught crawfish to eat. What rice we managed to get wasn't completely polished, so we put it in a glass bottle and pounded it with a stick. If there was any wheat flour and sugar, we combined them with rice bran to make dumplings.

It was popular then to make a kind of dark bread in a homemade oven consisting of iron plates set on wooden boxes. The bread crumbled when it cooled, but we thought it was awfully good. Some enterprising people made rice crackers out of palm flour and devised ways to prepare various simple confections out of whatever sugar they could get. The worst thing was the soybean pulp, which was really fit only for horse fodder. Since it did not cook well with rice, we prepared it by itself and added a little salt for flavor.

In those days many people went out to the country to try to trade their personal belongings for rice. Transactions of this kind were strictly forbidden, and there were police on guard at Osaka Station to check incoming passengers. Since some women bundled up bags of rice to look like babies, whenever I went to the station with my oldest son on my

WORSE THAN THE DEPRIVATION

back, the police would feel him all over to make sure he was what he was made out to be.

Just as there was a shortage of food, there was a scarcity of articles needed for day-to-day living. Clogs were coarsely made, lacked straps, and had strips of old tire stuck on the bottom to reduce wear and tear. Old newspapers served as toilet paper, and the slippers customarily positioned at the toilet door were made of either straw or bamboo husks. During the war my grandmother washed her hair with the pulp left over from making camellia oil or with the whites from eggs—only the broken ones—that our chickens laid. Sometimes she used the eggshells. To scrub our faces, we used bags filled with rice bran, and for toilet water there were cucumber and squash peelings or the juice from the sponge gourd.

Lime was used to wash colored cotton clothes, and the water left over from soaking rice for white clothes. After the war, bars of black soap were issued, but since they actually made the clothes dirtier than they had been, we didn't use them, and could not imagine what they might be made of.

During the war, gas supplies in Osaka were cut off. We cooked on wood burners stoked with what we could find. As part of our rations we received long pieces of hard wood that were a chore to cut and split. Whenever we burned some wood, we never allowed it to burn down to ashes but put it in an extinguishing pot, to make a kind of charcoal that could be used again. We went into the woods for brush to burn and walked the railway tracks looking for pieces of coal that had fallen from trains. Some people became so weary of the frequent air-raid alarms that they began burning their furniture as fuel, thinking that if it was going to be burned anyway, they might as well get some use from it.

Pots, pans, and even their rush and rattan handles were rationed. Newlyweds started out, not with new pots and pans, but ones that had been repaired and patched.

In about 1944, near the end of the war, people began leaving the big cities. Soon there were numerous houses for rent or left vacant in Osaka. My husband and I were in a new house, only two years old, at the time. But, being pregnant, I was eventually forced to leave the city for the safety of the country. When we returned to Osaka in 1946, after the war was over, we found an old house to live in. To a country-bred person like me, used to big farmhouses, it looked quite small. Still, looking back, I realize that it was big enough for a married couple and my mother-in-law: it had five rooms and a traditional ornamental alcove.

These were some of the inconveniences of the war. But far worse than all the physical deprivations was the spiritual oppression suffered by the common Japanese citizen.

Money changes hands at the Umeda black market in Osaka.

WORSE THAN THE DEPRIVATION

WOMEN WHO HAVE KNOWN HELL

A Life Long Ago Ruined

Kazuko Saegusa (54)

One of my younger sisters, who had once been a pretty little gird loved by everyone, died just five years ago. But her life had been ruined long before, when she was only eight, by a horrible air raid that took place thirty-seven years ago.

Before the war, the park near our house was a thickly wooded Shinto grove where it was dark even at high noon. Today, when the weather is good, old people take walks there, and young mothers play with their children. But for me that grove is filled with terrible, unforgettable memories. The children that I saw there the night of the air raid screamed in pain, and burned skin hung in tatters from the bodies of many of them.

Our neighborhood was full of military installations: a railroad brigade, a balloon corps, and infantry and antiaircraft schools. On Sundays the area was crowded with military men on liberty. Food was scarce then, and the local children loved to beg soldiers for the dried bread they were issued when on leave. But perhaps more important was the sense of security the children had from seeing so many military men in the neighborhood all the time. We felt that even if the Americans attacked, these men would protect us. Far from running away when the handsome B29s flew overhead, we stood and watched them unafraid.

This sense of security accounted for the confusion that hit us all on the night of July 7, 1945, when a squadron of B29s delivered a concentrated attack on our city of Chiba. In a frenzy people grabbed up useless things like dishes and mosquito nets as they fled out of doors in search of shelter.

When my family had recovered from the shock of the air-raid alarm, we noticed that the inside of the house was as bright as if it were broad daylight, though ordinarily the bamboo thicket around our house made everything pitch black at night. Putting on the first clothes I could find, I rushed outside and then stopped dead in my tracks, amazed to see the bamboo thicket ablaze.

Mother's shrill call for us to run for our lives brought me back to my senses. We had to escape, but flames roared at every turn. Terrified, we dodged among them.

As we tried to reach a main street, incendiary bombs continued falling. Full-grown trees toppled over to block our path. Embankments caved in. It took seemingly forever to cover a distance that ordinarily would take only two or three minutes.

I was exhausted by the time I reached the main street. Low-flying aircraft strafed us, and great waves of people, screaming and shoving, hurtled toward the grove, which was designated a place of refuge.

My eight-year-old sister, who was carrying the youngest girl, two years old at the time, was running about ten meters in front of me when suddenly she fell sprawling. The baby flew from her arms and rolled two or three meters. Fortunately, she was unhurt. But I was horrified to see that my other sister's head had split open like a pomegranate and was spurting blood.

It turns out that the parachute of an incendiary bomb cluster—they were apparently dropped in clusters of about twenty, which separated in the air as they fell—had hit a large cedar tree, and the impact caused the bomb attached to the parachute to explode downward, ripping my sister's clothing and cleaving her head.

For a few seconds I was too stunned to know what had happened. Coming to myself, I tied my sister's head with a small towel that was around my neck. But this wasn't enough to stop the bleeding. I called out for help, but no one paid any attention. They kept racing toward the grove. Beside myself, I suddenly found the strength to pick up my sister—who was nearly as large as I was, though two years younger— and put her on my back, then dashed forward into the sea of people.

Nearly two thousand men were said to have come back from Manchuria and be quartered in the balloon corps building near the park. But they all must have gone somewhere: not one of them came out to help us.

Knowing that something had to be done for my sister, I searched frantically for help until I heard that an emergency treatment center had been set up in the balloon corps air-raid shelter. Although my legs had lost all feeling, I carried her there, set her down at the entrance, and looked inside. I almost fainted at the sight. Corpses lay everywhere. Still, without strength to go any further, I carried my unconscious sister inside. Driven nearly mad by the moans and cries of the dying, I spent a long, wakeful night by her side.

When that hellish night had passed and my sister was still unconscious, I borrowed a pull cart from a nearby farmer and took her to a national hospital not far away. I shall never forget it. It was drizzling that morning, and low-flying planes continued to strafe anything in sight. Walking between the paddy fields made me a perfect target. Our family had gotten separated, and I had no idea where the others might be. Still I kept pulling the steel bar of the cart because I knew my sister had to have help as soon as possible. I had eaten nothing and was completely done in. How I made it to the hospital is a mystery to me.

At last at the hospital, it took a very long time before the doctors finally got around to my sister. Her wound was deeper than I thought and required twenty stitches. The shrapnel from the bomb had permanently deformed her spine.

The corridors of the hospital were packed with people burned past recognition. There were many young people whose arms or legs had been amputated. Though not a doctor myself, I could tell that some of them would soon die. The screaming was beyond description. It was July and hot. Maggots wriggled from the bandages that covered everything but the eyes. I stayed by my sister's side throughout all this, but sleeping was out of the question.

Before long the hospital became so crowded that we were moved to an emergency medical camp in a playground near the local Shinto shrine. Each time we were strafed, I would grab my sister and run for cover. Children burned by incendiary bombs often rushed into the grove howling in pain.

The wound to my sister's head deformed her whole face. Her hair could be combed down over the scar, but nothing could hide the curvature of her spine. Still, even with her body bent double, she sometimes managed to do the dancing she loved. Her poor posture eventually damaged her abdomen, and she later died of stomach cancer.

A LIFE LONG AGO RUINED

My Daughters

Yasu Takeuchi (78)

"It was you who killed our daughters! You killed them, because you didn't see they were safely evacuated!" These were the first words my husband hurled at me when he returned from the South Pacific after the end of World War II. I had struggled on in the hope that when he came back he would take me by the hand, pity me for the horrible experience I had gone through, and offer to share my sorrow and tears. But no matter how much I explained, he refused to understand what it had been like in Hiroshima the day the atomic bomb fell, the day we lost two of our daughters.

"You killed our daughters!" With his eyes red and swollen from crying, he tormented me for a very long time. Thinking back on it now, I realize that he was taking his suffering out on me because he had no other way to relieve his feelings. But at the time, each of his words was like a dagger in my breast, making my grief worse than it had been.

A long while after the end of the war, having heard about the bombing from many other people, my husband at last stopped berating me. He has been dead now for many years, and I no longer have anyone to whom I must explain. I really don't want to remember or to talk about what happened then. But we survivors have a duty to speak of it, so that the same kind of tragedy will never be repeated.

In the summer of 1945 I was living in Mizushi-machi in Hiroshima with my four daughters and my younger sister and her husband. Because of the military policy that kept students and working girls in the city, the three older girls could not be evacuated, but our fourth and youngest child had been sent to safety in the country. My husband was in the military in the South Pacific, and we prayed every day for his safe return.

On August 6, 1945, my oldest daughter, Kuniko, had gone to work at a savings bureau. Mineko, our third daughter, had left to work on what was called domestic evacuation. Our second daughter had a day off and was at home with me.

Some time after seeing Kuniko and Mineko off there was a blinding flash and then a tremendous blast that flattened our house, burying my daughter and me under it. It was instantaneous, and I had no idea what had happened.

My sister and her husband pulled my daughter and me from under the wreckage. We were covered with red dirt. When we had had a few minutes to collect yourselves, I washed my face and saw I had a large, freely bleeding wound on my head. There were burns all over my body.

But my little girl was in a much more pitiable condition. She had been sitting on the floor with her back to a large three-leaf mirror. When the blast hit, the mirror had been broken into tiny pieces, many of which had buried themselves in her back.

My daughter and I were taken to the Sumiyoshi Shinto Shrine, where we found many other wounded people, some of whom were barely alive. Soon I was told to go to Sumiyoshi Bridge and catch a boat taking people to a nearby island for treatment. At this point, I was separated from my daughter. A soldier had picked her up and taken her off someplace where the seriously wounded were treated. For many days I had no idea where she was, or even whether she was still alive.

When the boat arrived at Sumiyoshi Bridge, people rushed to get aboard. I waited for the next boat, and then for the next, until finally I found myself alone on the dock. Having gone three days without food or water, I fainted, falling to the ground like one of the dead. When I came to, I was assailed by worry and grief over the whereabouts of my daughters and sister. I wanted to go in search of them, but my body refused to move. I could do nothing but lie there, a hatred of the blinding flash welling up within me.

In a few days a nephew from Yoshijima found me, after having looked almost everywhere. Had he not found me when he did, I might have died. That night I was able to sleep in a bomb shelter, and the next day he took me to Yoshijima. The family house had been destroyed in the blast, but they had built a shack of boards and logs to keep out the rain.

The next day I went in search of my daughters. Sharp pains were shooting through my head, and I tried to keep it cool with a wet towel. I walked as fast as I could, but my legs, covered with burns and bruises, were not up to the task. Still I had no choice but to walk. There were no vehicles of any kind.

Only people who were there can know what Hiroshima was like.

Burnt-out ruins stretched as far as the eye could see. Everywhere in this hellish scene lay wounded people and corpses. But no matter how hard I searched, I was unable to discover where my children were. Nonetheless, I was determined to find them, regardless of what might happen to me.

After I am not sure how many days, my second daughter came back. After we had been separated at Sumiyoshi Bridge, she had been taken by the soldier to a hospital to be treated for her wounds. Then another soldier had taken her to an uncle's house in Itsukaichi. Though I was still worried about Kuniko and Mineko, it was a relief to have found at least one of my children.

But my relief soon turned to inexpressible grief and despair at news of Kuniko's death. She had been at work when the bomb hit, and as one of the seriously wounded had been taken to a hospital. She was naked, her face so badly burned and swollen that it was impossible to recognize her. Her uncle Shimizu from Itsukaichi was also at the hospital, helping the wounded as a member of the fire brigade. Hearing a faint voice call out, "Uncle Shimizu," he turned to find Kuniko lying on the hospital floor with so many other wounded people that it was difficult to walk without stepping on someone. Her clothing had been blown off in the blast, but around her waist was a wrapping cloth bearing the name Shimizu. This was how he recognized her. She died that very night.

Kuniko, dear daughter!
How you must have suffered.
How lonely you must have felt.
Mother will never forgive the bomb, Kuniko,
That tore and ripped you like an old rag.
No one to turn to, no one to tell your grief,
All alone, Kuniko, you departed this life.
On August 6 Mother lay unconscious at Sumiyoshi Bridge,
Unaware of your death.
Kuniko, forgive me!
Mother could do nothing for you.
Forgive me, forgive me, forgive me.
Even now the thought of you makes me breathless.

Kuniko was nineteen when she died. Maybe it's wrong to praise one's own child, but Kuniko was a fine, intelligent girl, especially good at mental arithmetic. I only wish I could have been with her at the end.

Although I had been unable to locate Mineko in all my searchings, I soon received news from her school. She had been at morning assembly when the bomb fell. Although Mineko and all the other children were injured, they managed to find shelter nearby in Hijiyama Park. Later the seriously wounded—including my Mineko—were taken by truck to a national elementary school at Fuchū. Unable to stand, Mineko was lying in the truck. Someone inadvertently stepped on her arm, and the burned skin popped open like a pomegranate. This hideous torture was inflicted on her several times during the ride. Each time she screamed in pain for her mother. She was only thirteen.

> Mineko, dear daughter!
> Over your raw arms flies swarm,
> Brazenly laying their eggs.
> Over your wounds maggots wriggle,
> Burrowing in.
> As if by right, they occupy your flesh.
> The thought of it maddens your mother.
>
> A stranger, a kind and blessed person,
> Plucks out the worms with chopsticks.
> Oh, thank you, thank you, kind person.
>
> Mineko, dear daughter!
> Though Fuchū is frustratingly far,
> My heart races to you.
> Wait for me! Live for me!
> Mother is coming.

My throat parched and legs dragging, I hurried toward Fuchū. My one thought was a prayer that Mineko would still be alive. When I arrived at the school, I found my poor child lying on the hard sandy floor of the lecture hall. Her face was so swollen that her eyes and nose were no longer recognizable. But I knew her voice when she called out to me. Her fingers had swollen so badly that it looked as if she were wearing

MY DAUGHTERS

a baseball glove. "My fingers are sticking together," she sobbed. I gently wrapped each finger in gauze.

Mineko had been clever with her hands and often made dolls out of leftover cloth. Looking at her fingers that day, she sadly said, "Mother, I won't be able to make dolls any more." I felt so sorry for her that I would gladly have changed places if only I could.

Burns covered her whole body, bleeding and festering. The doctor would hurriedly strip away the bandages, causing the blood and pus to pour forth, exposing the raw flesh. Each time she sobbed in pain. I couldn't help being angry at the doctor for inflicting such pain. To make things as easy as I could for her, before the doctor made his rounds I wet the bandages with antiseptic solution and then gingerly removed them bit by bit. Still, the burns kept her in agony day and night.

I have practically no recollection of what I ate and how I spent my time during those nine days of nightmare, when patients died one after another. I remained at Mineko's side until finally, on the night of August 29, in the murky darkness of the lecture hall, she died.

Not a light in the hall
As your thirteen years end,
My poor Mineko.
I cannot see your face;
Our eyes cannot meet.
I strain to hear
The fading beat of your heart.
Mineko, dear daughter!
Don't die, don't die!
In the darkness, only this.
With breath held,
I place an ear
To your budding breast.
Mineko, dear daughter!
Don't die, don't die!

At dawn, I gently cleaned the already cold body of my child and dressed her in pure-white cotton underclothes and a flower-patterned cotton kimono—her best clothes—which I had brought with me from the country. Other people tried to console me by saying how lovely she looked.

Kuniko and Mineko had been gentle, healthy girls. I couldn't be at Kuniko's side; she died alone. But at least I was able to care for Mineko for nine days, and to be with her at the end.

It rained heavily the day I was to start back from Fuchū. People urged me to stay another night and wait for better weather, but I had to leave. Drenched with rain, carrying the cremated remains of my child, I walked back to Yoshijima.

Thinking of how Mineko looked as a toddler, or of her excitement as she prepared for a primary-school picnic, I wept and talked to her, who was now no more than a few bones that rattled softly as I walked in the rain.

The pain from the wound in my head continued unabated. Finally all my hair fell out. Nonetheless, even bald, I was determined to have funeral services for my daughters. With a neckerchief around my head, I saw them to their final resting place.

When my second daughter returned from the hospital, she was unable to lie facing up because of the glass that had become embedded in her back. When I took her to the hospital to have the glass removed it had to be done without benefit of anesthetics. The pain was excruciating. No matter how many pieces were taken out, there were always more. She was only sixteen when she underwent this ordeal. I couldn't bear to watch. Some of the glass is still there and troubles her on rainy days.

Although my youngest daughter escaped exposure to the bomb, she has nonetheless had to suffer with me during the long period in which I have been afflicted with medullary leukemia. The scars of the atomic bomb are borne not only by the victims themselves, but also by their families and loved ones.

Although my husband is now dead, and two of my daughters were lost in the Hiroshima bombing, today, at the age of seventy-eight, I am glad that I survived. Even when marred with suffering and despair, life is good. I am sure that my daughters too wanted very much to go on living. For the sake of my living daughters and in memory of my departed ones, I hope to live out the rest of my life in a spirit of hope.

The Dream of Hide-and-Seek
Kikuno Egi (69)

In the summer of 1945 there was little food to eat, but still my husband and I and our three children—our son Tadahito, who was nine; our oldest girl, Sachiko, who was four; and our second daughter, Fumiko, who was only four months—were all healthy and living out each day as best we could in our home in Funairi Hommachi, Hiroshima. One day, however, our little happiness was obliterated in a flash of light.

I shall never forget the morning of August 6. I had just seen my husband off to the Japan Steel Works, where he had been conscripted to work, and the children and I were having the little bit of food we called breakfast. Suddenly there was an immense flash of light. I called out to the children to put on their protective hats and run for cover, but almost simultaneously a tremendous blast of wind rushed down on us, scattering everything in its path. Dust swirled in the air, blocking out the light and making it difficult to breathe. For a while I lay on top of Fumiko to protect her.

None of us had the faintest idea what had happened, but fortunately the children were not seriously hurt. Going outdoors, we saw old Mr. Arai, who lived across the street, pinned under his collapsed house. He was calling for help, and a number of people were trying to get him out. But he was hopelessly caught under a heavy post. His house had caught fire, and I can still hear his screams as he was burned alive.

Then I heard my husband's younger sister, who lived next door, calling out for help. She had been trapped in the toilet. Somehow I managed to pull a section of the wall aside and free her.

Running along the road, I could think of nothing but my husband. I wondered how far he had gotten before the flash. I prayed he was still alive and well. On the way I met him coming back. He was soaking wet from head to foot, and the upper part of his body was badly burned. He had been blown into the river by the blast as he crossed Meiji Bridge, and it had taken every ounce of energy he had to swim ashore. Staggering, skin hanging from his arms and face, he hardly looked human. Still he spoke in a firm voice: "Are you all right? There's still time to escape. Hurry to your family's home on Edajima Island. I'll be all right by myself."

When I hesitated to leave him alone, he scolded me and said to look after the children.

From that time on, I became like someone in a frenzy. I wrapped a diaper around the wounded leg of one child, told Tadahito to carry Fumiko, put Sachiko on my back, and started out for Ujina Harbor as fast as my legs would carry me.

The people we met on the way were mostly naked and burned reddish brown. Their skin hung from their faces, arms, and legs. Some trembled, cried out, and then, before you knew it, they fell dead. The dying stretched out their hands and called for water with their last breath. But no one gave them any. In their flight people walked over children who shrieked in pain at the slightest touch. We were witnessing not something of this world, but a living hell.

Still, we all had to run as fast as we could because the flames pursued us. Now as I try to put down my memories of that time, I realize that it is impossible to describe them in words. Only someone who was there can understand.

When we finally reached Edajima Island, the long summer day had ended. So much had happened that we could do nothing but cry all night.

The next day we couldn't return to Hiroshima, which was still a sea of flames. But we did return, with my mother, on the eighth. I carried Fumiko on my back. The city lay in total ruins. Only two or three reinforced-concrete buildings, like the Fukuya Department Store, still stood in the center of town. To the north and west, as far as the eye could see, nothing was standing. Near Yokogawa Bridge we saw a horse that had burned to death. From the Red Cross Hospital to Takano Bridge were mountains of bodies. No doubt relatives and loved ones were searching for each one of them. The river at Meiji and Sumiyoshi bridges were filled with bodies. Soldiers were pouring kerosene on the dead and burning them. What words can describe scenes like these?

I clearly remember the sight of a small girl about Sachiko's age who had died with her hands covering her eyes and ears. I could not help thinking how terrified the child must have been, how she must have longed for her mother, how she would rather have died in her mother's arms. I couldn't control the anger I felt. What had this child done? What had any of us done? I started crying and couldn't stop.

THE DREAM OF HIDE-AND-SEEK

At the west of Sumiyoshi Bridge I saw Mr. Miura, the rice dealer in our neighborhood, sitting beside a small fire. To my remark, "I'm glad you came out of it alive. How is your family?" he said in a despondent voice, "My son died. I'm cremating his body now. My wife was burned to death in our house." What could I say to him? Two days later, I heard, he died himself.

At Funairi I met my older sister—her child had died on the sixth—who told me my husband was in the Enami Army Hospital. I hurried there, but couldn't find him among the huge number of burned people. But finally I heard him call out, "Here I am."

Delighted to think he was all right, I turned toward the voice, but burst into tears at what I saw. He was practically unrecognizable. His skin had turned black, was dry, taut, and peeling. Still I was thankful he was alive.

That day he wept as he promised he wouldn't die. He said he couldn't leave me alone with nothing to eat, no house to live in, and three children to care for. That would be too much to bear.

I went back to Edajima that day and searched the whole island for tomatoes and squash to take to my husband. On the tenth, I returned to the hospital, this time taking Sachiko with me. My husband doted on all our children but was especially fond of Sachiko. He was overjoyed

Atomic Dome, Hiroshima.

to see us and for a while wouldn't let Sachiko leave his side. This was the last time we were to see him alive.

On the eleventh, Sachiko fell sick and we couldn't make it to Hiroshima. On the afternoon of the thirteenth, I took all three children with me, but by the time we reached the city we were so exhausted that we had to ask an acquaintance to put us up.

At about five o'clock in the morning on the fourteenth, Sachiko began crying and wouldn't stop. She said she was sorry but that she couldn't help it. "I want to stop, Mother, but I can't."

We had our breakfast and arrived at the hospital at about eight. We were shocked to find that there were only two or three people in the ward, which had been filled on our last visit. My husband was not among the remaining patients. A nurse who happened to pass by said, "Oh yes, I know who you mean. He had four false front teeth and kept calling for Sachiko." When I told her Sachiko was my daughter, the nurse held Sachiko tenderly in her arms and said, "Your father died this morning at about five o'clock. He was calling your name."

On my way to the morgue I silently asked my husband why he had broken his word, why he had left me and the children alone with nothing to eat, nothing to wear, and no place to go. At the entrance to the morgue I realized why there were so few patients in the ward: they had all been moved here. An indescribable odor filled the air. Somehow I was not afraid. Since he had died only that morning, my husband was not far from the door. He was completely naked, and I had nothing to cover him with. Two or three maggots wriggled on his face.

That night we kept a long vigil while soldiers cremated his body on the Enami Firing Range. When nine-year-old Tadahito said, "I'm sleepy. Let's go home," I suddenly realized that we had no home to return to. That fiendish bomb had determined our fate, thrusting me and the children into the life of misery my husband had foretold before his death.

We had no clothes but what was on our backs and two or three diapers for Fumiko. In a hut that we rented on Edajima, all four of us slept on a single mattress I got from my sister. We had no electric lights and no *tatami* mats on the floor. We had no land to raise food on, and no clothing to barter with. People all over Japan were going hungry. The best we could do was to go to the fields tilled by my parents and brothers and

THE DREAM OF HIDE-AND-SEEK

gather leaves, yam vines, and mugwort, making them into a kind of soup. In September it rained every day, keeping me from going to the mountains to find edible herbs or to the beach to hunt shellfish.

Tadahito cried desperately when he saw some local children eating steamed yams. Holding him close to me, I cried with him, wishing the bomb had never fallen and that my husband were still alive.

Rice rations were a month late, and the people in charge refused to sell me some of the piles of rationed squash and potatoes that were on hand. "You're not the only ones going hungry," they said.

With absolutely nothing to eat, my children and I would soon have starved to death. But one day we staggered to the rationing center in a neighboring village, and there our story found sympathetic ears. "It's a good thing you came, or Edajima would have had its first starvation cases," the man there said, and gave us some wheat flour and vegetable scraps.

We had no footwear. I improvised by putting thongs on any wooden clogs or pieces of board that I picked up on the beach. And on top of all this poverty and misery came illness. I developed an unidentifiable fever, my hair fell out, and I got very weak. Sachiko, who before the bombing had never been sick a day in her life, came down with a bad case of jaundice because, the doctor told us, her liver was in bad condition. Fumiko got boils on her head, something like érysipelas. At one point, all four of us were in the hospital at the same time.

Probably the most intolerable of all was the way the other villagers always suspected us when something disappeared. For instance, when someone stole yams from the fields that some sailors were cultivating, we were immediately suspected since we were the poorest people in the village. Once we were even called into the village office to be questioned. When I protested that I could never steal anything because my children were witnesses to everything I did, the investigator said, "Kids keep their mouths shut if their parents tell them to."

This was so humiliating and insulting that I decided to commit suicide. When I let this thought slip out, Sachiko said, "Mother, please don't. But if you have to, kill me first while I'm asleep." I never dreamed I would ever hear such words from a girl only four and a half years old. But none of the children objected to the idea of death. Life was so hard that they couldn't even say they didn't want to die. Yet they had patiently put up with everything.

Just thinking about it, I was overcome with pity and love for my children. I realized that instead of thinking of taking them with me in death, I should try my utmost to make them happy. I vowed to consider any future temptations to commit suicide as incentives to go on living, no matter how hard life became.

It was dawn by the time I reached this decision. Feeling myself very weak, I spoke to the children in my heart, saying that there was no longer any need for suicide. I asked their forgiveness and promised to do my best in the future.

At last I managed to contact the Japan Steel Works, where my husband had worked, and they sent some money for the funeral expenses and as a token of sympathy. I was specially happy and relieved to get the two blankets they sent. Winter was setting in, and I used the blankets to make warm clothes for the children. The year of the bombing, I made do with the cotton-crepe kimono my younger brother's wife had given me.

We went on living in this way until October 29, 1946, the day of the Hiroshima Festival. I had decided to take the children to see the festival since they had so little enjoyment in their lives. We all boarded the ferry connecting the island of Edajima with Hiroshima. The children had been excited and happy since early morning. It warmed my heart to see them smiling.

But at the pier, the boat became unbalanced and capsized. The hold, where the four of us had gone because Fumiko was still breast-feeding, was soon flooded. In spite of the excruciating pain I felt when my lungs filled with water, I did not want to be helped. All I could think was, "If we can stand the suffering a little longer, we'll all go to be together with Father."

But Tadahito's call for help brought me back to reality. He was still alive, and I could not leave him to be an orphan. I began struggling with all my might, and I soon saw a little light in a corner above me. I don't remember what happened after that. The next thing I knew I was on dry land. Tadahito had been saved. That morning Sachiko—whose name means "happiness"—died, followed in the evening by Fumiko. Sachiko

THE DREAM OF HIDE-AND-SEEK

was five years and four months old, Fumiko one year and six months.

They had first lost their father. And as a mother I had been too weak to do much for them. They had never even had good food to eat. Probably the best thing Sachiko ever had eaten in her whole life was the fresh green seaweed her father brought home from the sea off Yoshijima Prison, which I had combined with other things to sprinkle on steamed rice.

For months I thought of the pitifulness of their lives and of my own impotence. For hours on end I sat without moving, like someone insane. Then one night I had a dream. In it, my husband, Sachiko, and Fumiko were having a wonderful time playing hide-and-seek. Afterward I came to think that my husband had been unable to bear our suffering and decided to take the two girls to be with him. I looked at the children's deaths in a different light and came to know a measure of calm.

In 1949 I remarried. My present husband has been good to Tadahito. I still suffer from low blood pressure and constant inexplicable headaches and cannot go a month without a doctor. One bomb plunged countless people into a hell that continues even today. Because I know what Hiroshima was like, I abhor nuclear experiments by any nation whatever. I'm old now, but as long as I live I will go on speaking out against the misery of nuclear warfare.

The Scars Remain
Kikue Tada (56)

Hiroshima—a city proud of its abundant greenery, blue skies, and its seven rivers forming a beautiful delta—was converted in an instant to scorched earth by the atomic bomb. Even now, thirty-seven years later, I cannot forget the scenes I saw then, scenes beyond the power of pen or tongue to describe.

I was twelve in 1937, when the so-called China Incident occurred. Having been taught that dying for one's country was a great honor, I decided to become a nurse and tend soldiers on the battlefield. When the Pacific War began in December 1941, I had made the spirit of Florence

Nightingale my own and become a nurse at the Ujina-machi Joint Army Hospital (currently the Hiroshima Prefectural Hospital). I was then sixteen years old.

Then, on August 6, 1945, the first atomic bomb to be used against human beings was dropped on my beloved city. Only a few minutes earlier a brilliant summer sun shone in the sky, people came and went in the streets, and children played under the trees. In one blinding flash all of this became a living hell.

I had gone to my family home in the country to be with my younger brother, who was to enter the navy at a place called Kure on August 6. I returned to the hospital on August 8, two days after the bombing. A stream of trucks was carrying the wounded to the hospital, but the hospital itself was in a shambles, having been hit by a blast of wind from the bomb. The ceilings had fallen, and all the windows were broken. Shattered glass lay everywhere. Because the wards were full, we cleared up the glass from the corridors and lobby and put them to use.

Treatment began with simply determining whether the patient was alive or dead. But there was really not much else we could do. The medical supplies were soon depleted, and we were reduced to brushing the patients' wounds with oil provided by the army. The most we could do for the dead, who lay everywhere at our feet, was to cover them with straw mats. Their bodies were horribly mutilated. Skin hung in tattered strips, and raw bloody wounds gaped like split pomegranates. They were often naked or nearly naked, and yet it was sometimes impossible to tell men from women.

The only food we had to offer them was mush made of flour and water, served in lengths of cut bamboo. There weren't enough nurses to hand-feed the immobile patients; we could only put the food by their sides and have them fend for themselves. In doing this, I asked myself if I was being true to my calling as a nurse. Was it not my duty to help people who could not help themselves? But I had no choice but to steel myself against these doubts and go on with my work.

Making our rounds we lifted up the straw mats covering patients to see whether they were alive or dead. The dead ones were unceremoniously hauled away on stretchers like so much baggage.

Day after day, under a blazing sun, B29s seemed never to tire of flying over the city. Formations of five or ten enemy planes flew over the hospital on their way inland. Each time they came, we hurried the living patients into air-raid shelters. To get out of the heat and into the cool of the shelter, many patients pushed and shoved their way in, only to die there. We walked over their bodies as we carried in other patients. Because it was our duty to stand guard, the nurses had to remain outside the shelters, where every day we watched fighter planes burst into flames and fall into the Seto Inland Sea. It was oddly like seeing war films.

Added to everything else was the constant fear that our white uniforms would make us easy targets for enemy gunners. Our duty to the patients, however, would not allow us to think of our own safety. Instead, between air raids we had to pull a seemingly endless number of bodies from the shelters with hooked poles of the kind used by construction workers, and then haul them to the cremation pit beside the hospital. This pit, which was big enough to hold a building, was fitted with a kind of grill— resembling the grills used in roasting fish—made of heavy steel beams. The bodies were piled on this grill, doused with gasoline, and burned. These cremations took place constantly, day and night.

With no electric lights of any kind, we went about our tasks at night under the illumination provided by the bluish cremation fire and by the flames of still burning houses. All this was ghastly enough, but we encountered even more gruesome sights when we made our rounds.

I recall a screaming baby trying to nurse at the breast of its already dead mother. Could there possibly be any scene more inhuman than this? And once, as I was making a check of the corridors, someone called out to me. Walking toward the voice, what I saw took my breath away—a person so horribly burned that it was impossible to tell whether it was a man or woman. "Nurse," the person said, "my train pass is in my pocket. Would you take it out and look at the photograph. Do I look like the picture?" The person was unable to move, but was apparently desperate to know the answer. From the pass I learned that she was a fourteen-year-old girl named Kazuko Fukuda, a second-year student in a girls' school. The photograph showed a clever-looking girl with bobbed hair. But no words could describe her appearance now. She was like a piece of raw meat from which skin dangled. But I blurted out, "Yes, yes, you look just like this. Very pretty!" Then in broken phrases she said, "My address is written there. Please get in touch with my mother. I can't die without seeing her."

I identified very closely with this poor girl, and wanted terribly to do something for her. After all, there was not that much difference in our ages. Shortly afterward the girl became too weak to talk. I poured a little water in her mouth, and was trying to determine whether she had swallowed it when I realized she was no longer breathing.

I had seen many people die, but no death has remained in my mind as vividly and as long as that of this girl, whose final words were spoken to me. I can still clearly picture her face, and from time to time she appears in my dreams. Even today, I am plagued by the question of whether her family ever received her remains.

A woman with a baby strapped to her back stalked like someone half mad through the corridor, lifting one straw mat after another and shouting, "No! This is not him! No, damn it. No!" Then she lifted the mat from a corpse that was burned black and whose lips were horribly swollen. Turning the body over and seeing a piece of clothing adhering to its back, she shrieked, "It's him! I know this pattern. It's him!" Weeping hysterically, she fell on the poor body that was so disfigured that even a wife of many years was unable to recognize it except by the pattern of a scrap of clothing. For a while I just stood there, wondering why such things had to happen.

The victims who were still alive three days after the blast were in pathetic condition. Their wounds had rotted and oozed black fluid. Maggots crawled around in the joints of their arms and legs; unable to speak, the patients could do nothing but watch the maggots moving about.

Since the day of the bombing, the nurses had lived in the courtyard under a mosquito net. In three or four days, some of the nurses, falling victim to overwork, ran high temperatures, developed diarrhea, and then collapsed. There was no alternative but to send them home. Feelings of frustration and anger became overpowering. On any number of days I thought I had reached my limit. But, renewing my vows as a nurse, I was determined to go on as long as there was an ounce of energy left in me.

Ambulatory patients, constantly calling for water, wandered about like sleepwalkers. Their bodies were painted over with iodine and mer-

THE SCARS REMAIN

curochrome, adding to their unearthly appearance. As nurses we should have been able to remain composed in front of such people, but sometimes it proved impossible to suppress a gasp of horror.

Though I was subjected to massive doses of secondary radiation while at the hospital, I still hoped to lead a normal, happy life, and eventually I got married. Not long afterward, however, I began suffering from damage to my liver, kidneys, and abdomen. I had two operations on my ovaries. I became feverish and nauseous. Unidentifiable growths, nine or ten centimeters in diameter, began appearing all over my body. Surgery only caused them to multiply. Because I was constantly in and out of the hospital, my husband and I got a divorce.

Physically frail and with two dear daughters to raise by myself, I sometimes thought of suicide. But each time the children encouraged me by saying we would be all right if we all worked together.

Then when it came time for my girls, whose upbringing had caused me such suffering and effort, to get married, I was always asked about the health prospects of children of atomic-radiation victims. The only thing I could say was that they were perfectly healthy at the present time. Even after their marriages, I worried about the children they would bear.

Of course, other people suffered horribly too. A friend of mind, a nurse at the Red Cross Hospital at the time of the bombing, had been trapped under a house and her face burned. She underwent plastic surgery a number of times, but in the end she herself broke off relations with the man she hoped to marry. She now lives alone and works in a hospital.

The aftereffects of the atomic bombing still persist. Five years ago I began suffering from cardiac insufficiency and angina pectoris. Each year, from about October to May, when the weather turns cold, I have severe attacks of pain in the chest that last for an hour or so. My blood pressure rises to 200 over 140. I suffer, but have no idea where to put the blame for the suffering.

Every year on August 6, great crowds of people gather in the Peace Park in Hiroshima. I wonder if they really understand what we victims feel. Can their prayers really contribute to worldwide peace? I have my doubts. But, as one of the few remaining victims of the bombing, I intend to go on telling my story as long as there is life left in me.

Branded

Miyako Shinohara (36)

It is difficult to say how much pain, anguish, and frustration I have suffered owing to the fact that I was permanently branded with the words *prenatal atomic-radiation victim.*

When the atomic bomb was dropped on Hiroshima, my mother was in Kusunoki-machi, one and a half kilometers from the explosion center. She was pregnant with me at the time. She and my grandmother fled to Yaguchi, in the outskirts of the city, and then to Tokyo. On October 2, 1945, I was born in Itabashi Ward, Tokyo.

As a small child I always felt sympathic, but no direct involvement, when my grandmother told me stories of the atomic bombing. Both Mother and Grandmother were in good health, and it never occurred to me that I might one day suffer from the effects of the bomb.

In 1947 my family moved back to Hiroshima. One day, when I was in middle school and we were rehearsing a play for the culture festival, a classmate suddenly said, "You've got blood on your teeth." A look in the mirror showed that my gums were covered with liver-colored clots of blood. Several times I wiped the blood away with my handkerchief, but each time it returned. Later I noticed red spots all over my arms and legs. No amount of rubbing would make them go away. At home Mother and Grandmother told me not to worry. "It's some kind of allergy," they said. Still, for the rest of the day, I was puzzled and a little worried.

The red spots were still there the next morning, the day of the culture festival. I went to the family doctor and got an injection. By the time I had reached the hall where our play was to be given, the sleeve of my white blouse was soaked with blood. It had come from the tiny hole made by the injection needle.

The morning after the culture festival, our doctor said there was nothing he could do, and he called the Atomic Bomb Casualty Commission. An ambulance came to our house to pick me up, but always having been a healthy child, I couldn't understand why I should have to go. I had been having physical examinations at the commission hospital each year since entering primary school.

This time, too, I thought I would go to the commission hospital for a checkup and then return home, as I had always done in the past. But I was hospitalized at once and told that I had to remain absolutely quiet. I was even taken to the toilet in a wheelchair. Grandmother and Mother were restless and uneasy, and I cried a great deal, afraid that I might have atomic-radiation sickness. Mother looked pained but did not answer when I asked her why I had to be hospitalized if all that I had was an allergy.

One of my classmates was a so-called atom-bomb baby. Each year, on August 6, newspaper reporters flocked to her house to interview her. I always felt sorry for the girl, but never for a moment dreamed that someday I might find myself in the same predicament.

To my persistent questions, Mother finally told me that the name of my sickness was purpura. I had no idea what that was, but suspected it might be a fatal atomic-radiation sickness. Unable to understand why I had to go through such suffering, I began to blame Mother for having given birth to me when I was doomed to be afflicted with such a disease. Often when Mother came into my room, I would turn away and refuse to speak to her. Obviously, I was trying to escape my own torment by striking out at Mother. Now I can imagine the grief this must have caused her.

Praying that my purpura could be cured, I started making a thousand cranes out of *origami* paper, which is a Japanese custom when making an important wish. Just as I finished the thousandth, the blotches on my body faded away and the blood clots stopped forming on my gums. I was discharged after a month in the hospital and allowed to return home. But the medication I was under caused my face to swell to twice its normal size and made me allergic to penicillin and aspirin.

Mother, who had become extremely sensitive to the state of my health, rushed to buy medicine and tonics the moment I caught cold or became anemic. I myself dreaded a recurrence, and developed the habit of frequently examining my arms and legs to see if the blotches had reappeared.

My fears became reality four years later, in 1962. In my second year at high school I was changing into my school uniform one morning when I noticed a red blotch on my knee. With a gasp, I examined the rest of my body, and found many other blotches, on my arms and the rest of my body. Looking into the mirror, I saw blood on my gums. Everything seemed to go black. My chest throbbed, and my ears rang. The next thing I knew I had collapsed on the floor.

Once again I was ordered to stay absolutely quiet. But I refused to go to the hospital this time, and remained at home instead. The clots kept forming on my gums, and I daily passed blood that was not menstrual. I grew pale and suffered from dizziness. With no appetite at all, I soon became very thin.

Night after night, the fear that I might never wake again prevented me from sleeping. As time passed, I thought of death and suicide. I asked myself what use there was in going on living. I stood on the banks of Ōtagawa River, ready to throw myself in. I contemplated hanging myself, and I climbed Mitaki Mountain with the intention of leaping off a cliff. But each time the thought of the sorrow this would bring to my mother and grandmother held me back.

For some years, Grandmother had been a member of Soka Gakkai, the lay religious organization affiliated with Nichiren Shōshū Buddhism. At about this time, on Grandmother's recommendation, I joined too. Together she and I chanted the Daimoku (Nam-myōhō-renge-kyō) and prayed for my recovery.

Amazingly, as we continued the chant, I began to get better. The blotches began to fade away, and I came to see how strong religious faith is. Filling my handbag with tissue paper and cotton in case something should happen, I attended many different Soka Gakkai meetings and functions. By now a full-fledged member of society, in my own way I lived a full life as a young adult, and sometimes even managed to forget the atomic bombing and my own illness.

But before long I was shown that my fate extended to areas of life I had never thought it would touch. Like all other normal women, I dreamed of getting married and having children. I was shocked one day when the young man I was seeing asked me whether I was certain my children would be healthy and normal. I immediately answered yes, but gradually began to have doubts myself. Little by little, this young man stopped seeing me and finally broke off all relations.

Being branded a "prenatal atomic-radiation victim" had come to influence even my chances for marriage. Instead of holding anything against the young man, I repeatedly told myself that I could not hope for a normal married life and that I should give up the idea altogether. Of course, for me as a woman this was a fate harder than death. Looking at my wretched face in the mirror, I tried to imagine what my sin had been and came to hate the atomic bomb with all my being.

From that time, I turned my back on marriage and devoted myself quietly to my work and religious activities. It was while engaged in religious work that I met the man who is now my husband. When he proposed to me, I told him frankly of my two attacks of purpura. He only said, "It's not your fault. And if you ever get sick again, we'll fight it together." I wept with joy that my dream of getting married—a dream I had once abandoned—was about to come true. In 1974, in spite of the violent opposition he encountered from others, we were married.

Still, from time to time I regretted marriage. After all, I was branded. Would I be able to give birth to normal children? Six months later I became pregnant. As my time drew near, I was nervous and worried. I found no consolation in people's encouraging words that the baby would be all right, or that I should be strong no matter what kind of baby I had.

At just that time, Soka Gakkai held its general conference in Hiroshima. Bulky as I was, I attended and heard President (now Honorary President) Daisaku Ikeda say in his message, "The victims of the atomic bombing have the right to exist, the right to live!" This remark and my husband's encouragement gave me a more positive attitude. Until my delivery I continued confidently praying that my child would be normal.

In February 1976, I gave birth to a son, and the doctor assured me that he was the perfect picture of health. Before I could believe it, however, I examined my baby over and over. Finally satisfied that he was as healthy as could be, I wept for happiness. As for myself, I had hemorrhaged abnormally and was kept immobile on the delivery table for eight hours. Thereafter, however, mother and son grew strong and before long left the hospital. Today I am the mother of three healthy children.

In my youth, I had been unwilling to see or hear anything about the atomic bombing. As a mother, however, I realized that we must not turn away from the facts. One day, though it required courage, I took my children to the Peace Memorial Museum in Hiroshima. Seeing the displays there strengthened my conviction that we must never allow war to happen again. To this end, mothers must take the firmest possible stand in the name of peace and the protection of their children.

Momma Dead
Mayumi Yoshida (27)

I have written this for the sake of my older sister, Yuriko, who has suffered a fate more cruel than death. I have written in the hope that no other children like Yuriko, who is incapable of speaking in a human voice for herself, are born into this world.

Yuriko is one of twenty-two cases of severe microcephaly caused in fetuses whose mothers were exposed at close range to radiation from the atomic bomb. She limps because both pelvic joints are dislocated. She has a speech disorder. Her body is the size of a middle-school pupil, though she is thirty-six. Her mental abilities are arrested at the level of a two-year-old. She is a baby when it comes to taking care of herself. She is incapable of taking a bath, going to the toilet, or doing anything else unassisted. For more than thirty years, while raising three other children, my mother never missed a day caring for Yuriko, which was especially trying during Yuriko's menstruation period.

Yuriko has emotions. She smiles when she is happy and pouts when she is displeased. When she is out of sorts, she can be made to smile again by telling her the story of a television movie.

Television movies are her greatest joy, and she is never without motion-picture photographs from the newspaper or some magazine. Of course, she cannot read, but she finds pleasure in looking at the pictures, and takes the magazines or papers with her into the bath and to bed at night. I suppose she thinks of nothing else from the time she wakes till she falls asleep. After watching her glued to the television and pouring over movie magazines for more than twenty years, I have grown accustomed to her. Still, lately, I am sometimes overwhelmed with grief and pity for her and feel a sudden impulse to hold her in my arms.

Why has she been condemned to such a condition? Life is given equally to all. Who was it that twisted and deformed my sister's life this way?

On the day of the bombing, Mother was happily anticipating Yuriko's birth. But, then, in a flash of fiendish light, the bomb invaded even the sanctity of the womb and led a mother, an unborn daughter, a whole family down a long path of suffering.

Some houses were being dismantled at Nishi Daiku-machi, 730 meters from the hypocenter, on the morning of August 6, 1945. Mother, who was taking part in the work, had her baby boy, Masaaki, strapped to her back. Since she had a child to look after, she was given the light job of preparing lunches for the others. Just after she stepped under the eaves of the hut where the lunches were to be prepared, she was temporarily blinded by a sudden flash of light. When she had recovered the use of her eyes, she was amazed to find that both the buildings and the fifty workers who had been there just seconds earlier had vanished. Mother had been saved because she had stepped under the eaves of the hut.

As she looked about, Mother saw an immense fire heading in her direction. Forgetting about home and how things were there, she joined a frantic group of people fleeing toward the mountains. Before long a drizzle of black rain began falling. Mother dashed for cover in a toolshed that had survived in the middle of a field. But the shed was filled with other bomb victims, and Mother was forced to find what shelter she could in the doorway. From time to time, she was startled by the roar of explosions, some nearby, some further away.

Thinking that this would be a good time to nurse Masaaki, Mother took him down from her back, only to find that virtually countless slivers of glass were buried in his bloody head. She could barely keep from crying as she thought of the poor child huddled against her back, too frightened even to cry. Gingerly she picked out as many pieces of glass as she could, but some were too small.

After the rain stopped, Mother put Masaaki on her back again and started for home. The only things left standing were three metal barber chairs (Father was a barber) and the bathtub, all burned red from exposure to the heat. Her mother-in-law and her oldest daughter, Yaeko, had been at home when the bomb fell. Praying for their safety, Mother set out in the direction of Enami Primary School to look for them.

As it happened, she met them on the way. Grandmother's lip was swollen and bleeding from a cut she received when the house collapsed. But she was not burned. After the blast, Grandmother had found Yaeko crying under the entranceway floor boards, and had pulled her out. Miraculously, Yaeko had not suffered so much as a scratch.

After two days of living in an air-raid shelter, Mother decided to take the two children and return to her family home in Ōtake. Grandmother went back to her family in Mihara.

Though apparently uninjured, Mother fell ill a week later. Bloody pus oozed from her gums and her teeth came loose. She was nauseous and suffered from diarrhea and bloody fluxes. When her mother tried combing her hair, it came out in handfuls. Masaaki had diarrhea and was placed in bed beside Mother.

No one knew of atomic-radiation sickness at the time, and the local doctor treated Mother and Masaaki for stomach trouble. On August 29 Masaaki died, but his name is not listed among the atomic-bomb victims since the cause of death was reported as gastric obstruction.

For a while the doctor thought Mother would also die. But a neighbor said that she should drink an antidote to the poison she had taken in during the atomic bombing. From that day on, Mother drank a beverage made of boiled persimmon leaves. She did this every day until there were finally no more leaves on the persimmon tree. Whatever the reason, Mother gradually got better. In spite of her weakened condition, she had escaped miscarriage, and the child growing in her womb was some consolation for Masaaki's death.

I think it was five or six years before her death that Mother began complaining of pains in her back and increased the number of *shiatsu* massages she was receiving. This was the beginning of her struggle with the monster known as atomic-radiation sickness.

Putting up with her own pain, she never slackened in her attention to Yuriko. She said that she was the only person who understood Yuriko's needs. Certainly, after thirty years of life together, Mother could instinctively tell whether Yuriko wanted a new movie magazine or needed to go to the toilet.

The gravity of Mother's sickness came as a shock to all of us. In June of the year that she died, she went to a hospital for the first time and had X-rays taken. We were told that the lower part of her spine had been seriously damaged by a condition known as lumbar spinal deformation. A little later she complained of pains in her chest and side. Injections and plasters were tried, but her condition only worsened. Then X-rays showed that two of her ribs were broken.

In July the director of the hospital recommended that Mother have a thorough physical examination at a national hospital. But Mother decided against it, probably because she was worried about what would happen to Yuriko without her.

Walking became increasingly difficult. In October more X-rays showed that cancer had attacked her thigh bones, ankles, and scull. The doctor again suggested to Father that Mother be examined at a national hospital.

When Father told me that Mother had cancer, I felt as if someone had hit me on the head with a hammer. It was as if something had come crashing down inside me. Of course, we did not let Mother know.

The doctor cautioned us that Mother's bones were gradually dissolving and becoming so fragile that, ultimately, they would break from the exertion of walking. We were told to keep her in bed as much as possible, and the idea of a physical examination at a national hospital was abandoned. Mother was too weak for surgery, and there was no need to submit her to undue suffering and mental distress.

It was at this time that Mother entered the hospital for the last time. Her legs were very weak, but for a while she was able to go to the toilet adjacent to her room if she were helped. But before long even this became impossible, and the nurses put a bedpan at the head of her bed.

One day, when Yuriko was sitting next to her watching television, Mother stretched out her thin arm and took her by the hand. Laying it on her side, she said, "Yuriko, it hurts here. Rub my side for a little while, won't you?" There were tears in her eyes.

"Is it very bad, Mother—" I started to speak to her but stopped midway, realizing that the tears were caused not by physical pain but by love and worry for a child that would be left behind.

When the faded December page of the calendar on the wall had been turned, Mother looked at herself in a hand mirror and said, "My face's swollen." Swelling of the face or hands and feet of patients who have been hospitalized for a long time means that there is no longer any hope. Feeling hopeless, I nevertheless tried to sooth her: "That's because you slept face down." "No," she said again. "My face's swollen. Nothing can be done now."

Father tried to evade the issue by scolding her. "Stop looking in the mirror all the time and talking foolishness," he said. But he was deeply worried, and he often closed the barbershop to be at Mother's side. He and Mother had walked hand in hand throughout the misery and suffering that began on the day Yuriko was branded as microcephalic.

Mother and Father had to start all over again after becoming virtually penniless owing to the atomic bombing of 1945. What with repeated business failures and the problems of caring for Yuriko, they must have often been completely exhausted. But they could not give up. Nor was Yuriko a heavy cross for them to bear. On the contrary, I think she gave them a kind of psychological support.

They had been overjoyed when she was born on February 4, 1946, apparently a perfectly healthy baby. At the time there were no signs of anything wrong with her legs and certainly no indication of radiation-caused microcephaly.

Yuriko's first and second birthdays passed. My parent's third daughter was born, and still Yuriko neither spoke nor walked. With some worry in the back of their minds that she was developing slowly both physically and mentally, my parents went on with their busy lives, unable to give Yuriko any special protection or care. But when her younger sister was already prattling and toddling about, Yuriko still showed no signs of development. It was then that my parents began to be concerned.

With the passage of time, however, Yuriko was able first to crawl and then, with coaching, to stand up. But even then, she was unsteady in the hips and leaned to one side. When Yuriko was four, Mother and Father finally realized there was something seriously wrong with her legs and hips, but since she showed no sign of pain, they didn't have her examined.

Finally, however, when there was no improvement in her condition, they took her to the national hospital in Ōtake, where a doctor told them not to worry: "In infancy, the socket into which the femur fits is often too small, but then it enlarges with age. When this happens, the bone fits neatly and the limping disappears."

Later, however, doctors from the School of Medicine of Hiroshima University came to Ōtake to examine atomic-radiation victims and told Mother and Father that Yuriko had microcephaly. But this meant so little to them that they shrugged it off. Perhaps at another time, when it was explained to them in detail, they understood; but in those days few people knew anything about the effects of radiation. Mother and Father probably suspected that Yuriko's sickness was connected with the atomic bombing, but had no idea that it was an incurable state of mental and physical retardation. They went on hoping that some day— some day—she would speak and walk normally.

What a frightening thing ignorance can be. If my parents, with a child like Yuriko (and with Mother being a radiation victim herself), were this much in the dark, it is scarcely surprising that people who didn't experience the bomb have no inkling of the horror of radiation diseases. That is no reason, however, for saying that nothing can be done.

Stricken when they finally learned that her condition was caused by radiation, Mother and Father were soon compelled to struggle against the misunderstandings, discrimination, and curiosity the world has for people like my sister.

For instance, once when Yuriko was playing in Father's shop, a woman came in and tried to shoo Yuriko away as if she were a dog. On another occasion, Yuriko was standing in front of the shop when four or five primary-school children came along and mockingly imitated her limp. Not realizing that she was being made fun of, Yuriko smiled.

Worried about what would happen to Yuriko after their deaths, Mother and Father once sent a letter to the United States government by way of the American commander of the Iwakuni Air Force Installation, hoping to make arrangements to ensure Yuriko's livelihood. The Japanese government had passed a nominal law related to medical treatment for atom-bomb victims but showed no inclination to do anything to aid them financially. If organized groups had succeeded in eliciting no more than this medical-therapy law, the government would probably coldly dismiss an individual request for help. This is why Mother and Father decided to apply to the nation responsible for the bombing, even if their appeal was in vain. In the end, their request was shelved without action.

After this, Mother and Father participated in various movements in connection with atom-bomb victims. The suicide of a girl who had been exposed to radiation *in utero* inspired them, with the assistance of a member of the Hiroshima Research Association, to bring into the open the situation of microcephalous victims like my sister. Until then, many people with such afflicted children had hidden them from the public eye. Father became the first chairman of what was called the Mushroom Association (from the mushroom shape of the cloud formed by the atomic explosion). The association adopted three goals: (1) Official medical acknowledgement that cases of microcephaly were caused by the atomic bombing; (2) The creation of an institution to care for such children, whose welfare after the death of their parents is a source of great concern. (3) Reporting to the United Nations about the current conditions of microcephalous children.

As a consequence of these efforts, the Ministry of Welfare officially included among those illnesses qualified for therapy a group of people who had been embryos in an early state of development when their mothers were exposed to atomic radiation at close range. In June 1968 Yuriko was at last officially recognized as an atomic-bomb victim.

Thereafter, Mother and Father continued working to bring to the attention of the largest possible number of people the suffering that only a parent of a child afflicted with radiation-caused microcephaly could know. In the hope that it would help the drive to outlaw nuclear weapons, each August 6, when ceremonies are held to commemorate the bombing of Hiroshima, they took Yuriko to the site and passed out leaflets to passersby. I helped them on several occasions. Some of the people to whom I handed the leaflets looked annoyed, as though they were being pestered, and immediately threw the leaflets away. Others politely thanked me for the work I was doing. Looking at the leaflets that had been tossed aside, I felt a painful urge to pick them up and brush the dirt off. Thus, though it was only on a small scale, Mother and Father carried out their own peace movement. But all this didn't prevent Mother from falling ill herself.

In the middle of December, Mother had grown weaker and said she could

MOMMA DEAD

no longer see out of her left eye. I assumed that, since poor eyesight would normally affect both eyes, the cause must be cancer.

The suppositories she took for pain relief grew less effective, and we had to increase her daily allotment. She said that just before the suppositories began taking effect, the pain in her hips, back, and head actually became worse. Then, about three days before her death, the attacks of excruciating pain suddenly abated, and she grew so tranquil that we were unable to tell the exact time of her death. She passed away on December 26, 1978, at the age of fifty-eight.

Before the end she frequently told visitors that she had gone on living this long because of Yuriko. But at last her determination and strength were exhausted. I shall never forget watching Yuriko, who did not understand what death meant, sitting beside Mother and murmuring, "Momma sleep, Momma sleep."

On January 4 of the next year, Father received a letter saying that, though Yuriko had been recognized as an atom-bomb victim, Mother was not: she had not been sufficiently examined. The letter was dated December 25, 1978, the day before her death. What with caring for Yuriko, Mother just didn't have time to take all the necessary tests until her hospitalization. The irony of having such a letter delivered after a person has died of radiation disease symbolizes the heartlessness of government policy in dealing with atom-bomb victims.

Even today no system of aid has been established. The government rejects responsibility for all but those who were officially inducted into the military, and in this way blocks the creation of a sound aid policy, causing great anxiety for all concerned.

Mother knew the cruelty of weapons that can injure even the unborn. Unlike many victims who tried to conceal their condition, Mother turned directly to society, asking that people look at her and her daughter if they wanted to know the horror of the atomic bomb. Her desire for world peace led her to show herself and Yuriko before television cameras and the mass media up until shortly before her death. In her actions and thoughts I saw the determination to transform what had been an imposed fate into a chosen mission. I myself have resolved to continue her work in the name of peace.

Now, sitting alone with Father, Yuriko points to Mother's photograph and says over and over again, "Momma dead, Momma dead." Like a clock stopped for ever at 8:15, the moment the bomb fell, Yuriko, whose mind will never mature, is a living symbol of the atomic explosion. She and all others like her are proof that nuclear weapons can lead to the annihilation of mankind. They show how the misery of that abysmal moment persists into the future. All the millions of words spoken and written in the name of peace are necessary, but perhaps people should first come to see my sister and hear her murmur, "Momma dead, Momma dead."

The Hatanaka family (Yuriko far right) facing the Atomic Dome from the river embankment near Aioi Bridge. August 1955.

WOMEN IN
SEARCH OF
SAFETY

Biscuits from the Empress

Suzu Eguchi (49)

Five of my close relatives—my elder brother, my brother-in-law, my elder sister, and her two children—died in World War II. Some months before their deaths, I was evacuated from Tokyo and its air raids to Miyagi Prefecture along with other pupils in the third, fourth, fifth, and sixth years of Asakusa Kinryū National Primary School. Just before the train pulled out, Mother and I said a quick good-bye, and I clearly remember how excited I was. Along the way we were divided into two groups. My group, headed by a teacher named Itō, was lodged in an inn called the Suzuki, and the daughter of the owner was appointed our housemother.

At first, all of us sixth graders were determined to make the best of our last months in primary school. But in a week's time we had become dispirited, homesick, and ready to cry at the slightest provocation. We older children did our best to control our emotions and cheer up the younger ones. Often, however, first one child would finally break out in tears, then another, and before long all of us would be sobbing.

Ultimately what all the children wanted was to be with their mothers. This led to one little boy trying to run away. As soon as his absence was noticed, we joined our teachers in a search, but failed to find him. Suddenly one teacher had the idea that he might have set out for Tokyo. Sure enough, he was discovered waiting for a train at Kōriyama Station. Though he never stopped crying or saying that he wanted to go home to Tokyo, we managed to bring him back to the dormitory, comforting him as best we could.

As soon as the turmoil over the runaway had died down, a new one broke out over lice. When the luggage of a certain third grader was opened, it was found to be crammed with dirty clothes covered completely with the creatures. The sight of them crawling around sent chills down my spine. We laundered the clothes, poured boiling water over the wicker suitcase, and aired everything out in the bright sunlight. Then we paired off and inspected each other's luggage. By this time it was not at all unusual to find two or three lice walking around on one's body. We girls spread newspapers on the sunny veranda and combed out our hair, sending showers of lice dropping to the floor. We picked lice eggs from each other's scalp with our fingernails. Then we washed our hair with soap and water and felt much better. But the lice were usually back in two or three days. Indeed, we were never able to get all of them out of our hair and eventually carried them home with us as souvenirs.

One day the plum-flavored lozenges I had been saving up were stolen. This was a serious matter in those days when candy of any kind was simply unavailable. I searched frantically but without success. The next thing to be missing was soap, but the culprit was never caught. I began to grow suspicious of the other children.

In communal life such as we were living, bosses inevitably emerge. Especially among the girls, groups tended to form that had a sinister aspect. One such clique teased and harassed me for a long time for my suspiciousness. They would blame me for such things as having received a persimmon from a local student or being treated kindly by one of the teachers. It was at this time that I first became conscious of the ugly side of female nature.

Since food was in short supply, we were constantly hungry. To satisfy our longing for sweets, we searched for various substitutes, the first being medicine. We ate and drank all the palatable medical preparations we could find until finally the local pharmacy was completely sold out.

Next we consumed large quantities of flavored dental powder, which tended, however, to leave a sandy, cleanserlike taste in the mouth. Also, since we needed dental powder for brushing our teeth, we were more restrained in its consumption.

One day a child scorched his cotton bath towel when drying it over the charcoal brazier. The smell given off by the towel was very much like that of a popular honey cake called Castella. Soon, ten or more children had gathered around the brazier, savoring the aroma. In our daily battle with hunger this became a favorite pastime, and before long we had burned thirty towels.

The evacuees were allowed to use one room in the ramshackle country school, but we city children never fit in very well with the local children. Some of the more calculating pupils did succeed in ingratiating themselves, and secretly received little gifts of persimmons or chestnuts. I remember a school athletic day in autumn when local children and evacuees alike ran and jumped to their hearts' content. As a prize for participating we were each given a patty of rice with a chestnut inside. It was the most delicious thing in the world. The evacuees ate their single patty in no time, but were still hungry. Looking around, we saw the local students eating any number of salt-flavored rice patties, which made us extremely envious.

We only went to class a few days of the week; the rest of the time was spent working in the fields. When the rice began to ripen, it was our job to protect it from the locusts. We vied with each other to see how many we could catch until we had filled a hemp bag. Our teacher later cooked the locusts for us, a great novelty for a native of Tokyo like myself. After the harvest was in, we went to the fields to salvage any rice left behind, and thereby supplemented our own food supply.

Another one of our jobs was to gather firewood from the mountain behind our lodgings. It was a five-kilometer walk to get there, and on the return trip we carried the wood on our backs. On the way, there was a narrow suspension bridge made of logs. One false step would have sent us tumbling into the valley below, but we always made it safely.

Compelled to provide for ourselves, we were kept very busy. But not all was unpleasantness and hard work. For instance, we enjoyed beautiful snow-covered winter scenery never seen in Tokyo. We improvised skis from split green bamboo and were soon able to manipulate them with considerable skill. Children learn very fast.

At the end of our sixth year in primary school, we made a trip of two days and one night to a hot-spring resort, where a splendid geyser shot up to a height of forty meters at regular intervals. After our baths we were served a meal consisting of three dried fish, some pickles, bean-paste soup, and as much white rice as we could eat. Unfortunately perhaps, never again have I enjoyed rice as much as the four servings I ate that night.

From my mother's letters I learned about the situation in Tokyo. Warning sirens sounded almost every day and night, making sleep difficult. The house behind ours was hit by an incendiary bomb and had burned to the ground. This was the tenor of Mother's letters. Regardless of the danger, however, I still wanted to return to Tokyo to be with her.

I no longer remember what the occasion was [editor's note: it was the celebration of the eleventh birthday of the crown prince on December

BISCUITS FROM THE EMPRESS

23], but one day each of us was given six biscuits as a present from the empress. Most of the children wolfed them down. But I stopped after eating only three, thinking I would give the rest to my niece and nephew when I got back to Tokyo. I wrapped them carefully in paper and put them away. Now and then, I would take them out to look at them, my mouth watering. Sometimes I even nibbled a little from the edges, giving them a jagged appearance. Still I managed to keep my vow not eat the biscuits until I had returned to Tokyo after graduation.

In the meanwhile, the war was going from bad to worse. B29s were even appearing in the sky over our safe country retreat. Finally, on March 9, 1944, we sixth graders graduated and, each occupied with his own thoughts, said good-bye to the younger students and boarded a train for Tokyo. An air-raid alarm sounded as we reached Kōriyama, halting the train. This happened to be March 10, the day of the air raid that turned the part of Tokyo where my family lived into a sea of flames. Our house was reduced to ashes.

When we reached Tokyo, I immediately went to the grounds of the Kinryū Primary School, where my mother, a sooty bandage covering the wounds on her face, came to meet me. After nine long months away I could finally call out "Mother!" and receive an answer, but I found myself too overcome with emotion to say anything else. And I was among the lucky ones. Half of the students who came back with me waited in vain for their parents and relatives. They had become war orphans.

Mother and I first went to the ruins that had been our house and then to an air-raid shelter, where we spent a sleepless night. The air around us grew steadily smokier. From time to time a charred telephone pole would crash to earth. Smoldering heaps of corpses lay everywhere. The hellish sights I saw then have never left me.

The following morning my brother-in-law showed up, wrapped in a quilt soaked in water as protection against the flames. He had been on the run all night to escape the fire, and had now come to get his wife and children. His eyes bloodshot, he couldn't conceal his distress when we told him they weren't with us. When the fire had started, he had sent my sister, who was nine-months pregnant, and the two children on ahead, to what he thought was the safety of our house. This decision turned out to be a tragic one. No amount of searching did any good;

they were never found. I suspect my sister must have died trying to protect her two small children, my niece and nephew, for whom I had saved the empress's biscuits. Taking them out of the paper wrapping, I imagined the happy faces of the two children and my sister as I gave them the biscuits so carefully preserved for them all those months. Tears filled my eyes. I kept the biscuits until well after the war ended because I continued clinging to a faint hope that they would return. Finally, I put them in the empty grave erected for my sister and the children.

In the days that followed the firebombing, you could see soldiers casually tossing on an endless line of trucks the bodies of people so badly burned that they looked like charred logs. The Sumida River was filled from bank to bank with bloated corpses. Half-demented people dashed from place to place searching for their loved ones. No one must ever look on sights like those again. And what happened to my friends whose mothers and fathers never came for them that night after our return to Tokyo from the country? I can only pray that somehow they found happiness.

Evacuated to the countryside, students go over their books on the veranda, personal possessions piled in front of them.

BISCUITS FROM THE EMPRESS

Neither Flowers Nor Fruit

Yoneko Moriyama (50)

On the morning of December 8, 1941, when I was in the third grade of primary school, Mother did not begin the day with her usual phrase, "Hurry up or you'll be late for school." The household seemed to be in a turmoil, and my still sleepy ears caught snatches of conversation: "War's started! War's been declared! Pearl Harbor's been attacked!" With no real understanding of what all this meant, I nevertheless felt a certain foreboding that something very serious was taking place.

I went to school in low spirits. At morning assembly the principal told us that war had been declared with England and the United States, and urged us to study hard so that we could be of service to the country. Since life at school went on as usual that day, I wondered what it meant to be at war.

From my parents and grandparents I had heard of such things as war memorials for Japanese victories in the Russo-Japanese and Sino-Japanese wars and tales of hardship during the Manchurian and Shanghai incidents. I had also heard stories of patriotism and valor like that of Kohei Kikuchi, who, even in death, maintained a tight grip on his bugle. And I knew of the loyalty and devotion of General Nogi and Fleet Admiral Tōgō. All the parades and celebrations I had seen in commemoration of war victories had been colorful and gay. What was there for all the grown-ups to be so serious about? Motivated by a mixture of curiosity and apprehension, I began trying to figure out the nature of this thing called war.

Daily news broadcasts, opening with the cheerful strains of the "Battleship March," reported the results of the day's fighting. They always ended, "And our casualties were light." The adults got excited about the news, but never looked especially cheerful. In my child's mind I wondered just how much "light casualties" were.

During physical education at school the boys were instructed in kendo fencing and the girls in the use of the halberd. Later we were to be taught how to use the bayonet. The prevailing mood was one described as "One hundred million hearts beating as one heart of fire." I particularly remember the less robust children, who could not keep up with this kind of training, standing in a corner of the school playground and looking forlorn.

In my fourth year in primary school, I joined what was called the Seas Youth Corps because I was attracted by the idea of participating in the war and sailing on a battleship to the South Sea Islands. The South Pacific loomed large in my dreams since I did my best during cutter-boat drills. On the maps of the time the Japanese empire appeared in red, and one by one, as the empire spread, the islands of the South Pacific were painted in that color.

Large numbers of Japanese went to live in the newly formed nation of Manchukuo on the Chinese mainland. We were taught that everything taking place in Asia was in the name of Universal Brotherhood and the Great East Asia Coprosperity Sphere, both of which meant all Asians were to live in prosperity under one roof. We were further told that the war had started because England and the United States were opposed to this idea. In posters about the "American and British devils," Roosevelt and Churchill were depicted with the faces of demons. We thought that the United States and England must be the epitome of barbarianism and that the war was being fought for justice in Asia.

In my fifth year in primary school, we children sometimes read compositions or sang songs on a short-wave evening radio program for the men at the front, which was broadcast by the Japan Broadcasting Corporation (NHK). This was a serious matter, for some of the students had seen fathers and older brothers off to battle. As the war situation turned increasingly grave, however, we were no longer called upon to appear on the program. I remember that as a reward for participating, I once received a crayon box. I was overjoyed since crayons were something I had wanted for a long time. But my joy was immediately followed by disappointment as I found that all I had was the box, without any crayons. For the first time it occurred to me that war was a pretty sad affair.

Ever since the war started, food and clothing had been rationed. There was nothing to buy even if one had the money. Restaurants put up signs identifying themselves as food-coupon dining halls, and people lined up to buy the thin rice soups they served. Good citizens frowned upon colorful clothing, which was eventually branded as unpatriotic. Everyone ended up dressing in somber colors. Posters put up around town an-

NEITHER FLOWERS NOR FRUIT

nounced that luxury was the enemy. My mother, who was a good dresser, made her silk kimonos over into covers for mattresses and quilts, saying, "Just like a feudal lord," as she snuggled under this brightly covered bedding.

One evening I found my mother and father in a closet with a quilt hung over the door. They were listening to classical records and then sorrowfully breaking each one as it was finished. When I asked why, they said that Western music had been banned. I could not understand what was wrong with Beethoven and Bach; they were not our enemies. But when I said something like that, or laughed because the commonly used word *posuto* (mail box), derived from English *post*, had been replaced by the pure Japanese *yūbinbako* as part of the campaign to eliminate foreign words from the Japanese language, Mother and Father would scold me and say that the secret police would come to get me if I wasn't careful. As a result, I began to think that war means not being able to say what one thinks.

At about this time a happily married White Russian couple and their charming baby disappeared from our neighborhood. It was rumored that they had been spies. I couldn't believe that this was true, but the ominous word *spy* stuck in my mind. I came to see that war is secretive.

Although all factories were given over to meeting military needs, raw materials, including those for munitions, were extremely short. This resulted in bronze statues and the iron window frames from ordinary houses being confiscated and melted down. Precious metals and even children's savings had to be turned over, in return for which we received slips of paper expressing the government's gratitude. I assumed that this was the way things had to be if we were going to win the war, but I was somewhat worried about what would happen when all the window frames had been made into bullets and those bullets had been fired. With talk of the imminent "decisive battle on the home islands," my romance of the South Seas soon evaporated. What was left was a painful general mood of willingness to sacrifice everything for the sake of victory.

More and more children began requesting permission to leave Tokyo and live with relatives in the comparative safety of the countryside. Almost every day we said, "Goodbye, take care of yourself," to one or two classmates, whose departures left gaping holes in the classroom seating arrangement. Children without relatives in the country were sent in groups to government-designated evacuation zones. The evacuation zone for our school was in Nasu, Tochigi Prefecture.

Parents often had a hard time deciding whether to part with their children. For instance, my family debated what would happen if I survived in the country while everyone at home was killed in an air raid. Grandmother said, "Let's all die together in Tokyo." Mother said, "Who's says we're going to die?" And Father said, "Let's at least try to save the children." The disagreement was resolved when it was decided that if worse came to worst, the government would surely take orphaned children under its wing. It was only then agreed that I should be evacuated. Mother, who was still against the idea, relented when a maiden aunt who was a nurse agreed to go with us as a housemother.

Only children in the third year of primary school and above were eligible for evacuation. My younger brother just squeezed under the line. Because we had no notion what evacuation would be like and thought we were going to live in some dormitory, he and I were in a happy mood as we packed our things.

I can still remember the last night we spent at home. Every good thing to eat that could be found in the house was put on the table, around which we all sat with faces that seemed to prophesy the end of the world.

The baggage of people leaving the city overflowed the train stations in those days. And since priority was given to military freight, there was no saying when it would reach its destination. Even worse, both at the stations and in the baggage cars, things were often stolen, with the result that sometimes nothing but wooden boxes or wrapping paper found their way into the hands of the addressee. Still, there was no way of preventing this from happening.

At our evacuation zone we assembled at a house in town and were divided into groups: children who would stay at inns in the vicinity of the train station and children who would go to Buddhist temples in the outskirts. My group was assigned to the Bakurō-juku, a small inn with an immense barn.

The local people greeted us warmly when we got off the train at Kuroiso, which commands a view of the vast Nasu mountain range. Our group consisted of a male teacher, who was in charge of the group, two

NEITHER FLOWERS NOR FRUIT

housemothers, and thirty-two children, including nine sixth graders. We were told to consider the male teacher our father, the housemothers our real mothers, and all the other children our brothers and sisters, and were urged to do the best we could under the circumstances.

Although special schools were apparently set up for children on the outskirts of town, our group attended classes at the local school. The children there were a little worried by the "evacuees" and "Tokyo kids," as they called us, but we fit in before long, as children will. In the end, our teachers and housemothers had little cause for concern. Of course, if trouble arose, the locals and the evacuees stuck to their own side, regardless of who was right or wrong. The locals were physically stronger, but the evacuees were cleverer with words. I think our teachers took great pains to keep things running smoothly, and I recall few instances in which we city children were reprimanded.

Since most of the able-bodied men had been drafted into the military or conscripted to do factory work, we children were called on to help with the farm work. It was all new to us city children, but not wanting to be ridiculed by the locals, we did our best, even covering for the slower, younger children. We did fairly well in digging potatoes and threshing wheat, but reaping the rice with a scythe proved agonizing.

Cooperating with the farmers also enhanced our dinner table. Our quota of rationed food was insufficient, and our leader and the house-mothers were kept busy trying to make up the difference. Owing to their efforts, our comparatively small numbers, and help from the farmers, we managed to overcome the early days of hunger.

This is not to say we ate white rice and delicacies from the mountains and the sea. Seafoods were unavailable in the inland Nasu Highlands, and all meat was appropriated for military consumption. To provide some animal protein, butter cut into dice was put on top of rice that had been eked out with diced *daikon* radish and yams.

The main dish usually consisted of vegetables, mostly locally produced Chinese cabbage and *daikon* radish. When dried fish, fried *tōfu* balls, or eggs appeared on the table, they were a source of great delight. Since sugar was precious, this was the period in which I learned to appreciate the natural sweetness of vegetables. Though the portions were usually enough to fill children's stomachs, psychologically we craved the favorite foods we had eaten before the war. Our teachers would sometimes caution us about taking or accepting other people's food, no doubt after they had heard rumors about "evacuees" stealing food or a local feeding some pitiful child from Tokyo. They were hoping it wasn't one of us.

With the older children taking the lead, we all helped with the cleaning, laundry, and cooking, and took turns at feeding the furnace to heat the bath water. I remember how we sometimes picked up yams and chestnuts on the way to school and then cooked them in the bath furnace. I also remember how bad roasted green tomatoes tasted, turning me forever against tomatoes. We tried hanging persimmons out to dry, which makes them quite sweet, but someone ate them all before they were ready, leaving nothing but the strings.

Our first winter in the country was exceptionally cold. Our fingers were so numb that, when scrubbing the floor, we couldn't wring out the rags properly, with the result that a thin film of water remained on the floorboards. This froze, turning the corridors into an excellent place for skating. One morning a child still groggy with sleep urinated in the footwear cupboard, and all our wooden clogs were frozen over. Another child, who had wet his bed, quietly folded and stored the damp bedding the next morning, as if nothing unusual had happened. That night, forced to sleep in a icy bed, the boy started crying, which sparked sniveling and sobbing from all around the room till there was a great lugubrious chorus.

Family visiting days were scheduled on an equitable basis for all children, but the fact that some parents had difficulties in procuring train tickets or simply couldn't find the time to make the trip inevitably led to disappointments. Also, there were strict rules against eating in the sleeping quarters, but doting parents nevertheless brought treats to give secretly to their children. The frequent result was that children ended up crying from indigestion after their parents returned to Tokyo.

My mother grew impatient with the fixed visiting days and came whenever she wanted to. Perhaps feeling guilty for having sent me off to the country, she would fill her rucksack with hard-gotten food and gave it all to the dormitory. In general, both parents and children were hypersensitive about both visiting days and food.

I especially disliked letter-writing days because of the memories of better times that they evoked. As if by malicious chance, on those days I

NEITHER FLOWERS NOR FRUIT

always clearly heard the heart-rending whistle of the Tokyo-bound train which carried the mail. One day a child managed to get on that train. Everyone said he was running away from home, but I disagreed. He was trying to *return home*.

It was during this period that, for the first time in my life, I heard the word *lice*. Since we slept with our pillows side by side, the lice spread until everyone's head itched. The eggs fairly glittered in our hair. The boys could solve the problem by shaving their heads, but the situation was much harder for us girls. We rubbed mercury ointment on our scalps, waited for the lice to die, then washed our hair and took turns brushing one another. In the eyes of an outsider, we must have looked like a pack of grooming monkeys.

At first a general sense of tension in our new circumstances made life run smoothly. But we soon grew tired of the monotonous life there and the stern restrictions placed on our activities. We were at an age when children love to play, but instead we had to work. With no recreation of any kind, the work pressed heavily on our minds, and the regimentation grew ever more stifling.

Our teachers became concerned and tried to cheer us up, organizing concerts, games, and excursions to gather chestnuts or play in a nearby river. And it may be true that children are generally geniuses at devising amusements, but still we remained despondent and spiritless. What occupied our minds was how long the war was going to last, though none of us put the question into so many words.

It was now time for those of us in the sixth grade to take entrance examinations for middle school. Since Tokyo was already being bombed then, we were urged to remain where we were, and not to return to the city to take examinations for schools there. But since we were ignorant of the devastation being wrought by the air raids, most of us were unwilling to give up our plans for going back to Tokyo.

Just before we left, probably as a kind of going-away present, our teachers told us we could do anything we liked. I decided to take a bath with my night robe on. Nothing has ever felt so unpleasant. The cotton cloth clung so fast to my body that I could not raise my legs to step out of the bath. Everyone had a good laugh, and so did I. It was the first time I had felt really free since our stay at the evacuation site began.

Things were worse in Tokyo than I had expected. At night, under an enforced blackout, everyone went about the house almost stealthily. Conversation was rare, and we were forbidden to go out of doors after dark.

I was waiting for the results of my entrance examinations into middle school when on the night of March 9, 1945, Tokyo became the target of a massive bombing raid. B29s flew brazenly overhead, dropping showers of oil incendiary bombs. Flames shot up immediately from where the bombs fell. Looking up at the bombers in the night sky, I felt a deep horror, as though I were watching some great nocturnal demons. It was then that a tiny Japanese fighter attempted to crash into one of the huge B29s. They seemed to make contact but only the fighter burst into flames and fell to the earth. Gritting my teeth, and with my eyes opened so widely that they hurt, I joined my hands in prayer for the pilot of that little plane. Tears trickled down my face.

The people in our neighborhood tried frantically to put out the fires that arose everywhere, but there was little that could be done with hand-driven pumps and bucket brigades. Grandmother and I ran for safety first. Nearby Ueno Hill was safe, but it had already been encircled by the fire. To reach it we had to dash here and there through the flames and against blasts of hot wind. I do not remember where we ran throughout that night, but by dawn we had reached Ueno Hill. We pushed our way through mountains of corpses. There was a mother with a baby strapped to her back: the infant was on fire. Wounded people called out for help, but no one heeded. "So this is what war is like," I thought. From the hilltop I turned in the direction of our house. A vast plain of smoldering ruins was all I saw.

Later, at the burned-out site where our house had stood, I met a friend named Yasuko. She was crying, and said that her mother was missing. We later learned that her mother had taken refuge in an air-raid shelter in the basement of the Japan Salt and Tobacco Monopoly building. Following the burnt tracks of a train line, we went to find her mother. What we found were smoldering ruins heaped over the shelter. Firemen were pouring water on it because they were afraid that the fire would break out again if the doors of the shelter were opened too soon.

The shelter was finally opened the following day, but there were no survivors. Yasuko turned over one corpse after another, but none of them

NEITHER FLOWERS NOR FRUIT

seemed to be her mother. I tried to encourage her by saying that her mother was bound to come back soon. My father even offered to take her in as his own daughter. But Yasuko only looked sadder and sadder. Then, a few days later, she vanished without saying good-bye.

Though I was supposed to be going to middle school, nothing remained standing in our part of Tokyo, much less a school. We decided to ask our relatives outside Tokyo for help, and thereafter moved to Mito in Ibaragi Prefecture. At about this time Father was drafted, and Mother and I spent our days and nights running from air raids, offshore bombardments, and strafing attacks by carrier-based aircraft. With no time to sleep or cook, we were soon completely exhausted, both mentally and physically. When the end of the war was announced on August 15, 1945, we were not so much saddened by defeat as relieved that the war was finally over.

The immediate postwar period was marked by extreme chaos, and in some respects life was harder than during the war. In addition to material shortages, there was endless inflation and the constant turmoil created by revolutions in education and the Japanese way of life.

We evacuees all went our separate ways, with no attempt to keep track of each other. There was nothing much to eat at the time, and clothing was so short that everyone wore patched underwear. This was simply not the time to worry about other people and their affairs.

Ueno Station and its underground passageways were filled with war orphans, some of whom froze to death in the cold of winter. The indifference toward such children showed how the war had burned out human hearts in the same way that it had burned down cities.

About ten years after the end of the war, I accidentally ran into Yasuko in front of Shinjuku Station. Overjoyed, I embraced her and blurted out several questions about what had happened to her since we had parted. She said not a word in reply, but simply stared at me coolly as if I were a total stranger. Wondering if she could have forgotten what I looked like, I continued trying to get a response. Then, without changing the expression on her face, she roughly pushed my arm away and said, "Don't you see I'm different from you?" Then she briskly walked away. I stood for a while in amazement. After I had recovered, it struck me, for the first time, how coarsely she had been dressed and made up.

A girl just out of primary school, she must have undergone great hardship to keep from starving. The memory of those days was far too bitter to be the subject of lighthearted reminiscing. Apparently the grimness of Yasuko's life then wouldn't allow her to respond to my foolishly sentimental questions. I only hoped that my thoughtlessness had not caused her fresh suffering. My heart ached with sharp resentment against that war, that it should have erected so impassable a barrier between Yasuko and me.

On March 25, 1976, our group of evacuees finally came full circle with a primary-school graduation ceremony held thirty-one years after the end of the war. At the time when we should have graduated, our school had been burned down along with our graduation certificates. In 1976 volunteers from the group discovered the whereabouts of seventy percent of our classmates, and we assembled once more. We were all forty-four years old at the time, and our faces showed both the strength and the strain that were the products of those dark days. There was no need for words. Looking into each other's faces, we saw the paths we had trod. Merely taking each other's hands, we could hear what the heart was saying. Of the nine people who had been in my dormitory room, only three had survived. Some had died of illness; the whereabouts of others were unknown.

In the past, as children, we had cried tears of sorrow, suffering, bitterness, love, parting, and regret. On that day, we knew the heartwarming joy of shedding tears in gratitude for our survival and in praise of life itself.

No Regrets
Mitsuko Ōoka (56)

AT THE START

When war was declared in 1941, I was about to graduate from the Takehaya Women's Teachers' School in Tokyo. The following spring, with great hopes for the future, I began teaching at the Tabata Shimmachi School in Takinogawa Ward (now called Kita Ward), about fifteen minutes' walk from our house. That year all primary schools became known as "national schools," and emphasis was placed on the militaristic education that was supposed to be fundamental training for citizens of the Japanese empire. An air-raid shelter was dug under the school, and the children wore padded hoods during frequently held air-raid drills. When soldiers left home for duty overseas, we took the children to the nearby train stations to see them off, waving small Japanese flags.

In April 1944 it was decided that younger children should be evacuated to the safety of remote rural areas, in that they were an important human resource that would shoulder the burden of the country's future. So-called group evacuation was available only to children in the third grade and above, those without relatives in the countryside who could provide for them individually.

Though reluctant to part with their children, one after another parents applied for permission to send their children away from Tokyo and the danger of the air raids. Many of the faculty, however, had personal reasons for not wanting to leave the city, and requested to be allowed to stay in Tokyo. In my case, for instance, my family's country relatives lived near an airfield: there would be little sense in evacuating to a place as dangerous as that. Aside from that, my older brother had gone to war, my father was old, and I had four younger brothers and sisters. Naturally I did not want to leave my family. Still it seemed a great pity that so many students were applying to evacuate but so few faculty members were willing to accompany them. Finally I convinced my parents that it was my duty to go, fully realizing that I might not see them alive again.

While negotiations were under way with people from the Sawatari hot spring area of Sawada Village in Gumma Prefecture, we held repeated meetings with the children's parents to work out all of the details at our end. The evacuation staff eventually consisted of four teachers, ten housemothers, and one health specialist, who were to be responsible for roughly two hundred students.

At last, on the morning of August 19, we assembled at Ogu Station to depart for the country. Carrying my baby brother on her back, Mother joined Father in coming to see me off, and urged me to do my best in looking after the children. After a tearful farewell, the train pulled out, and I became acutely aware of the heavy responsibility I had undertaken.

Traveling on the Jōetsu Line by way of Shibukawa, we detrained at Nakanojō and took a bus for Sawatari. As we rode along, I was struck by how remote and uninhabited the region was. The occasional house came as a surprise. But we were given a warm welcome by the local people, and the foliage of the surrounding mountains was certainly beautiful.

Our group was split up at this point. Sixth-grade boys and girls were sent to the nearby Buddhist temple, Eirin-ji. The group that I was to supervise (one hundred and fifty students in all) was to be housed in three inns in the hot-spring town: fifth-grade boys and girls and fourth-grade girls in the Marumoto; fourth-grade boys in the Yorozuya; and third-grade boys and girls in the Ryūmeikan. Each grade had its own teachers. There was a man for the sixth, but young woman teachers were in charge of the third, fourth, and fifth. The fifth was my responsibility. Until we

Students being evacuated to the countryside are given a send-off by their classmates.

got settled in, a member of the local faculty acted as the head teacher. Two or three housemothers were assigned to each grade.

We immediately set about assigning teaching and work assignments, organizing the children into groups, designating group leaders, and drawing up a schedule of classes. City-bred and totally ignorant of the way things were done in the country, we were very unsure of ourselves.

The local schools allowed us the use of their classrooms. The fifth and sixth graders attended the district school, which was about two and a half miles away, and third and fourth graders went to a nearby branch school. The children's meals were prepared in the kitchens of the inns where we stayed, but a cook was hired for the children at the temple.

THE FOOD SITUATION

The local people in our village were largely charcoal makers, and thus could only provide the children with the standard ration of rice. Soy beans were usually added to the rice to make it go farther. Besides the rice, all we had was some salted cabbage and thin bean-paste soup. Since I had heard that chewing your food thoroughly leaves you feeling full and satisfied, I encouraged the children to chew each mouthful thirty times.

Soon a number of children came down with diarrhea. And shortly after that our intake of food was reduced to three bowls of rice gruel a day. All of the canned and dried foods that parents had provided at departure time were soon exhausted. Our group was no longer merely suffering hunger pangs; we were on the verge of starvation. I knew the situation was bad in Tokyo, but was convinced it could be no worse than with us. A check with the other group at the Buddhist temple soon showed why. The inns in our village still had official permission to operate commercially, and it turned out that they were using for their own purposes some of the rice, other foods, and seasonings that were supplied for the school children. The children at the temple were actually receiving everything that was intended for them.

Negotiations with the inn owners brought about no improvement. They assumed the attitude that they were doing us a favor by taking us in, and if we did not like the way they did things, we could get out. We were trapped in the hands of unscrupulous people. The children's parents soon learned of the situation and sent what food they could; but owing to the times, we knew their assistance could not last long.

I couldn't bear seeing the children go hungry, so I went around to the farmhouses in the region and asked for whatever they could spare. What I got were sweet potatoes, corn meal, and dried pumpkin. The wretchedness of our condition brought tears to my eyes as I trudged up and down mountain roads in search of food. A lump would develop in my throat when I saw the hungry children catching small crawfish in the river and roasting them on bamboo spits.

ILLNESS AND INJURY

Other problems were caused by the unfamiliar surroundings the children found themselves in. The difference in water and food plus mental anxiety made many of them sick. We were kept busy caring for cases of headache, stomachache, fever, toothache, sore throat, and so on. As long as we knew what was wrong, we could do our work confidently. But when inexplicable aches and pains developed, we became frightened that something might be seriously wrong and immediately made the long walk to the doctor. The line of fresh complaints never seemed to cease. Cases of congenital asthma and epilepsy developed. Bed-wetting occurred. Some children malingered to get out of the wearisome trek to school. Others pretended to be sick in order to gain affection and attention. Only a week or so after we arrived, one after another the children grew weak and despondent because of homesickness. Our evacuee camp was quickly turning into a sick ward.

Then there was the time when the children were attacked by wasps. We had gone on an excursion to a statue of the Buddhist deity Acala, which was located near a waterfall. As we mounted the path leading to the top of the falls, a swarm of wasps attacked and stung practically everyone on the face or arms. One girl was stung on the throat, which swelled so that it was difficult for her to breathe. After we had given what first aid we could, we immediately took the children to the doctor. Fortunately everyone recovered, but later I was horrified to learn that people have been known to die of shock after being stung by wasps.

THEFT

What with the children always being hungry, the next thing to happen was the disappearance of food. The first things to be stolen were the little treats that parents sent to their children. This would often happen at night when everyone was in bed. Or sometimes it would take place when everyone was away at school or at the bath, the perpetrators being malingerers who remained at the inn with a feigned illness. It usually proved impossible to discover the guilty party. Food was sometimes taken from the kitchen of the inn and even from neighboring farmhouses. There were even cases when housemothers stole food that was intended for the children's mid-afternoon snack.

WORK

Another aspect of our life as evacuees was the fact that the local villagers were short of help and expected us to do our part. Consequently, though raised in Tokyo and unaccustomed to such work, the children were required to carry firewood, charcoal, and vegetables for long distances. For example, we would go into the forest, bind up already cut firewood with coarse ropes, and carry it on our backs out to the prefectural highway, and from there to the kilns where charcoal was made. The way was long, and the loads were heavy. Some children were stronger and walked faster than others, and this made it difficult to keep all of them together in a group. Most of the children worked hard at first when it all seemed like a game, but later began shirking so much that we could not meet our quotas. Some of the children quickly saw that if they exerted themselves too much, it only made them hungry.

The work of the housemothers was also very hard. They had to haul things up to the inn, do the cleaning, and climb up and down a hill to do laundry in a mountain river.

CORRESPONDENCE

Writing letters home should have been a source of pleasure, but this too had its problems. We preferred that the children not write home about their hardships and thereby upset and worry their parents. But a check of the children's letters showed that they all contained pleas to be allowed to go home and urgent requests for their parents to come for them, or at least to visit and bring some food.

BATHING

As for the children's baths, they were allowed to use the inn's hot springs. Unfortunately, since its medicinal water was said to be good for venereal diseases, afflicted guests also used the baths. Though some people said that germs would not be transmitted in mineral baths, we couldn't help but worry about it. Our concern was aggravated by a rumor that some children had contracted gonorrhea from bathing in other hot springs. Furthermore, some of the inn's guests said crude things and made obscene gestures to the little girls and to the housemothers in the bath, where the sexes were not segregated.

VISITORS FROM HOME

Nothing made the children happier than visitors from home, but these calls were infrequent because of the difficulty of obtaining train tickets. Nor could parents or relatives stay long. Generally they remained only long enough to give the children the clothing and food they had brought. The children who had received a visit usually settled down for a while, but those who hadn't became depressed.

ILLNESS AMONG STAFF MEMBERS

Overwork and inadequate food and sleep eventually took their toll among the staff members. Our health specialist fell ill about two months after we arrived in the country and finally had to return to Tokyo. Thereafter, we had to rely on the local doctor and the wife of the head priest at the temple where some of our students lived. She was a nurse and a great help. In addition to the health specialist, two other staff members were forced to return to Tokyo. One of the housemothers suffered a recurrence of tuberculosis, and another became mentally sick with something like schizophrenia.

This was a terrible blow since we had been shorthanded even before these three departures. This meant that the children could not go to school, but had to study at the inns, where teachers doubled as housemothers. It was only after we acquired two more housemothers that the teachers were able to return to their educational duties. But by this time, living conditions in our evacuee camp had greatly deteriorated.

A Precious Experience

In spite of differences in grades, my constant contact with the children led me to think of them not as being inferior or superior, but as all being basically the same. On a fundamental, nonrational level, I became aware of the dignity of life, the respect due to human nature, and the equality of all individuals. Superior intelligence does not necessarily make a superior person. Children with poor mental capability and bad grades in school often have splendid personalities. Looking at the children while they slept, I keenly felt the uniqueness of each and every one of them.

Bosses

To my utter surprise, however, our evacuee camp spawned bands of miniature gangsters. At some time or another, the children split up into groups, and each group had a leader, or boss, who bullied the weaker members and engaged in rivalry with the bosses of other groups. The more timid children did as their bosses told them, to the point of turning over their own food and most prized possessions. They would give the bosses their good clothes, and wore in turn the boss's dirty castoffs. If the parents of these children had known about it, they would undoubtedly have been very sad.

This phenomenon occurred among the girls as well as among the boys. And sometimes the boss, who exerted great power in secret, was a child no one would have ever suspected. A boss had to be assertive and have enough pluck to win the reliance of others. But these bosses never misbehaved in front of the teachers; on the contrary, they kept up the appearance of being cooperative. Questioning the children of a certain group failed to supply grounds for reprimanding the boss, for the children simply replied that they gave things to the boss of their own free will. Apparently these groups also practiced ostracism and carried out corporal punishment.

Lice, Scabies, and Malnutrition

All the children lost weight from malnutrition, and lice sucked blood from their thin bodies. On sunny days we stripped the children naked and boiled their clothes to kill the lice. The water would turn red from all the blood the lice had sucked. Having dried the clothes, we next had the irksome task of picking out all the dead lice. The situation got so bad that we found the lice reproducing even in the laundry baskets.

The lice in the children's hair multiplied so rapidly that no amount of combing or mercury ointment could keep them down. In very bad cases, we had to shave even the girls' heads and then apply ointment and bandages. The girls hated it and made a big fuss, but it couldn't be helped.

It is said that itching is harder to bear than downright pain. This was certainly true with our children. Even while sleeping they continued to scratch themselves. In many instances, they broke the skin and made small wounds that festered and turned into scabies. Caused by filamentous bacteria, scabies can occur on any part of the body, though it is apparently most common in the soft skin between the fingers. Practically all our children came down with it. We tried using sulfur-spring water as a cure, but to no avail.

Under such circumstances the teachers and housemothers had to be tough in order to survive. But a toll was taken on our physical appearance. Our chins became pointed, our eyes sunken, our complexions sallow, and our fingers as bony as those of old women. In the past, I had always been round-faced, but during this period my face became pointed and foxlike. I lost so much weight that I could encircle my waist with my two hands. What with the responsibility I had and the endless work, I was sustained by will power alone.

GRADUATING STUDENTS RETURN TO TOKYO

Tokyo was laid low by a massive air raid on March 10, 1945. On March 11, according to plan, I accompanied the newly graduated sixth graders back to the devastated city and handed them over to their parents and relatives in front of Tabata Station. In my own mind I could not rationalize the absurdity of sending these children, whom we had taken such pains over at the evacuee camp, back into the ashes and smoking ruins of Tokyo.

At the same time, I picked up a fresh group of third graders and took them back with me to Sawatari. There, in preparation for the new school year to commence in April, the staff was reorganized and lodgings rearranged.

Wildfire

The living conditions of the evacuees, already hard enough, were dealt a particularly devastating blow when a forest fire broke out and destroyed the entire village. The fire had been accidentally started by the owner of the Yorozuya Inn, who was trying to clear and cultivate more land in order to provide the children with more food. It blazed for three days and three nights, taking the lives of three people. The evacuees escaped unharmed, but were unable to salvage anything but what they happened to be wearing; everything else was destroyed. It was a terrible misfortune, but I was still thankful that none of our people had been injured.

Relocation

Thanks to the unstinting help of many people, we were relocated not long after the fire, about the time the cherry blossoms were falling: my group went to Ōei-ji Temple, in Iwashima Village, Azuma District, and the other group to Rinshō-ji Temple in Nakanojō Village. Our temple was near a train station and commanded a beautiful view of the valley.

The villagers were good enough to share their bedding, dishes, and other things needed on a daily basis. From Tokyo we received blankets, of the kind set aside for air-raid victims, as well as clothing and rubber shoes for the children.

The villagers in Nakanojō were farmers, raising vegetables, devil's tongue, and flax on terraced fields beside a river. Our work there consisted of carrying vegetables from one place to another; we were relieved of the need to haul firewood and charcoal.

There were no hot springs in the village, and so part of our daily routine consisted of taking the children some way up into the mountains to bathe in open-air hot springs. Having lost our textbooks and writing materials in the fire, we were forced to extemporize in such ways as practicing penmanship in the sand. As before, we had to do battle with lice, scabies, and hunger. The very little rice we received had to be augmented with sweet-potato vines, vegetables, soybean dregs, and kaoliang.

Clearing New Land

To vary and supplement their diet, the children went into the fields and mountains to eat wild strawberries, mulberries, walnuts, akebis, gingko nuts, and chestnuts. In an organized attempt to increase our food supplies, we cleared new fields on a hillside and planted buckwheat—which we later ground in a borrowed stone mortar—and also sweet potatoes, which, however, grew no bigger than the size of a mouse. In the end, this proved an invaluable experience. Of course, it was extremely heavy work for people in our weakened condition, but we felt it better to try our hand at something, as a sort of test of our spiritual reserves, rather than to sit around idle.

Needless to say, clearing new fields proved no small task. Farming in the mountains entails much more work than farming on flat land. The hours of available sunlight are fewer, and irrigation, fertilizing, and harvesting are more difficult. Even the wear-and-tear on tools is greater.

For the children, merely making the round trip from the temple to the fields was exhausting enough. There was little energy left for working. Seeing how dejected and dispirited the children were, we teachers felt the pressing need to do something, anything, to revive their spirits.

RUNAWAYS

Children had occasionally run away from the camp from the very beginning. They seemed to have the idea that they could get to Tokyo by merely following the train tracks, and we usually found them and brought them back. In some cases, however, the process was less simple. One third-grade girl was gone for three nights before we finally located her, drenched by the rain, hiding in the mountains. Two fifth-grade boys showed amazing cleverness when they managed to get as far as Shibukawa by hitching rides in ox carts and trucks. As more and more of the runaways were brought back in failure, the number of attempts gradually diminished.

THE END OF THE WAR

In the early days of the evacuation we did all we could to keep the children's spirits up. We recited a poem written especially for evacuee students by the empress, did calisthenics in conjunction with a radio program, and sang military marches. In addition, we held wrestling matches, had school festivals, and put on various kinds of performances. But after we had been burned out of our first lodgings and as malnutrition grew worse, it proved impossible to carry on these activities.

Soon, even in our remote area, we began to see P51s flying overhead and to hear the sound of air-raid sirens. No doubt enemy aircraft came this far inland because of the pine-oil extraction plant that had recently been completed not far from us, or perhaps because of the iron-ore works in Naganohara.

The head priest of our temple, who was an intellectual and a graduate of the University of Tokyo, told me that Japan would be defeated and that the war would soon be over. Being young, I refused to believe him, and made up my mind to continue doing my best until Japan had finally won.

On August 15, 1945, I had taken the children out to look for vegetables and did not hear the emperor's radio broadcast announcing the end of the war. When I returned to the temple and heard the news, I felt as if every bit of energy in my body had drained away. I was at a loss to know what to think or do.

In practically no time, we began experiencing the confusion that marked the postwar period. First of all rumors began flying left and right. For example, one story had it that we must take the children up into the mountains and push them off cliffs, for the Americans were going to come and lay them out on thick steel plates to be crushed by steamrollers. Fearing there might be a grain of truth in this, I myself wished I had a sword with which to defend my honor should the worst happen.

After we were informed that our school district in Tokyo had been completely destroyed, it was decided that the children should be kept in the country until their parents came for them.

THE OPERATION CONCLUDED

Almost every day one or two children were overjoyed at having their parents come for them, but the other children looked terribly forlorn. Our numbers gradually diminished until, in late autumn, we closed down our camp at the Ōei-ji Temple and consolidated at Rinshō-ji. As snow began to fall, we asked all parents to come for their children. The three who were left without parents were enrolled at the Higashi Kurume Orphanage. In the middle of February our evacuation operation was closed down completely.

All in all, I have no regrets about this phase of my life: I dedicated my youth to helping a group of children whose lives might otherwise have been jeopardized.

Helping the Handicapped

Aiko Matani (57)

My father was the proprietor of a public bath called Matsunoyu in Tokyo. My younger sister, Toshiko, was a congenital deaf-mute. She passed the entrance examinations for the Tokyo Municipal Shinagawa School for Deaf-Mutes when she was thirteen. Father had waited until then to have her enter the school because by that time I had graduated from high school and was able to accompany her to school and look after her. Father did not want to entrust her to strangers. Every day, rain or shine, we commuted to the school in Ōimachi. There I studied about deaf-mutes and their problems, and at home I helped Toshiko with her homework.

As the war intensified and Japan proper was threatened, the school decided to relocate to Kanagawa Prefecture. Students were grouped by age and sent to Buddhist temples in four parts of the prefecture. We got special permission to allow Toshiko to stay with her class, where most of the students were younger since she had started school late, rather than being grouped with a lot of children her own age that she did not know. She was sent to a temple called Zenshō-ji in Chigira Village, Kanagawa Prefecture. The evacuation took place about a year earlier than the ordinary primary schools in Tokyo.

After our house was burned to the ground in the big air raid of March 10, 1945, Father and I took the large rice-cooking pot and went to Kanagawa to see Toshiko. When we got there, the teacher in charge, a Mr. Imanishi, urged me to stay and help with the children. Father, however, was opposed to the idea; he felt that since I had never lived among strangers before, I would be of no use. Toshiko, of course, was overjoyed that someone in the family should be nearby. Mr. Imanishi pointed out that my life would not be worth much if I stayed in Tokyo during the air raids, and stressed the importance for the handicapped of having as many relatives as possible survive the war. Hearing this, I resolved to help out.

I was appointed an employee of the city of Tokyo, my official duties being to look after the daily needs of the roughly fifty children at Zenshō-ji Temple. This appointment was made in Tokyo, after which I returned to the temple, accompanied by Father on May 5, 1945. Train tickets were hard to buy then, and the ones we got took us only part way. We had to walk the last leg of the journey loaded with heavy baggage.

The temple was located deep in the mountains in a region where rice could not be grown. The village was a poor one, subsisting on wheat cultivated in terraced fields that had been laboriously carved out on the mountainsides. The school staff consisted of ten people: three teachers from the school, Mr. Imanishi's wife, four people hired from the village, one parent, and myself.

There is nothing more wretched than not having enough to eat. In our case, the rice rations were particularly small. Each morning, at six o'clock, we got up and prepared a mixture of rice, dried radish leaves, sweet potatoes, edible fungi, and other things. We stirred the mixture with an immense wooden paddle, allowed the rice to cook partially, then removed the pot from the fire and let it stand covered till all the water had evaporated. This was the children's breakfast. When one of them discovered that his or her bowl did not have a slice of sweet potato in it, there would be a great deal of complaining in the characteristic tone of deaf-mutes.

To conserve our ration of rice, we would bake little cakes made of a combination of wheat flour and vegetables. Usually we set about making approximately sixty of them for lunch immediately after clearing up the breakfast dishes. Apparently we went too far with the cakes, however, for everyone soon got thoroughly tired of them.

Birthday parties provided a bright spot in our daily routine. And the children were very good about remembering each other's birthdays. On these occasions we always cooked pure white rice—a great treat—plus whatever other good things that the teacher in charge had managed to purchase on trips to Hachiōji or from nearby farmers.

Water was a big problem. It was drawn from a few mountain streams and piped to the temple through bamboo poles. The problem was that these pipes got clogged up very easily, sometimes by as little as a few leaves. In the daytime it was easy to find where the pipe was congested. But at night it was absolutely terrifying to go out with a flashlight and check the pipe, even though the boy students would help me. A city girl at heart, I could not help recalling with some nostalgia how convenient life in Tokyo had been.

We bathed twice a week, but this too was a problem because of the shortage of water and fuel. To heat both the cooking and bath water, the children gathered twigs and cedar needles from the mountains. Sometimes, however, what they brought back was not dry enough, and I had to blow through a short length of bamboo to get a fire started. While I was doing this, the kindling would suddenly flare up, and as a result my bangs were always singed.

On certain days we prepared balls of cooked rice and took the children into the woods to hunt for fuel and anything that was edible, such as lily roots, mountain yams, butterbur, and chestnuts. The rice balls were enough to stimulate student enthusiasm for these outings, but the real purpose was to increase our food supply. We also rented a field and raised our own vegetables, and perhaps because we had raised them ourselves, they tasted the best of all.

Despite the teachers' unremitting efforts, however, there was simply never enough to eat. Hunger finally drove some students to stealing tomatoes or fruit from the neighboring farms. This brought the villagers down on us in a rage. I remember one boy vehemently denying having eaten a farmer's mulberries, though his mouth was still stained purple from their juice. If we scolded the children, they turned against us and had their parents come to take them home. On one occasion, however, it was a parent that caused the trouble. A mother who came to visit her child stole some rice and, concealing it in the *tabi* stockings she wore, tried to take it home with her. This made it very embarrassing for the child to continue with us.

At the end, only about fifteen remained of the original fifty students. As their numbers dwindled, the remaining students grew increasingly lonely and homesick. Sometimes a full moon would set them to thinking about Tokyo with such longing that they would eventually burst into

HELPING THE HANDICAPPED

tears. Whenever we saw the night sky over Tokyo glowing from the fires of an air raid, the students would invariably write home on the following day to see if their family was all right.

On fair days the area where we aired our bedding would take on a cheerful look from our colored quilts. That night the quilts would be nice and warm, but this did not compensate for the vicious lice that sometimes woke the children from their sleep. When some of the children developed sores and infections, we followed the advice of a villager and prepared a remedy from the dried leaves of a plant called *dokudami* (*Houttuynia cordata*). It was kept ready to hand in a special kettle marked with a red ribbon. This same concoction was said to prevent bed-wetting too. When the weather was good, the girls would sit on the veranda and comb out each other's hair in an attempt to delouse themselves. To kill the lice eggs in our clothing, we would boil clothes in a drum can almost on a daily basis. Some of the students were so fascinated by the lice that they would put some in a jar and show them to me. At the beginning it was enough to turn my stomach, but before long I got used to them.

Sunny days were laundry days as well as days for airing the bedding. We had no soap but made an effective substitute by filling buckets half full of ash, adding water, allowing the mixture to stand overnight, and then using the clear water at the top. The older girls helped with the rinsing, which we did in a swift stream that flowed down into a marsh. It was virtually impossible to buy clothes in those days, and so when a girl let a garment get away from her and float downstream, she would have to wade in to retrieve it, even though it meant getting drenched herself. I was as relieved as the girl when she had stalked down the runaway clothing, coming back with a look of quiet triumph on her face.

Physically handicapped children are often extremely sensitive to small things, as was demonstrated by the praise they lavished on me one day for managing to sew a particularly stubborn button on an old shirt. The more I came to appreciate their impressionable and grateful natures, the more I was determined to do everything I could for them.

From our straitened living conditions I learned some very basic lessons. For instance, when we received a large supply of *daikon* radishes, we had to devise ways of storing and making maximum use of them. We cut off the leaves from the top, parboiled them, and hung them to dry on a rope stretched around a hall in a corner of the temple grounds. The radishes were then cut into thin slices and dried. I learned that sweet-potato vines and taro stalks keep well when dried and can be used as food. And sweet potatoes can be easily stored in mountain caves. Carrot tops can be eaten with sesame-seed sauce, and watermelon rind are good when pickled.

Our temple was located not far from Atsugi airfield. When enemy air-craft began flying over the home islands, P51s frequently appeared overhead and carried out bombing raids not far from us. Once a P51 dove suddenly down toward us, and there was no place to hide but under the temple gate. Later some of the children found empty shells in a field and brought them home as souvenirs.

After a serious air raid on Hachiōji, I took a leave of absence and hur-ried home to see if my parents were all right. On the way we passed a train coach standing beside the tracks. I was horrified to see human hair and flesh spattered all over it. It must have been attacked as it emerged from the tunnel we had just passed through.

From the end of the war till the time our group was disbanded, the food situation got even worse than before. Still, I remember how pleased I was to find that I had gained a little weight, probably from emotional relief that the war was finally over.

Training with wooden swords becomes a part of school routine.

HELPING THE HANDICAPPED

WOMEN WHO STUMBLE

The Ashes of Youth

Mitsuko Noritake (57)

As I write this, in 1982, Japan enjoys both peace and prosperity. People can generally get what they want, and it is unlikely that there is even a single person on the verge of starvation. I doubt that many of the young people who stroll happily among the skyscrapers of Shinjuku have any idea of how precious peace is. As the numbers of such people increase, people who have no firsthand knowledge of the war, the horrors of war and the wretchedness of the immediate postwar years are gradually forgotten. This is true, for example, in Yokosuka, a city where there is an American naval base and the place where I have spent half my life. The hunger and misery that I experienced there in my younger days were such that it is extremely difficult for me to talk about them.

In 1945 my family and I were living deep in the mountains of Gifu Prefecture. Our home in Nagoya had been totally destroyed in an air raid. Our house in the mountains was a converted barn. While we could be thankful that the roof did not leak, we were continually plagued, summer and winter, by fleas in our bedding. Hunger was our constant companion, and malnutrition ate away at our bodies and minds. Our rations, which tended to arrive late, consisted of no more than a daily handful of rice. To eke out our existence, we received vegetables and yams from the parsimonious farmer on whose land we lived, in return for helping with the chores. But this was barely enough to feed ten people, and, sad to say, we often quarreled over food.

One day, during a squabble over food, I suddenly shouted out that I was leaving. Since no one tried to stop me, I started walking down the village road, driven by my own words. The road to the station was a long one, and there were no buses. Only my youngest sister, her eyes red from crying, followed me to the station and saw me off. The times being what they were, everyone was too worn out to concern themselves with what anyone else did.

My only prospect for making a living depended on a newspaper clipping I had in my pocket: it was a help-wanted ad for dancers to perform in front of Occupation troops and included room and board. On the strength of this alone, with no possessions but a small suitcase, I had set out on my own at the age of twenty-three.

With the end of World War II, American army, navy, and air force personnel were stationed at strategic points throughout Japan. These military bases, overflowing with soldiers and sailors, were always surrounded by swarming crowds of Japanese eager to make a living off the Americans: women working in cabarets, nightclubs, and brothels; touters; and black marketeers in American dollars, cigarettes, liquor, and food. Should a base be relocated, all of these people followed it like parasites. Any man or woman who entered this world immediately lost all sense of right and wrong and wallowed in the mire of these people's way of life. For a few years I was one of those people.

Some years had passed since my leaving home, and the United States had started sending troops to fight in the Korean War. One day I found myself standing in front of the main gate to the American naval base at Yokosuka. To the right of the gate fluttered the flag of the United Nations and the Stars and Stripes. Beyond the high wire fence, I felt sure, was a utopia, brimming with all kinds of wonderful American things that I had never so much as seen before.

Yokosuka was a quiet town of low, one-story houses, its streets lightly traveled. Though I was a little uneasy at being in a strange place, I resolutely entered the back streets where the bars and nightclubs were. I optimistically imagined that a nice dress and fashionable shoes would get me a job at once. To find work in a place like this, there was no need for references, education, or experience. I had already given up hope of finding a decent job.

I was nearly thirty, had no savings whatsoever, and at the moment was solely concerned with making enough money for lodgings that night. The shabby back streets of towns like Yokosuka were crawling with women in the same desperate situation.

As soon as it got dark, Motomachi, the bar district in Yokosuka, came alive with flashing red and green neon lights, and recorded music boomed so loudly it could be heard clearly out on the street. The touters, whose job it was to entice customers into the red-light district, were like predatory animals stalking their prey. The streets were overflowing with sailors, for whose attention the bar girls competed.

The girls working in the bars did not receive a guaranteed salary. They simply got half of the price of the drinks they cajoled the Americans into buying. It was just a matter of keeping the liquor flowing. The whiskey was cheap stuff poured from unmarked sake bottles. Girls who could not hold their liquor drank barley water, which is the same amber color. The stronger girls could hold fifty to a hundred drinks, occasionally going to the toilet to induce vomiting and empty their stomachs.

One way of making more money was to go out with the customers. The bars permitted this, provided the customer paid a certain fee that was added to the tab. The management was indifferent to what a girl and her patron did off the premises. Depending on how much had been paid, the girl decided whether they would go to a movie, have something to eat, or go to a hotel. So many of the girls were doing this that there seemed to be nothing wrong with it.

My life went on in much this way until one day I began taking narcotics. Holding the clear ampules up to the light, I could see things floating in the liquid, showing how contaminated it was. But that made no difference. Once the injection was finished, my body seemed to expand infinitely, my mind to float upward. But before long, signs of addiction appeared. I heard all kinds of strange sounds and saw vague flut-

Bar girls work hard to attract customers. Courtesy of Mainichi Newspapers.

tering black objects. I became irritable and would fly into a rage over nothing with a perfect stranger. Life became more and more miserable, and any money that came into my hands vanished immediately.

It was the people who ran the bars and the brothels who were having a big laugh. Despising the girls on the one hand, they nevertheless got rich off of them. And among the GIs these women were known as "yellow latrines." In spite of the scorn and contempt heaped on them, the girls went on trying, somehow, to make a living and survive. Today very few people know what happened to most of the more than a thousand women whose youth was wasted on the streets of Yokosuka. Those few women who are still known to me are reluctant to talk about the past. The memory of those years remains an oppressive weight on their hearts.

Some of the women I remember have now disappeared forever. A certain Sumie (these names are fictitious), though not very pretty, was extremely good at entertaining men. She had no time for the young boys, always choosing middle-aged men of higher rank, usually ones who were already extremely drunk. And when she latched on to a man, she stayed with him till his wallet was empty. Her dream was to build an apartment house and live a life of ease. She kept her money in bank accounts registered under fictitious names so as to avoid paying taxes. But just as she was about to realize her dreams, she had a hemorrhage of the lungs. She was hospitalized for a week and then died. They say that an old chair in her room was bulging with money she had not managed to put in the bank. Some distant relatives took care of her personal effects, but they did not bother to give her a funeral. Where is her dream now?

A certain Eiko, a clever girl who could read and write English, suffered from poor health but always ate the best foods she could afford. She had a cute little boy of mixed blood, though no one, probably not even Eiko herself, knew who the father was. She left the boy with foster parents and then, without contributing a cent to his upkeep, vanished completely.

In contrast, a girl named Harumi tried desperately to raise her child without any help. (It has only been in recent years that the Japanese system of social welfare has improved.) Conditions were such that Harumi could not worry about appearances, and her child could sometimes be seen crouching outside the locked door of Harumi's room waiting for

Harumi to finish her business. My heart still aches whenever I think of how Harumi must have agonized at such times.

Of course, situations like these resulted in frequent abortions. It is sad to think of how many lives were lost in this way. I often went with these women and sat beside their hospital beds, waiting for them to come out of the anesthetic. Their faces distorted and glistening with perspiration, they seemed somewhere in their unconscious minds to be asking forgiveness for violating their maternal instincts.

I sometimes wonder if happiness finally came to those many women who struggled out of the mud and filth of this way of life to go to the United States as war brides, some to black Americans and some to white. But one woman, who is now an American citizen and has grandchildren, says that when asked how and where she met her American husband, she is hesitant to tell the truth.

Time passes, and the world changes. If it had not been for the nightmare of war, all of these women would have lived perfectly ordinary lives as wives and mothers. This thought now seems to haunt the quiet desolation that was once the old Yokosuka pleasure quarter.

But even now, thirty years later, the Yokosuka Naval Base is still a berth for huge American aircraft carriers and battleships. There has been agitation for reversion of the base to Japanese control since 1972. But it is unlikely that the United States will withdraw completely, and under current circumstances it may be impractical for the Japanese government to demand that they do so. Nonetheless, we citizens are deeply aware of the glasslike fragility of a peace that must coexist with bases of this kind. This is why I think the Japanese people must join hands with their friends throughout the world and work for peace, never forgetting how cruel war is.

From Town to Town
Anonymous (50)

I arrived at Yokosuka in 1958, after having left my home in Osaka and spent time in Asakusa, Tokyo, and in Misawa, Aomori Prefecture. I was then twenty-six years old. Now at an age when I can reflect calmly on the past, I see that, whether I care to admit it or not, most of my life has been spent in the company of American soldiers. My life can be compared to a small leaf blown here and there by the winds of war. If it had not been for war, I would have had no contacts with the American military, and my life would surely have been very different.

In February of last year my husband, who was an American, died of myocardial infarction, and I now live alone with a dog named Julie that he befriended. This is no doubt the most tranquil period of my whole life. My one wish is that young people nowadays will not have to go through what I did, that no matter how hard life gets, they will live in a way they can be proud of.

War brought great misery to Osaka, as it did to the rest of postwar Japan. In contrast to the well-fed, healthy American soldiers who swaggered about town, we Japanese were a sorry-looking lot with empty bellies. With an eye on the unbelievable amounts of chocolate, cigarettes, and other good things the soldiers had, many girls my age began going out with them. I even knew of a girl who dated American soldiers so she could buy penicillin for a brother who had tuberculosis.

My troubles began one day when a girlfriend invited me to go to a movie. Unknown to me, she had arranged for two American soldiers to join us on the way. Though I felt betrayed, the evening ended with my not going home.

From that time on there was a change in the way my parents and the neighbors looked at me. Still, for two or three years I kept working at a small factory. But once people begin thinking about a girl in a certain way, they practically never change their minds. With no one to talk to about it, I soon found the situation unbearable. Then a friend wrote suggesting that I come to Tokyo and live with her. Since I had always wanted to go Tokyo, and more so now with the trouble at home, I finally decided to go.

When I told my parents, they were taken by surprise and, in the end, absolutely opposed to the idea. There was a lot of shouting and even some physical violence, which I now realize was about the only way they could show their love for me. On the other hand, though, I am sure they felt I would be an embarrassment to them if I stayed in Osaka.

In Tokyo, my friend took me to a place not far from the famous

Kokusai Theater, in the Asakusa district. It turned out to be a brothel. The main street was lined with perfectly ordinary shops, but behind them, down a narrow alley, were ten or so crudely built shacks, each of which housed five or six girls. The alley seemed to have girls coming and going at all hours. The shacks were filled with the smell of alcohol, smoke from foreign cigarettes, and the sound of voices yelling out to each other. It was like nothing I had ever experienced before.

Asakusa was thriving then. The celebrated Takiko Mizunoe and the Armstrong Show played at the Kokusai Theater. People thronged the lane of shops called Nakamisedōri and the road lined with movie and strip theaters.

From the day of my arrival, I put on some gaudy clothes, had my hair done up, and sat around waiting for the phone to ring, like all the other girls. In those days it was all the rage to have your hair done like Marilyn Monroe or Audrey Hepburn. With my thick black hair, I chose the Monroe style.

People are bound to be influenced by their environment. And once you gave up your self-respect, it didn't require any special courage to fit into this new way of life. Sooner or later, you felt no sense of shame at all.

We were on call twenty-four hours a day. When the madam answered the telephone, there would be a familiar voice at the other end: "Five girls for the Azabu Hotel." And we would quickly make up a party, recruiting girls from next door if necessary, and catch a taxi.

Arriving at the lobby of the hotel, we would see four or five American soldiers talking loudly, obviously on leave from the Korean War. The manager of the hotel would line us up in front of the men like so much merchandise and introduce each of us. Of course, the Americans never caught our names and merely indicated the girl they wanted by the color of her dress. When everything was settled, the soldiers would pay a week's hotel bill on the spot, plus an extra fee for being introduced to us.

Most of the men we came into contact with in those days were on leave from the war. We said they were Korean punch-drunk. They had all been exposed to imminent death for six months and had no assurance that they would return home alive. From their standpoint, a week's leave meant getting their washing done while the sun shined. As so-called one-week wives, we had to see that the soldiers had as much fun as possible, entertaining them night and day. And money was no object. They would take us to the Ginza district and buy us shoes, hats, and clothes of the kind I had never even seen close-up before.

These soldiers had more money than they knew what to do with, and they spent it all on the girls. And the hotels did everything they could to encourage them to spend. But the end of the funds was always the end of the fun, and the hotels drove away soldiers who had run out of money. Or sometimes they would tell the Americans to go out and pimp. This meant going to Camp Dream, where R-and-R troops first landed, enticing them with tales of how nice the girls were, and bringing them back in groups to the hotel. Though the war between Japan and the United States had ended, representatives of the two countries continued fighting over the dollar. Sometimes military personnel who knew nothing of Japanese currency would pay a thousand yen for a ride in a tiny buglike taxi, the standard fare for which was sixty yen.

For their part, the soldiers were convinced that money was power and carefully eyed the girls to make sure they got the one they wanted, or the best looking one. Intellectual types and the finicky boss type took longest in making their choices. There was nothing but money in these transactions, and not a scrap of human feeling. Fights and quarrels were rife. An unsatisfied soldier would scream for his money back or demand a different girl. An irate girl would shout that under no circumstances did she intend to spend a whole week with this damned Yankee. In spite of everything, I accepted the job for what it was and worked hard. There was no emotional involvement. I did not think about the future, partly because I was still young but also because there was no time for it.

I do remember, however, one emotional experience. Most of the soldiers were twenty-two or twenty-three, but this particular man was older. As he looked up at the starry sky, he started crying and said, "All my buddies have been killed. And I don't know what's going to happen to me from one day to the next."

Though I had no clear notion of what a battlefield was like, I felt sorry for this man and, nodding in agreement, listened to his broken story. "On the battlefield, you send out dogs first. You don't know whether it's mined or not. Some of the young guys are so scared they won't take a step. And you have to smack them and drag them forward..."

It is only logical that no one wants to kill another human being for the fun of it. These American men, all of whom had lives of their own back home, had been sent across the Pacific to the Far East to fight against their will. They were victims too. In war, the winner and the loser are both victims.

In a sense, the girls at Asakusa were the GI equivalent of the "solace girls" provided to the Japanese army during the war. One person sarcastically said that we were engaged in the human-flesh trade. The girls were merchandise trying to sell themselves to the highest bidder. The people pulling the strings behind the scenes were also out to get as much as they could.

In fact, the business was only able to remain a going concern because the military, the police, and the house managers cooperated with each other. True, I could buy expensive winter coats and wear eight-panel flared skirts when I went out with GIs to do the latest dance steps, but

Sailors on R and R from Vietnam have a night on the town.

ultimately the years I spent in Asakusa were empty of everything but disgrace. Finally, hooked on drugs, a mental and physical wreck, I left Asakusa for Misawa in Aomori Prefecture, where there was an American base.

Misawa was a quiet town, but there was little chance that a half-sick woman like me could make much money. I got deeper and deeper into debt. Sometimes I even propositioned GIs on street corners to make extra money. But still my debts showed no sign at all of dwindling. After thinking the matter over for a long time, I decided to run away from the "house" where I was working. I knew I would be in for a lot of trouble if I got caught, but I had sunk so low that there was really nothing more for me to lose. I made my plans in advance.

A girl named Kazuko wanted to go with me. Women like us were not allowed to go anywhere we liked in the town; people from the brothel were always on the lookout for wayward girls. But we arranged ahead of time for some GIs to pick us up and, on the pretense of going for a ride, take us to Misawa Station. There we could board a train for Yokosuka, where we had friends.

On the appointed day, I told the madam of the house that I wanted to take Kazuko to the doctor's, and that on the way back we would stop off at the public bath. I put a bar of soap and a towel in a wash basin, and the two of us set out. Along the way, the GIs picked us up as planned and we headed for the station, throwing the bath basin out of the window on a country road.

We arrived at the station without any trouble, only to find that the train had just pulled out. We had an hour to wait for the next train, and spent it hiding behind an *oden* vendor's, hoping against hope that we would not be spotted.

If we had dressed as usual, it would have been clear what we did for a living. So we had carefully chosen the least flashy dresses we owned, wore coats over them, and had rubbed off all our makeup. Certain things about the trip I shall never forget. First was the delicious bowl of noodles we ate at a stop where we had to change trains. Second was the way the people stared at the two of us throughout the long ride.

Yokosuka was incomparably brighter and more open and free than Misawa. For my first few years there, I either worked alone or lived in a house, doing much the same kind of thing I had done in Asakusa and Misawa. My friend there eventually followed her boyfriend to America and later, I heard, committed suicide.

It was after my fortieth birthday that I met the kind, cheerful American man who brought me happiness as a woman and as a human being. He was fifty-five at the time. We had a simple wedding ceremony and I was so happy that, for his sake, I was at last able to give up the cigarettes and liquor I had relied on for more than twenty years. We had been together for about ten years when, as I have said, in February of last year he died of myocardial infarction in the naval-base hospital, leaving me to a solitary life once again.

I think it is true that women are the greatest victims of war. My youth was spent during the war and then in the postwar upheaval caused by the war. It is only because of my religious faith that I have managed to survive.

Death in war is cruel and horrible, not the swift clean thing that young people nowadays see on television programs and in motion pictures. Even those who survive a war must endure the wretchedness and starvation that follows. To prevent this from happening again, we must make sure today's young people understand what war is really like. This is why I intend to go on telling my own story.

WOMEN IN
SEARCH OF
A HOME

Over an Ocean
Nobuko Davis (67)

My two sons by my first husband, who died in a Siberian concentration camp, live in Japan. My third son, by my second husband, lives with me in the United States. Since September 1961 Japan has been a distant homeland for me. As I think back on my past, I feel two emotions well up in me: one is that war must never happen again, the other is a kind of angry hope that no other woman will have to go through the same experiences that I have.

In 1934, when I was nineteen, my parents forced me to marry a man with whom I had never even spoken. He was the head priest of a well-known Shinto shrine in the city of Yokosuka.

The times became more and more troubled. The so-called Manchurian Incident, which took place while I was still in school, had developed into war with China. The Ladies Defense Guild began to conduct air-raid drills on almost a daily basis.

In 1945 my husband received his draft notice and was mobilized on March 2. At the time our older son was seven years old and the younger one three months old. My husband said, "The war must be nearly over if they've gotten around to drafting Shinto priests. I imagine I won't be back, so this is good-bye." And it turned out just as he had said, though I never dreamed that those would be the last words I would hear him speak.

On August 15 the emperor announced the end of the war. While there were no more air raids, it proved terribly hard for a lone woman to provide for two old people and two children. For a while we lived by selling personal possessions. But soon there was nothing left to sell, and I had to go to work as a cleaning woman on the Yokosuka naval base. In addition to my work, I had to look after the house, care for two old people and two children, and go out into the countryside in search of food. I barely had time to catch my breath.

My mainstay in all this was the hope that my husband would soon return. But on January 5, 1946, I received word that he had been taken by the Russians to a concentration camp in Siberia, and there he had died. With my one prop gone, I fell into a daze for a while, unable to do anything. To make matters worse, my mother-in-law wanted me to get out of the house, and began treating me very coldly. Her daughter had gotten divorced and wanted to come back to live with her family.

Considering how hard the times were, it was understandable that they should want to reduce the number of mouths to feed, but still it was very hard on me, having lost the family breadwinner. Realizing that I could not stay much longer, I made up my mind to return with the children to my own family home.

But even at home everyone was worried about having enough to eat, and I did not receive a very warm welcome. I ended up staying with this friend or that for a month or two each. But I was always anxious about what would happen next. The world did not look kindly on a widow with children.

Just about this time I got a job as a maid in the home of an American major with whom I had been acquainted when I worked on the Yokosuka base. Not long afterward an American sailor with a group of seven or eight Japanese workmen came to repair the steam pipes. The sailor's name was Davis, and he later became my husband.

The workmen continued to come to the house for about ten days, and little by little I began to talk with Davis. He turned out to be an only child. Though cheerful in general, he had a sad side to his character and liked to have a good time with lots of people. Gradually we became good friends.

I wanted to invite him to my house, but it was out of the question. In my two sons' eyes their father had been killed in the war with the United States, and so all Americans were as good as their father's murderer. Davis was an upstanding young man of high principles, but this made no difference: he was still an American.

Nonetheless, until his four-year tour of duty came to an end, Davis did what he could to make our way of life better. When time came for him to go, he promised to return and handed over a large sum of money for me and the children to live on. I hesitated at first, but finally accepted the money when he said it was not a gift: he was merely putting me in charge of it.

During the year following his departure from Tachikawa Air Base, he sent me a hundred dollars a month without fail. And I was not surprised when, at the end of that year, he started talking of marriage.

I had two children and was twelve years older than he. In spite of my doubts, however, he insisted. The children, however, flatly rejected the idea. "Why do you have to marry an American when it was the Americans who killed father?" they asked, and began looking on me too as an enemy.

Davis took a different view. He said, "You're worried about nothing but the children now. But when they've grown up, they'll get married and leave you on your own. That's why I say you should get married now for the sake of your own future."

My children looked askance at me, and my family disowned me. I was too confused to know what to do. Finally, however, the loneliness and helplessness of my position as a war widow and Davis's enthusiasm and personality made up my mind for me. We were married in 1955. But for the next three years Davis was stationed in southern Africa, and I saw him only once a year when he came to Yokosuka on leave.

My third son, Johnny, was born in the hospital on the Yokosuka naval base. Perhaps because of my age, his delivery was so hard that I thought I might die. With Johnny's birth, the emotional rift widened between me and my two older boys. The youngest was in primary school and still somewhat dependent on me. But the older boy, who had just graduated from middle school, went out and found a job without even discussing the matter with me. He lived in the company dormitory and went to high school at night. When I learned about this from the school, the news saddened me more than it surprised me. In a way I was happy that my son had become old enough to stand on his own two feet. Still, it grated on me that the war and national differences, things over which I had no control, should cut off normal, open communication between parent and child.

When my husband was transferred to the United States in September 1961, I decided to join him. I wanted to take all the children with me so that we could start a new life together. The two older boys, however, would not hear of it. No amount of talk could bring them around to my view. When I had done all I could, I left them with relatives and, with little Johnny, reluctantly boarded a plane for the United States.

In the United States everything was not necessarily easy. My husband, who had to live on a camp some distance away, left us with his parents. My surroundings were completely new, and my English was far from perfect. I lived as quietly as possible.

Then one day I received a letter from my second son in Japan. Though leaving the two boys on their own had been unavoidable, it had been an indescribably difficult decision for me. And for the boys the days that followed were undoubtedly very hard. My heart nearly broke when I read the letter: "Every time I see an airplane flying overhead, I think that that could be the plane Mother took to America, and tears come to my eyes."

Added to the uncertainties of my new surroundings, I soon found that I could not get along with my father-in-law. Language problems were not the only reason. One day, things became so unbearable that Johnny and I left the house and made a four-day bus ride to the camp where my husband was stationed.

In the eleventh year after Johnny and I came to the United States, my kind, warmhearted husband died of heart failure. Because he had been a military man, we have been completely provided for, and I live in relative security.

Ten years after leaving Japan I made my first trip back. I was pleasantly surprised when my two sons came to meet me. My older boy had just married a charming girl. His younger brother was working in Osaka, but he came to join us in Tokyo when he heard of my return.

The decade we had been separated must have been hard for them, but fortunately they too had become believers in Nichiren Shōshū Buddhism. I myself had become a believer while still living in Japan. Faith had obviously strengthened the boys. In ten years they had grown big and strong, not only physically but also in their outlook on life. A willingness to take a kindly view of others showed in their faces. Though separated by an ocean, we were fellow believers in the same religious faith as well as parent and children. I said nothing while I held their hands, the warmth filling the vacuum of ten years.

The boys said, "It's so much better that you married a good American than it would have been if you had married a bad Japanese."

I Never Call Her Mother

Jōji Sakai (29)

I will never forget it. It happened in 1964, the year of the Tokyo Olympics, when I was in the fifth grade of primary school. I was taken to the Elizabeth Saunders Home for orphans in Ōiso, just three weeks after going with my aunt to the Child Counseling Bureau in Sagamihara, Kanagawa Prefecture. (At the time I had no idea what being taken to a child counseling office meant.) I can still see the mountains rising clearly into the beautiful blue sky.

My mother worked at night in bars and nightclubs. By the time she got home from work I had usually left for school, and when I returned in the evening, she had already gone to work. That is why I didn't think it particularly strange that, with my book satchel strapped to my back, I should be taken to the counseling office without my mother. Even at the counseling office, when I heard voices shouting, "Run away again, has he?" and then the sound of feet running down the hall, I attached no special meaning to it.

But by the time we got to the Elizabeth Saunders Home I had a vague idea that it was an orphanage for children of mixed blood, and that I would never again be able to live together with my mother as other children did.

I was born in 1953. My father was a black man. Mother was a kind person, but she shut up as tight as a clam at the mention of my father. My only memories of his face date from early childhood.

A violent man, he sometimes came to our house and beat Mother. When I was still small, I once saw him in a rage. In the room upstairs he was slashing her clothes with a razor. I hated him for what he did to Mother and also hated his country, America. After a while he disappeared; perhaps he went back to the United States. Mother had to raise me alone. But I was happy. She was good to me, and all the people in our neighborhood were kind.

Sometimes the other children in school made me cry by teasing me about being a half-breed, but instead of just sympathizing, Mother would bolster me up by telling me to fight back.

We were poor, and I often played with a bad group of kids who were always skipping classes. But since I was living with Mother I was satisfied with our way of life.

The day before I was taken to the Child Counseling Bureau, Mother said she was going shopping and asked if there was anything I wanted. I said I wanted a new book satchel, and she actually brought me one. I didn't know what the tears in her eyes meant as she handed it to me, although I was puzzled that she had gone to such expense when we had no money. Now that I look back on it, I realize that she was probably already thinking of going to America. As a matter of fact, she once asked me if I would not like to go to America before she did.

On the day my aunt took me to the counseling office, I was so happy about my new satchel that I shoved into the back of mind any suspicions that I might be parting with Mother for good. Even after I entered the Elizabeth Saunders Home, I still believed that she would come for me some day. Even later I readily accepted the story that she had gone to study in Europe.

Mother's occasional visits and the gifts she brought made me very happy, but it also caused trouble between me and the other children. Most of them had been born during the confusion of the immediate postwar period, when they had been abandoned in places like train-station passageways. It was most unusual for a child of ten—my age at the time—to be enrolled at the home. I was among the younger black half-breeds: most of the others had been born in 1946 or 1947. Their parents practically never visited them. When they did, it was not from love but with the hope of somehow making money off their children, who were now young adults. It was only natural that I should be envied when Mother came to see me.

As far as life at the home was concerned, I enjoyed myself in a way. I played in the tree house in the garden and made what we called telephones out of paper and twine. In summer we went swimming at the head mistress's beach house in Tottori Prefecture. At New Year's and on our birthdays we received five hundred yen extra spending money and were allowed to go into town.

No matter what anyone said, though, there was one thing in which I was determined to have my own way. Throughout my middle-school years I flatly refused to study the English language. "Who wants to study

I NEVER CALL HER MOTHER

a language the Americans use?" I asked myself. This feeling was deeply rooted in me, and I never changed my mind.

I went on living more or less like this until my compulsory education was almost finished. Shortly before graduation ceremonies from the home, a letter from Mother arrived telling me that she had married an English engineer.

When I finished reading the letter, I made a vow that contradicted all those years of having thought of nothing but her: I vowed that from that time on I would not think of her anymore, that I would never call her "Mother" again. She became a much more distant person than she had ever been in the past.

After graduation the home found me a job with room and board in a boutique in the Asakusa district of Tokyo. I stayed there six months and then began studying in a dressmaking and design school in nearby Ueno, working in the meanwhile at a number of other boutiques. Coming out into society like this, I realized what a disadvantage it was to be a product of the Elizabeth Saunders Home. Being a half-breed was handicap enough, but being from the home—which meant that you were an orphan, a foundling—made social barriers even higher.

Most of my classmates at the home ended up working in bars or cabarets. I knew of a girl from the home who married a pure-blooded Japanese, but was divorced when she had a baby. The child was then sent to the Elizabeth Saunders Home. And such cases were not uncommon.

Even my own relatives were cold toward me. For a while I failed to understand what they meant when they said that if I wanted to visit, it should be at night, and if I was asked who I was by the neighbors, I should say I was a company acquaintance. When I finally realized what they meant, I was furious.

On the other hand, I have been fortunate in having a lot of good people as colleagues and friends, people who are not related by blood. I am extremely grateful for the warmth they have shown, which has enabled me to go on with my work as a fashion designer. I am twenty-nine now, and it is about time to start thinking of marriage. I have been lucky in meeting a lot of good people, but I cannot shake off a kind of uneasiness whenever I think of the difficulties that people of mixed blood must face in Japan.

Recently the mass media have been devoting a great deal of attention to the Japanese children who were abandoned by their parents in the last phase of the war in China; these people, now middle-aged, were brought up by Chinese foster parents, and now they want to come to Japan and search for their parents and relatives. When I heard of this problem, I wanted to cry out: Under no circumstances, even if face to face with death, should parents abandon their children the way those Japanese did. Naturally, this silent cry is a reflection of the fact that I had to live apart from my own mother.

The wife of the English engineer comes to visit my office several times a year now. True to the vow I made on graduating from the Elizabeth Saunders Home, I have never once called her "mother."

For my own part, I see that it is now time to take a hard second look at my life, and to accept the responsibility of being a parent and building a solid home life of my own.

At first, children of mixed blood had no trouble fitting in at school.

A Son without a Country

Shizuko Kamiya (49)

In 1954, after graduating from high school in Okinawa, I went to find a job on the main Japanese islands but soon came back because I wanted to be near my family. I hoped to make as much money as possible, but since most jobs—generally work related to the American military establishment—paid poorly, I decided to work in a bar. As it turned out, the soldier who was later to be my husband was a regular customer there.

After the end of World War II, MPs had frequently come to our house. They always had plenty of food and their babies were as cute as dolls. My young heart gradually came to look on them as a wonderful people. This infatuation prepared the ground for my later marriage to an American.

He was eighteen and I was twenty-eight. I could tell from my parents' faces that they disapproved of our seeing each other. When I became pregnant and the ninth month approached, I went to them for the first time to ask if they would be witnesses at our marriage. Taking one look at my big belly, they disowned me on the spot.

On October 2, 1963, I gave birth to our first child, a boy. For a while my husband and I were very happy, and our second boy was born in April 1965. But two months before this, my husband had been sent to Vietnam. After a year there he returned a totally different man. My handsome, gentle husband now had such a demonic look on his face that the children were afraid to go near him.

He rarely spoke of his experiences in Vietnam. In fact, the only thing he ever said was that he had had to kill a five-year-old child who was running toward him with a hand grenade in its hand. This memory was a permanent scar on his mind.

After a while he was sent to Vietnam again, and the fighting was even more intense than before. By the time he returned to Okinawa, his mind was completely deranged. Before long the army forced him to return to the United States, and his wife and two children were left behind. At the time, there was one thought that went through my mind like a repeated cry: in war the winner and loser are both victims, their homes and families mercilessly broken.

As if in answer to my longing to be with him, my husband wrote any number of times saying that he wanted us to come to the United States. But I grew very uneasy at the prospect. He was disabled and unable to work and support us. I myself was unfamiliar with the American way of life, and then there was the language problem. I even considered the possibility that he might someday divorce me and take away the children. Finally, fully aware that I was letting myself in for a lot of hardship, I decided to remain where I was and raise the children as Okinawans.

The money I had received from my husband had long ago been spent, and my own savings were now depleted. Life grew more and more difficult. When we were down to our last two dollars, I once more started working in a bar at night. I had to do all I could for the children—one who was now three years old and the other only one. This period of my life was so hard that my memory is blank about many things that happened then.

At about this time, the immigration authorities informed me that I was to register my children as aliens. But when I went to the American consulate to get the boys' passports, I was told that my older boy had no citizenship and that a passport could not be issued. It seemed that, because my husband had been under age (nineteen) when our older boy was born, under paragraph (a) (7), article 301 of the Immigration and Citizenship Law of the United States of America, the boy was ineligible for citizenship. My younger son, who was born after his father had come of age, automatically acquired American citizenship. I was amazed to learn that the older boy, whom I had implicitly assumed was a United States citizen, actually had no country at all.

After the interview I dragged myself home in a daze, physically drained. But I was not ready to give up yet. Whenever I could take time from work, I went to the Domestic Court and the International Welfare Bureau to see if something could be done. The officials there had no idea at the time how to arrive at a fundamental solution to the problem, though they did say it would take time and money. Living from day to day, I was in no position to get the large sums they said I would need. Though I realized that I was not doing as well as I should by my son, I gave up all attempts to pursue the matter.

I was unable to ask help from my own family, so I left the two boys at home by themselves while I went out to work. Thinking they might be trapped by a fire, I always left the door unlocked. Sometimes my younger son would mistake a bright moonlit night for daytime and go out to play at two or three in the morning. The neighbors told him to go back inside or the bogyman man would get him.

When I took the boys to the beach, I was usually so tired that I would fall asleep while they played. Once an American saved one of the boys from drowning. The children were so lonely for a father's attention that they clung to the American's legs, calling "Daddy, Daddy!" The American picked the boys up in his arms and bought them a bag of candy.

If we were going to survive, I had to work. But no matter how hard I worked, our way of life never got better. Sometimes I wished I were a dog. Dogs do not have to pay rent and can sleep anywhere they like, eating what they find. The social welfare system was of no use to me, and I did not have the money to find someone to care for the children while I was working. They were alone much of the time. Harassed and run-down, I had reached the end of my tether.

It had been my own decision to work in bars, but the pride I felt at being a high-school graduate meant a nightly battle with my sense of self-respect. I also began to lose confidence in my ability to raise the children. All of these things, plus the fact that my work demanded that I do a certain amount of drinking, resulted in neurosis, insomnia, and alcoholism. Things got so bad that I sometimes fell asleep, drunk, by the roadside. I was also bothered when some of the women I worked with, though basically good, kind people, began talking behind my back.

I had fallen about as low as I could and was almost ready to give up, but one part of me still wanted to make a new start. I was looking for something that would save me. It was then that one of the girls I worked with explained the meaning of true Buddhism to me. I was particularly struck by the energy she showed in her life, the conditions of which were very much like my own. On February 18, 1968, I accepted faith in Nichiren Shōshū Buddhism.

Thereafter, whenever I met soldiers about to be sent to Vietnam, I always begged them to come back alive, and without having killed anyone. I would then give them leaves of the holy *shikimi* tree and say, "If you kill, you'll end up like my husband!" Some of them looked at me

A SON WITHOUT A COUNTRY

suspiciously, as if I were a spy of some sort. But I always rejoiced when one of these men returned safely from the war and, showing me the *shikimi* leaves they had kept with them, thanked me for my concern.

After curing my alcoholism, I began to apply myself to my work with much more energy. One evening—it was Saturday, December 19, 1970—I was sitting in the bar having a drink with an American serviceman when I heard a commotion outside. Looking out, I saw that the road leading to the main gate of the base was crowded with taxicabs—at first ten and then twenty. I could not figure out what was happening.

It seems that some drunken American servicemen had hit an Okinawan pedestrian and, without stopping to help, had tried to drive away. Some Okinawan taxicab drivers had seen the whole thing and were doing their utmost to prevent the soldiers from getting away. Soon a crowd of angry people had gathered around the soldiers' car, shouting and threatening violence. This was quite different from the usual docile Okinawan attitude.

By this time I was part of the crowd. Soon an MP car arrived on the scene, its sirens shrieking. The crowd was growing angrier. "I suppose the Americans are right again and the Okinawans wrong! It's the Itoman

During the Koza Riots, seventy-three American cars
were set afire.

business all over again," someone shouted. I turned to an Okinawan policeman and shouted, "What are you, some kind of American spy? You're an Okinawan, aren't you? Why don't you stand up for the Okinawans?" When the policeman turned his flashlight on me and stared angrily into my face, I felt a shiver run down my back.

Okinawa was under American control then. In the many cases of robbery, murder, rape, and other crimes committed by American soldiers, the MPs took charge, and invariably decisions favorable to the Americans were handed down.

Instead of quieting down, the trouble grew worse. Americans were dashing everywhere to keep out of harm's way while the Okinawans turned over automobiles and set them afire. It was as though a war had started. I told our American customers to go home and stay there if they valued their lives.

When I heard that the Okinawans were beating up Americans and burning every car with an American license plate, I felt a sudden pang of fright. My children were half American. They might be killed!

I do not recall how I did it, but I somehow managed to get home. The children were safe. I held them to me, relief flooding my body. That night the long pent-up emotions of the Okinawan people flared up in what later came to be known as the Koza Riots.

My children grew up quickly, and soon it was time for them to go to school. Although at first they were enrolled in the Catholic King's School, I later decided they should have a Japanese education. But when I tried to enroll my older boy in a Japanese school, I was turned down because he was stateless. But then the principal of the Koza Primary School, moved by my story, took a personal interest in the case and overrode the objections of other members of the faculty. He agreed to let my son attend school on what was to be a provisional basis.

In 1971, at the age of eight—two years late—my older boy enrolled with his younger brother in primary school, where he soon made friends and became better and better at speaking the Japanese language. He enjoyed going to school, and when his classmates would sometimes tease him by calling him American, he would reply, "I'm not an American, I'm a half-breed." A carefree child, he had no idea what the words meant.

Seeing his shining, open face, I became determined to solve his citizen-

A SON WITHOUT A COUNTRY

ship problem and started making the rounds of consulates and the Ministry of Justice again. I was told to submit thirty-seven different documents in order to have him naturalized. This seemed so forbidding a task that for five years I did nothing.

With the reversion of Okinawa to Japan on May 15, 1972, the question of children without citizenship came into prominence. This issue and the movement for women's rights ultimately forced the slow-moving Japanese government to do something about the problem.

For years I had wanted to stop working nights for the children's sake. And, at last, I did take a day job. Though the salary was only a third of what I had formerly made, the children did their part by delivering papers and helping with meals and the laundry.

Before long I was asked by the human-rights department of the local office of the Ministry of Justice to come and discuss my older son's citizenship. Once again I was told to submit all kinds of forms and papers, but I sent in nothing but a birth certificate.

After this, we heard nothing. Then, just as my son was about to take his high-school entrance examinations, I decided to try again. I felt it would be much better if he could have all of this settled before he went on with his education. When I called the local office of the Ministry of Justice, I was told, "Oh, you never showed up again, so we just went ahead and completed all the paper work. Your son is now a Japanese citizen."

For a second I felt this must be some terrible joke, and could not believe it. Why had they let me suffer for eighteen years if the matter could be settled so easily? Why had they failed to do something like this earlier?

Just to check, I went to the city hall and found that my son's citizenship had been recorded as of February 2, 1981. Overjoyed, I immediately went home and prayed before the Gohonzon, which has been the sole support of my lonely life.

Some time later I received an unpleasant telephone call from the immigration authorities, asking me why I had taken it on myself to have my son made a Japanese citizen. I referred the person to the Ministry of Justice. I had done nothing myself but submit one paper, a birth certificate. I still could not understand how a situation like this could have happened.

After a long struggle, one child was granted citizenship. By telling my story I hope that some light is shed on the lives of other Okinawans who are still officially without a country.

Alien Blood

Anonymous

During World War II my grandmother and mother were on the South Pacific island of Tinian. Grandmother's husband had died in the war, and she was engaged in a life-and-death struggle to survive, along with her daughter (my mother) and a younger son. Finally, however, she took the boy and ran away, leaving behind my sobbing mother, who was twelve at the time. Mother was an illegitimate child born before my grandmother's marriage, whereas the boy was born in wedlock. When all of their lives were threatened at the end of the war, my grandmother had apparently decided that my mother could be dispensed with.

Ironically, however, all three of them were captured by the Americans and sent to the same prison camp, where inevitably they met again. Even today, my mother cannot forget the sorrow and anger she felt at being abandoned by the woman who had born her.

When Grandmother returned to Okinawa after the war she gave birth to a child by an Okinawan she had met while in the South Pacific, thus having a total of three children fathered by three different men. Though they had safely returned to Okinawa, they had neither land nor house. When my mother reached the age of fifteen, she had no choice but to support grandmother and her two younger half-brothers. It was hard enough for a young girl to earn enough in those days to keep four people in food, but matters were made worse by Grandmother, who had taken up with another man to whom she gave money. To this day, Mother has never said what kind of work she did, but now I think I know.

I was born when Mother was eighteen. My father was an American, although no one on earth but Mother now knows the particulars of the relationship. My first memories are of living together with two uncles, one ten and one three years older than I, and with Grandmother. I remember going with my younger uncle several times to get money from

Mother, who worked in a bar catering to American servicemen. These trips were a bright spot in my life because Mother always treated us to something good to eat. I had no idea what Mother's job was, but once recall being puzzled when she gazed at me with tears in her eyes.

Though silent about herself, Mother often talked about Grandmother. She said it would have been bad enough if all she had had to do was leave me with Grandmother and work to provide for the family. Actually, however, she had to support Grandmother's boyfriend too, whom Grandmother had promised to build a house for. A flashy person by nature, Grandmother went through money like water. And when Mother did not bring enough money, Grandmother refused to look after me any more and would order Mother to take me away. Later, however, this willful woman would always come and take me back again.

Once, lonely for Mother, I went with my two uncles to see her. When she saw our pinched faces, Mother asked what kind of food we had been getting. We replied that we had had nothing but plain noodles. "And how about Grandma?" she asked. Instead of answering, we glanced furtively in the direction of a telephone pole, behind which Grandmother was watching everything we did. Things like this made Mother feel so sorry for me that she had no choice but to go on working, making as much money as she could.

Mother sometimes went so far as to say that she no longer thought of Grandmother as her mother. She blamed Grandmother for the life she had had to live. Grandmother's affair with the boyfriend especially disgusted her. The man beat Grandmother from time to time, and Mother tried to persuade her to leave him. On one occasion, when delivering money, Mother found the two of them in bed, the man in nothing but his underwear. Infuriated, she grabbed the man's trousers, threw them into the sewer, and stomped on them. Grandmother's immediate reaction was to throw me out of the house, and Mother and I ended up running through the streets at night to get away.

When I was eight, Mother married an Okinawan without telling him or his family of my existence. For a long time after that, I saw her only when she came to visit us. Fortunately for Mother, her husband paid all her debts, and she was able to set up her own bar catering to foreigners. At last, she had begun to know a little human happiness.

I myself, however, was far from happy. Whenever I visited Mother, she introduced me as her niece, and I had to call her "Aunt." It was from this period in my life that I began harboring feelings of resentment towards Mother and have doubts about her way of life.

In the third or fourth grade of primary school, I started suspecting that my father had been an American. If we happened to go shopping together and someone asked if I were not half American, Mother would grow angry and flatly deny it. Apparently our neighbors also made malicious remarks, but I was not aware of them. As I grew older, my classmates would often ask if I were not an American, and when there was an argument, they would call me an American as an insult. In this way I became increasingly aware that I was different from the others.

In order to hide her own past there is no doubt that Mother treated me somewhat strangely. And by the time I entered middle school, I actually felt a deep hatred for her, though I was then helping her in the bar by cleaning up and washing dishes. Mother took great pains to prevent me from becoming too friendly with the live-in girls at the bar, who, I now realize, slept with foreigners to pay their debts. But when Mother was out, they frequently sent me on errands. I often went to a nearby drugstore with a slip of paper on which was written "condoms." At other times, though I did not understand its significance, I had to keep a record of the number of customers the girls took and the amount of money due: three dollars for a limited amount of time and five dollars to stay all night. Sometimes girls were actually sold to bars catering to foreigners for five hundred or a thousand dollars, and I would have to help them move in. Now, I can hardly bear to think about it.

The older I grew the more I disliked my mother. I was ashamed to introduce her to my friends and disgusted by her habit of smoking constantly regardless of time or place. And gradually I lost interest in school. Almost against my will I found myself feeling unwanted and growing gloomier by the day. Mother and I fought frequently, and I often hurt her by saying that I wished I had never been born.

As soon as I finished middle school I was made a permanent helper in Mother's bar, though a very unwilling one. At the age of seventeen, I was without a future and had no reason for living. Finally I attempted to commit suicide by cutting my wrists with a kitchen knife.

It was about this time that I happened to come into contact with Nichiren Shōshū Buddhism. Although a warped personality like mine could hardly be straightened out overnight, thanks to the attention and care of other fellow believers I came little by little to see that I too had a mission in life. This gave me the hope to go on.

When I was twenty-two, I was introduced to and married my present husband. About a year after our wedding, one of his friends asked him if I were half American. At the time my husband laughed off the suggestion, but when he asked me about it, I told him it was true. The news seemed to stagger him for a moment, but since we were not only husband and wife but also believers in the same religion, he has never brought up the matter again.

Now a married woman myself, I have come to understand Mother's position a little better. She was one of those women who did what they had to do in order to eke out a living in extremely difficult times. After a while, she gave up the bar and even stopped smoking for health reasons. Gradually we have found that we can communicate with each other.

Now realizing how hard her life must have been, I regret my attitude toward her when young. Robbed of her own youth by the war and then put in the position of having to provide for a family after the war, she had no choice but to sacrifice herself for others. We have agreed that the past should be put to rest. For my part, I am determined to do nothing in the future that will hurt her.

But the past will out. I have four children, and my oldest son has fair hair. It is more conspicuous even than my own, which is reddish, and not at all like the black hair of the rest of the family. Mother was more shocked by this than I. Still, we have tried to make a joke of it, saying that it is a good thing the boy lives in our modern world, when young people all over the country are dyeing their hair different colors. When my son asks about the color of my hair and my American father, I can now answer, "Yes, I have American blood in my veins and so do you. That's why your hair's so fair."

Mother had other children by her Okinawan husband, and it was not too long ago that they learned I was their sister. In fact, I once remember quickly changing the subject when my younger half-sister asked, "Sister, why is your hair so red?"

Perhaps because of the way Mother brought me up, I rarely asked about my father and never felt his absence. For the sake of Mother and my half-brother and half-sister, I have tried to forget him. Recently, however, I was proud of my own frankness when in reply to a friend's question, I said that, yes, I would like to meet my father if he were still alive.

If there had been no war, the lives of Grandmother and Mother would no doubt have been very different. Now, however, I want to forget the past, and that is why I was very reluctant to write this paper. But I hope that perhaps Mother's experiences and mine can make a small contribution toward preventing another war. And when my children have grown up, I want them to know that their mother did something for the cause of peace.

WOMEN LEFT
ALONE

A False Report

Aiko Inaba (55)

Many people from many countries were victimized by World War II. I also carry scars from the war. In fact, just recalling the suffering of those times is enough to make my hair stand on end. But if telling my story will help prevent the recurrence of war, I am willing to write it down.

Born in 1927 in Shimo Suwa, Nagano Prefecture, I was the oldest girl in a family of five boys and two girls. In 1943, at the age of sixteen, I married into a family that lived in Iida in the same prefecture. Because of the war most of the men had been drafted or mobilized, and young women were called on to work in munitions factories. After a while, the only people left in our town were children, wives, and old people.

Only four months after the wedding, my husband, who had been working in a spinning mill, was drafted into the army. Pregnant at the time, I returned to my family home, and five months later gave birth to a girl, whom I named Kazuko.

With all my brothers off to war, I was afraid I might be a burden on the household finances and decided to find work. Since I could not take Kazuko with me, I left her in Mother's care while I worked in the fields. On my first payday, Mother said, "You've gone off to work, right? If it weren't for me, you'd have to pay someone to watch the baby. There's also the cost of electricity and food. Besides that, you'll owe me for a pair of clogs each month since I'll wear them out taking the baby out for walks. So I'll just take all that out of your pay."

I couldn't believe it. Did getting married and then returning home mean that I had to be treated like this by my own mother? Maybe it was just my imagination, but from that day on Mother seemed very cold toward me. I made up my mind that as soon as my husband came back I would leave home and never return again, not even to take care of Mother if she happened to get sick.

Life continued in this way for some time, and then one day Mother came to the fields and told me to return to the house at once. Wondering what could have happened, I went into the living room, and there Mother told me that word had just come of my husband's death in battle. Everything went black. My one little thread of hope had snapped.

Who could I rely on now that my husband was dead? A widow at seventeen, how could I go on living? I sobbed uncontrollably.

From a chest of drawers Mother took out three bank books and put them on the table in front of me. "I know you think I've treated you coldly. And you have borne it all bravely, without shedding a tear. Actually, though, it was harder on me than on you. I haven't used any of the money I took from your pay. I put it all in these accounts that are in your name and Kazuko's. Of course, I had no idea the savings would be used on a funeral..." Mother took my hand in hers and wept. Apologizing in my heart for the hatred I had felt toward her, I began to realize how difficult it must have been for her to maintain a hardhearted attitude toward her own daughter. I ended up crying as loud as I could.

As she stroked my back, Mother said, "Cry it all out. You've put up with so much. But now you've got to be strong for Kazuko's sake, and there won't be time for crying."

In the autumn of 1944 we held a funeral, although there were no remains. All I received was a box with a memorial tablet in it.

Then came the defeat and the problems of trying to raise a small child in those hard times. When I had almost entirely recovered from the grief of my husband's death, I had a proposal of marriage.

My husband's older sister had frequently sympathized with me for being widowed before I was twenty. She offered to take Kazuko into her care, and advised me to remarry. It would set my mother's mind at rest, she said, and that was what a dutiful daughter should do. Since I had a child, the idea of remarriage had never crossed my mind. But when it was put in this light, I decided to accept the proposal.

My fiancé was a head carpenter in the city of Shimizu, Shizuoka Prefecture. It was his first marriage, and Mother thought it a bad idea to start a new marriage with a child from a previous one, so she decided to register Kazuko as her adopted child. The arrangement was made with the understanding that once we were settled down, my husband and I would take Kazuko back. This was in the spring of 1946, when I was nineteen.

My new husband's family raised tea plants. He was very busy with his own work, and since there was nothing for me to do in the house, my mother-in-law asked that I go into the fields to help pick the tea leaves. One day, when my husband had been called away to do repair work on Yasukuni Shrine in Tokyo, my own mother, looking extremely pale, came to the fields and told me that my first husband had not died in the war at all. He was still alive. I asked her if she was absolutely sure. After all, we had even held a funeral for him.

"Anyway, come back home with me," she replied. Unable to think clearly, I simply did as I was told. When we reached home, there he was in the flesh, sitting in the living room with Kazuko. No words can describe the complicated emotions I felt at the sight of him. All I could do was express my sympathy for the hardships he must have gone through during the war.

A few days later, he and I took Kazuko with us to visit his parents' graves near his family home. Though Kazuko still had not gotten used to him, he did all he could to please her. With perplexed looks on their faces, my husband's older sister and her husband welcomed us. After our greetings had been concluded, I went into the kitchen to help. My husband and his brother-in-law sat in the living room talking.

Though we had planned to spent the night and make a trip to the family graves, my husband came into the kitchen after a while and told me to get ready to leave.

His mood had changed completely. He did not say much or even smile at Kazuko. When we reached Mother's house, he asked if she would look after Kazuko while we went out for a private talk. Mother offered to leave the house to us, but he declined the offer. We went to a nearby inn, where a maid led us to a small separate guesthouse.

As soon as we sat down, he said, "You're hiding something from me, aren't you?"

My whole body went cold. I had intended to settle matters with my second husband and then explain things to him.

"What makes you say a thing like that? I'm not hiding anything," I replied.

He asked me over and over, but I gave the same answer. Finally he asked if I had not noticed a change in him after he talked with his brother-in-law. "That's when I heard about your marriage. Until then I'd believed you when you said you left Kazuko with your mother and went to

Shizuoka to work. I felt sorry for you. I wanted the three of us to live happily together. How can this have happened? It's like I came back to Japan just to have mud slung in my face. Think of what went through in the war just to come back to this. I should have died over there. I suppose I can understand how you felt when the notification of my death came. But why did you have to go away and leave Kazuko behind? Didn't you think of her? Or were you just out to find happiness for yourself? That's what I can't forgive!"

I asked him to listen to my side of the story, but this was like throwing oil on a fire. "You weren't like this when I married you! What kind of a fool do you think I am?" He became more and more excited and finally said, "I'm going to kill you first and then myself." He pulled out a knife he had been hiding.

I tried to get away from him, but since I knew nothing about the layout of the building, I just kept running from room to room with him chasing after me. Finally I came to a room with a shuttered window. The shutters looked solid, but when I pushed against them with my elbow, they gave away, sending me sprawling into the garden. Unluckily, my head hit a large rock and I was stunned. Before I could recover my senses, he had straddled me and was slashing at my face with the knife. I tried to ward off the blows, and once the knife pierced all the way through the palm of my left hand.

The next thing I knew, I was in a hospital. Since I had fled to the rear garden, I couldn't be seen. But a man who happened to be passing by heard me moaning on the other side of the wall. It was he who called the police. The first doctor I was taken to had refused to help. He took one look at my face and said there was nothing he could do for me. Three other hospitals also refused to take me in. Finally, one of of policemen told a fourth doctor, "The woman's still alive. You can't just leave her like this. Do something for her!"

The doctors had to make thirty-seven stitches in all. Fortunately, one eye just escaped being permanently damaged. But my face and head were so heavily bandaged that for about three months I couldn't hear or see.

During the trial my husband claimed that he had intended to kill himself as well, and the newspapers treated the case as a suicide pact. Since my written evidence and his didn't agree, and since he would not tell where he had hidden the knife, the trial dragged on for eight months. In the end he was sentenced to prison for six years and seven months.

Some time later I received word from the prison that my husband wanted to see me. Mother was completely opposed to the idea, but I went secretly to see him anyway, taking Kazuko with me. My husband said, "Forgive me. I lost my head. I didn't know what I was doing. By the time I had calmed down, here I was in prison. I thought I'd killed you. But when I've done my time, can't we start all over again—the three of us?"

I could not bring myself to see things his way. I told him to pay his debt to society and, if later the right person came along, to remarry. "I'm not coming again," I concluded.

"Well, at least let me hug Kazuko," he pleaded.

I was willing to let him, but Kazuko was not.

The man in Shizuoka who was to have been my second husband magnanimously understood my position and invited me to come back whenever I was ready. Thanking him, I declined the offer. I could not stand the idea that my first husband might get out of jail and come brandishing a knife in the home of people who had been kind to me.

After the visit to prison, my physical condition began to improve. But the psychological wounds were deep. Constantly harassed by the thought that my husband might attack me again, I became so neurotic that I had to reenter the hospital.

Finally, however, when I had at last calmed down, I made up my mind to leave my mother's house and, taking Kazuko with me, go out to find work. But times were hard. Discharged soldiers were everywhere, and it was hard enough for a strong man to find work. A woman with a small child had little chance. Ultimately, through an introduction from a friend, I found a couple—I will call them the Komines—who were willing to act as Kazuko's foster parents. They were clearing new agricultural land in a village called Kiyosato in Yamanashi Prefecture, and had lost a child of their own. Leaving Kazuko with them, I went to work as a cook in a construction camp on the site of the Sakuma Dam in Shizuoka Prefecture.

Kazuko was three at the time. Until then I had always kept her by my side, and my only thought was to have her back as soon as possible. I worked hard, sent money for her upkeep exactly on time, and looked forward to the two or three times a month when I could visit her.

When she was four, I tried to make up for not celebrating a special holiday for children who are three, five, or seven years old: I had a nice set of special clothes made for her and took them with me to Kiyosato. The Komines looked displeased when they saw me. "Are you ready to take Kazuko back?" they asked. "If not, don't come around so often. We've gone to a lot of trouble to get her used to us, and each time you come she gets upset. Ask her, if you want, who her mother and father are."

When I asked Kazuko, she looked fearfully at them, lowered her head and said, "Sakujirō Komine is my father and Saku Komine is my mother."

The words cut into me like a knife. They must have been very strict with Kazuko to get her to say such a thing. How I wished I could take her back with me that very night.

When the Komines had gone out to work in the fields, I put Kazuko on my back and went to the nearby home of the friend who had originally introduced me to them. On the way I kept telling Kazuko to be a good girl and I would someday let her ride on a choo-choo train and would bring her whatever she wanted to eat. As she put her arms around my neck, she touched my breasts and said, "I used to drink this milk." She knew I was her mother. The fact that she knew I was her mother but still could not call me "mother" was so pitiful that my whole body shuddered.

When we reached my friend's house, there were tears in her eyes as she told me that I must take Kazuko back with me as soon as possible. No matter how hard times were, she said, parent and child must stay together. She said that the Komines had punished Kazuko when she refused to acknowledge them as her mother and father by giving her only animal fodder to eat. It broke my heart that I was not able to take Kazuko away that very night. When I left, I was determined to do so on my very next visit. Returning to the camp, I worked harder than ever.

Not long afterward, I received a letter from the Komines saying that since Kazuko was growing bigger, they needed more money to take care of her. Because I wanted life to be as good for her as possible, I immediately sent the extra money.

In the meantime, the construction camp established facilities to care for workers' children. I immediately wrote the Komines saying that I wanted Kazuko back. In their reply, they said that a year earlier, after a bout of measles, Kazuko had gotten acute pneumonia and died. I was too stunned even to cry. Why had they not let me know? And why had they gone on accepting my money? It turns out they used it to buy farming equipment.

In a state of shock, my stomach would not even accept water, much less food. Some kind people around me saw that I was put in a hospital, where I was kept alive by intravenous feeding. For many days I lay in bed like a vegetable, calling out my daughter's name.

I was like a living corpse, no longer with a reason for existing. The Komines were put on trial, and the police came to talk to me from time to time. But since each visit made my physical and mental condition worse, the hospital soon refused to allow any callers at all. Unable to go to Kiyosato to find out for myself what had happened to Kazuko, I remained only partly convinced that she had actually died. Perhaps the Komines had plotted all of this just to keep her for themselves. All the information I had came through third parties, and then the Komines moved from Kiyosato, leaving me with no way of discovering the truth.

In 1979, when I visited my family home in Shimo Suwa for the first time in years, I heard from my younger sister that a woman named Kazuko Inaba from Kiyosato had married a man in Shizuoka. Could this possibly be my daughter? It was too much of a coincidence that two girls of the same name should come from a small village like Kiyosato. I wanted to meet her. If it were my daughter, she would be thirty-six. Even if I could not identify myself as her mother, I wanted to see her. But when I had the matter looked into, she turned out not to be my Kazuko after all.

In my album, I have only one photograph of Kazuko. It was made when she was two. Each time I look at it, I am stricken with my own failings as a mother and with grief over her sad death.

When the Sakuma Dam was finished, I moved to another camp in Nara Prefecture to go on working as a cook. Although I had long since given up any idea of marrying, a man did proposed to me. That was ten years ago. He had five children, who are all grown-up now, and we have grandchildren. My husband is healthy, our life is stable, and at last, after all the troubles I have been through, I am happy. But the scars are still there on my crippled left arm and on my face. If I do not look in the mirror, I can forget the scars on my face, but my arm is a constant reminder. War and one false notification of death robbed me of my husband and my only child. The war wounds on my mind are as irreversible as the keloid scars from the atomic bombings.

The suffering that my generation went through is enough. It must never happen again. This is why those of us who experienced the war must tell our stories to those who have not.

A Telegram
Ikuko Yamane (56)

On December 1, 1944, I was living in a quiet and peaceful mountain village on the island of Shikoku. A little after noontime a telegram arrived from my fiancé, who was supposed to be in Manchuria: "Return 2, leave 3." It was signed "Akira."

The man I was to marry, a newly appointed officer and the object of general envy, was to summon me to Manchuria at any moment, or so I had thought. But now he would be arriving in our village the next day. We hastily made preparations to welcome him and for the wedding.

He arrived on schedule, looking very imposing in his uniform. The wedding was the barest formality, during which we exchanged ceremonial cups of sake. On the very next morning he left again to join an air squadron in Tochigi Prefecture.

I joined him a month later, and we began our life as newlyweds in a boarding house. At the time, although the fighting was growing ever more intense, no one imagined that suicide missions would someday be employed to stem defeat. January and February slipped past like a dream. Then, on March 10, my husband received change-of-duty orders. He was being sent to Ibaragi Prefecture for special training as a member of a special-attack unit (what is sometimes referred to as a kamikaze unit). Once again he set out alone.

A few days later I made up my mind to try to see him at least once more before returning to Shikoku. Just as I was considering how to carry out this decision, I received a thick, special-delivery letter containing both permission to live in off-base housing and detailed instructions on how to get there.

Overjoyed, I set off in the cotton trousers (*mompe*) that women wore during the war, carrying a rucksack on my back. After walking over fifty miles, I found a farmhouse near the base which accepted boarders. It was April 2, 1945, and the cherry buds were swelling and getting ready to burst into bloom.

Our happiness was very short-lived. On April 9 my husband was ordered to take part in a bombing attack on the island of Iwojima. Although I had tried to prepare myself for it, I prayed over and over that the orders were not true. I cannot say how happy I was when an air-raid alert that day postponed and then canceled the mission.

Praying that he would be spared another day, I lived on the borderline between happiness and grief, savoring gratefully every scrap of time allowed us.

We got safely through April 10. But as I lay half awake on the night of the eleventh, I had an evil premonition. I heard heavy footfalls and my husband's voice calling out, "I'm home!" I leapt up, only to find that it had been a dream, and then dozed off again. This was repeated a number of times. But at two in the morning the footsteps and the voice were real: "I'm home. Get up! I've got my orders. We're going to attack Okinawa. Seven in the morning. Wake everybody up, and we'll have a farewell drink."

He was unable to conceal his excitement: it was to be the last drink before his final mission. "There will be twelve of us under Captain Sawato," he said. "We'll fly in ten planes to a base in Kyushu and then transfer to the smaller craft. Then we go up and crash-dive."

He blurted out these pieces of information in rapid succession. Then he set about making preparations. He wanted to thank the people at the boarding house for the kindness they had shown us and to leave some mementos for his family. "There'll be no ashes to send back," he said with a wry smile, but with no sign of a tear. "So give this to my parents; this is for you." He gave me two envelopes containing clippings of his fingernails and hair. Then, with a blank look, he handed me his will and the grommet he always wore at his waist. In response, I tried to live up

A TELEGRAM

to the ideal of a good soldier's wife. A scarf was considered essential to a pilot's uniform in those days, and I improvised one from a silk *furoshiki* wrapping cloth. My husband said that the scarf was unnecessary, but I urged him to take it. Then I gave him the new underclothes I had prepared to be his death garments.

Finally, before dawn on the twelfth, we bade each other farewell: "Take good care of yourself." "Sayonara!"

What more could have been said? He set off on foot down the two-kilometer road leading to the base, and soon his figure vanished in the distance.

Left behind by myself, I could not remain still. Like a sleepwalker I left the boarding house and, inquiring the way as I went, finally reached the spacious airfield. I could not give him up so easily and clung to the faint hope that I might see him just once more.

I stopped an officer I happened to meet and told him I was the wife of Okada, who was to go out on a mission that day. "Okada?" he asked and then disappeared. It all seemed unreal.

Suddenly, in the distance, I saw someone riding toward me on a bicycle, waving and shouting out. It was my husband dressed in his flight clothes, ready to take off on the mission that would be his last. More than the joy of seeing him once again, I felt the grief of having to lose him. I just stood there smiling, unable to speak, my body all atremble.

"You made it!" he shouted. "It's that plane over there. The one with the blue tail. You can see me off from here." Then he turned and rode away, a small could of dust following after the bicycle.

Before takeoff there was an air-raid alert, and the aircraft withdrew into the hangars. Over and over I prayed the alert would never be lifted. The thought crossed my mind of rushing to the hangar, finding my husband, and spending the last moments together. But I decided it would be better to wave to him quietly from a distance. I took shelter in a farmhouse for the duration of the alert.

All too soon it was lifted, and the aircraft rolled back on to the field into takeoff position. From a window of one plane, someone was vigorously waving a branch broken from a cherry tree. The sole family member among a small band of local people, I unashamedly waved my handkerchief, and between sobs shouted "sayonara" at the top of my voice.

With a tremendous roar the first plane lifted from the ground, and then the second. It was no longer possible to see any of the passengers. The third plane took off and then, after having flown no more than two or three hundred meters, burst into flames and crashed into a pine grove. It never occurred to me that my husband might be on that ill-fated craft. After seeing all the planes off I returned to the boarding house.

Hardly hearing the words of comfort spoken by the people there, I lay down in bed almost at once, clasping the grommet my husband had left behind.

That evening a messenger from army headquarters came to see me. After asking me to remain calm, he said that my husband had been on board the plane that had crashed. He then handed me the belongings they had salvaged: a charred and misshapen saber and his personal boots, which he had worn instead of issue ones. What a pitiful sight they were.

Like the blossoms of the cherry tree, and yet without even fulfilling his mission, my husband had fallen all too soon. I was so overwhelmed by the futility and waste of it all that I shed barely a tear. At the time he was twenty-five, and I was twenty.

Eleven days after his death I returned home with a box containing his ashes. In August of that same year, the war was over.

Owing to the haste of his transfer and the general turmoil of wartime, it turned out that our marriage had not been officially registered. After the war, in the ugliness and poverty following defeat, my in-laws told me I was still young enough to remarry, and they sent me back to my family home. The survivors' pension went to his old parents. In a defeated nation both the law and the people become completely heartless, and the times required that all energy be focused merely on staying alive.

The following words, from my husband's diary, have sustained me for the last thirty years, and are as fresh in my mind now as when they were written.

> Suspended by nature from the heavens,
> Fed by perpetual flames,
> The stars,
> Ablaze in the sky,
> Are the true guiding light

For the lonely wayfarer.
To those who implicitly trust
In the spiritual nature of all being,
Life is without end.

My Sister Stayed on Sakhalin

Shigeko Sugawara (47)

Today, with Japan experiencing a period of economic prosperity, many people tend to forget the mass murder that was World War II, but for some of us the scars remain unhealed. For instance, my older sister, Haruko, now lives on Sakhalin, and we are unable to meet when and where we like. Ironically, she was born on Hokkaido and yet lives in what is now a part of the Soviet Union, whereas I, who was born on Karafuto (the Japanese name for Sakhalin, half of which was Japanese territory before the war), now live on Hokkaido. I pity Haruko for the checkered life she has had to lead since the end of the war, and for my own part, I sometimes feel homesick for the place where I was born.

When the rest of the family left Sakhalin in 1948, Haruko remained behind, waving to us, having promised to follow us on the next available ship. After reaching Hokkaido, we expected her to appear any day. We waited and waited, but there was no word from her at all.

For a while Mother grieved about Haruko, but gradually she resigned herself. Still she set an extra place at the table for my sister, prayed daily for her safety, and, addressing her photograph, frequently expressed the hope that Haruko would always have enough to eat. From time to time I tried to reassure Mother, saying that as long as Sister was alive we would certainly see her someday.

Then in 1959, after a silence of eleven years, a letter and a photograph from Haruko were delivered to the town office in Bishin, where we used to live. The handwriting was undeniably hers. She said she was well and gave a little information about why she had not followed us. It seems a friend who the family was obligated to had pleaded with her to stay behind. She had agreed to do so, apparently feeling that even if she did not return to Hokkaido immediately, someday relations between Japan and the Soviet Union would be reopened and people would be able to travel freely back and forth. At last we knew the whereabouts of the sister who had been on our minds constantly for over a decade. In one of her later letters, she asked that we try to make arrangements for her to visit Japan. My older brother and I undertook the task, which led us to the city hall, the police, a foreign-language center, the prefectural office, and other places. We filled out and returned all the forms required by the officials on Sakhalin. But perhaps because of different ways of doing things, they kept asking us for more and more detailed information. The situation was aggravated by a mistaken entry in our papers. During the confusion of the postwar period, someone had registered Haruko's surname as Tazaki instead of Tsūzaki. It is difficult to make alterations in official documents in Japan but infinitely harder when one is dealing with the government of a foreign country. The Russians were very reluctant to recognize the woman whose name was Tazaki as a daughter of the Tsūzaki family.

Our hope of bringing Haruko to Japan while both our parents were still living was frustrated when Father died in 1970, at the age of eighty. At one point we were ready to give up, but at last, on February 15, 1978, after fifteen years of agitating, my two older brothers, a welcoming group from the Hokkaido Prefectural Office, and I went to greet a small, middle-aged woman descending the gangplank of the Soviet ship *Khabarovsk*. One of my brothers called out, "It's Haruko, it's Haruko!" Without a doubt, it was the sister with whom we had parted thirty years earlier. Choked with emotion, I could only wave my hand.

Our meeting was an emotional one. We wept and embraced. Haruko seemed to have grown smaller than she used to be. Feeling the warmth of her body, I knew for certain that our long-cherished wish had at last been fulfilled. At the same time, I recalled what had happened in August 1945 as clearly as if it had been yesterday.

When World War II ended, I was a third grader in primary school, eight years old. We lived in a village called Ushiro twenty-four kilometers south of Esutoru, on the west coast of the island that we called Karafuto, but which is now known as Sakhalin.

On August 10 the Soviet army suddenly attacked. Esutoru was set on fire, and for several nights the sky was dyed red by the conflagration.

All of us were worried about Haruko, who, twenty-five at the time, worked as a midwife in the hospital of the Mitsui Coal Mines in Nishisakutan. The hospital was only forty kilometers from the border separating the Russian half of the island from the Japanese half. Since I was the last of eight children, Haruko was actually old enough to be my mother.

When they heard of Japan's defeat, Haruko and her co-workers in the hospital decided to take poison rather than be killed by Soviet troops. But because of the confusion of the moment, the injections they administered to themselves were too weak to be lethal. Suddenly recalling her parents, Haruko fled homeward, though still groggy from the injection. The Russians were shelling from the sea and from the air, and there were bound to be Soviet soldiers along the way. To stay out of view Haruko chose a mountain path. It took her five days to cover the more than a hundred kilometers separating Nishisakutan from our home.

I remember that she was completely exhausted when she finally reached home, just managing to open the front door before collapsing in the entranceway. Her feet were covered with blisters and blood. Her clothes were spattered with mud. But Mother was immensely relieved to see her alive.

For a while the six members of our family were together: Mother and Father, Haruko, my two older brothers, and me. The village doctor had already left, so there was no one to care for the sick and the dying. This meant that Haruko was invaluable. A person who takes her responsibilities very seriously, she cared for all who needed her, even spending nights in patients' homes when necessary. When there was no medicine, she improvised. For instance, she busily sought out medicinal herbs and gave kidney patients a tonic made by brewing dried watermelon rind. Never idle for a moment, she sewed for our family at night.

The Soviet army now occupied the whole island. We had to live with them for the three years that passed before we left Sakhalin. Haruko even cared for Russian women in labor. And we children learned what it means to be the citizens of a defeated nation. At school, when there was any cleaning or hauling of supplies to be done, it was always we who had to do it. But children forget things like that easily. On the playground the Japanese children swung on the swings and played happily with their Soviet classmates.

At last, in May 1943, the time came for us to leave our home on Sakhalin. I was convinced that all six of us would go together, but Haruko said she would come on the next boat: she still had work to do.

For several days Haruko cooked dried bread for us out of flour and eggs and mended old clothes to provide me with a big enough supply, she said, to last three years. Then one day in May the five of us got on a truck headed for Esutoru. As we drove away, Haruko, her apron fluttering in the May breeze, stood waving in front of the house till we could no longer see her. My child's mind entertained the strange notion that I would never see my older sister again. I cried all the way to Esutoru.

At Esutoru we boarded a Soviet cargo ship that took us to the evacuees internment camp at Maoka, where we were plagued with lice and fleas until, in July, we boarded the Japanese evacuation ship *Shinkōmaru* for Hakodate. Deeply saddened to be leaving my sister and my home behind, I stayed on deck until our island could no longer be seen.

At Hakodate my mother's younger brother came to meet us and took us to Bishin, where we settled down with his help. We were all convinced Haruko would return before long. But in 1950, when her name did not

Repatriates from Sakhalin land at Hakodate.

MY SISTER STAYED ON SAKHALIN

appear on the final list of evacuees, Mother became frantic, then fell ill for a long time at the loss of her daughter. Father concealed his tears in anger. When I mentioned the foreboding I had had in Sakhalin, Mother shrieked and asked why I had never told her of it before. I could not have told her; I was afraid to.

Thirty years later, we could at last see with our own eyes that Haruko was alive and well.

Haruko's first remark was that everything she saw was wonderful. Still, although she could read all the Japanese signs and posters, she felt she was in a foreign country. Perhaps it was because she had become a Soviet citizen. In any case, hearing her say it made me very sad.

The next day we set out for Bishin, where Mother and my other brother waited. Because of my work, I had to stay in Sapporo, where I watched on TV the first meeting between Mother and Haruko in thirty years. Mother wept and trembled for joy. I myself could not see the screen properly for tears. Mother was eighty-five at the time, and the daughter who had been twenty-eight at their last meeting was fifty-eight.

We applied to the Soviet consulate to have Haruko's stay extended from two months to four. We were thrilled when her friends and acquaintances arranged a welcoming party for her. They reminisced about the hard times they had shared. Some of the women wanted Haruko to visit the grown men and women who had been only children when she had known them. Some of those children already had children of their own, and Haruko herself had a son twenty-seven or twenty-eight.

Haruko said little about life in the Soviet Union, except that there were inequalities, that there were the rich and the poor. When we asked why she had not followed us, she said that she had been ready to leave when a very close friend, to whom she was obligated and who could not go to Japan because she had a Soviet husband, had pleaded with her to remain. Haruko had always thought and acted for herself and was the kind of loyal person who could not refuse a request. Probably this is why she stayed on Sakhalin for a friend's sake without discussing the matter with her family. The rest of us, who had worried about her intensely, were saddened that she offered no more detailed an explanation. However, when she learned that I had suffered from tubercular meningitis after leaving Sakhalin, and that I was still afflicted with oculomotor paralysis, she cried and said that it would never have happened if she had been with us.

Soon it was time for Haruko to leave. During her four months with us, though I detected Japanese elements in her, I came to see, to my deep sorrow, that she had become a Russian. At our parting, she thanked us for the good time she had had, and said she hoped that we would invite her to Japan again. We offered our wishes for her good health and promised to meet soon.

But at Sapporo Station, where we said goodbye, I seriously doubted that I would ever see her alive again, in light of the current international situation. As a going-away gift I gave her a decorative paper plaque with drawings of Sapporo lilacs. On the plaque I wrote the following clumsy verse: "Partings remain limitless in the heart."

On her way back she was infinitely more chic than she had been when she got off the *Khabarovsk*. She left behind the bulky black coat, fur hat, and boots she had arrived in and was elegantly outfitted with necklace, earrings, and other finery that were gifts from friends.

Some time after she had departed, I received this letter:

"Although I was with you for four months, I came home without saying what I wanted to say. To tell the truth, when the ship pulled out of the harbor, I would have thrown myself into the sea if I had no children. Now I live for my responsibilities as a parent and have no desire to live a long life. Ironically, things may turn out quite that way. I am in bed as I write this.

"I always think of you and your husband Kunio as still in your twenties. And whenever I hear of an automobile accident on the radio, I think for a moment that it might be him. Please be careful.

"Give my thanks to Kunio and to all of my friends who held the party for me. Both of you take the best possible care of yourselves. I am looking forward eagerly to our next meeting. Haruko, July 1978."

Her letter expressed the thoughts that she can now neither write nor utter. "When you left Karafuto, I wanted to go with you and now regret staying here." But since the Soviet authorities censor letters, it is amazing that she said as much as she did. The recent tragic Soviet shooting down of a Korean Air Lines plane seems to have made the distance between my sister and me even greater.

WOMEN WHO
TRIUMPH

Don't Call Me a Widow

Kiku Arayama (69)

In 1938 I married a policeman. My first child, a daughter, was born the following year, and my first boy in September of 1940. Though we lived with my husband's sickly younger brother, we were happy. But World War II destroyed everything.

When she was about eighteen months old, my daughter, Noriko, fell off the porch, and from that fall she developed an incurable bone disease called caries. For a while I was too busy caring for my baby son to notice it. But one day a neighbor told me that the way Noriko walked was odd and that I should take a close look at her the next time we went to the public bath. By this time the disease had advanced. War had everything in such turmoil that we could neither care for her satisfactorily at home nor take her to a hospital.

On February 1941 my husband's brother died. Before we had time to get over the sorrow of his loss, my husband was drafted. I saw him off as bravely as I could, and then stayed up all night crying. Although it was an honor to be the wife of a serviceman on duty, I could not help wishing he would come home safely.

Air-raid alerts occurred at all hours of the night and day. All the young men had been called up, and there weren't enough men to work in the factories. Women with children and young girls were mobilized to fill the places of the men who had gone to war. We didn't get paid for it, but it was considered unpatriotic not to work. While my mother took care of my sick daughter and baby son, who was still in diapers, I went to work and did the best I could.

We slept with our clothes on because of the constant night air raids. I would have been so happy if the children could have gotten even one full night's sleep. But they rarely did.

After four years away with no word, all of a sudden my husband came home. It turned out his ship was in port for repairs. For a while he commuted between the shipping company and home. I prayed that the war would end without his having to return to regular duty. But that was not to be. And when his ship left harbor, I was pregnant with our third child. His parting words were that he realized how hard it would be for me, but that I should be brave and do my best.

The confusion of wartime continued. There was little to eat and hardly a peaceful moment, but we struggled on, nevertheless, day in and day out. With three children, one of whom was courageously battling a serious illness, I suffered indescribably, but I told myself it was for the sake of our homeland, and did my best.

The only people left where we lived, in Kawasaki, Kanagawa Prefecture, were women, children, and the elderly. Factories everywhere had been bombed and burned to the ground. Then, on August 15, 1945, we were told to assemble to hear the emperor's declaration of surrender. We all cried, wondering why we had gone to war at all and what the future would hold.

Postwar food shortages made life all the more difficult, but more than that, people had lost their reason for living. Seeming to be more dead than alive, they wandered about aimlessly as if in search of something. I can still see their faces, full of insecurity and wrath, sorrow and suffering.

On the postwar black market, it was necessary to barter things like kimonos for rice: money was usually unacceptable. As the wife of a policeman, I could scarcely go to such places, so I relied on Mother to buy what rice she could. My poor children were always hungry. Our issued rations consisted of dry, tasteless sweet potatoes and a very small amount of canned goods and sugar. We had to make the rice last by adding potatoes, *daikon* radish, and other things so that sometimes it was hard to tell where the rice was.

My husband had returned but was so sick that he had to be hospitalized. In February 1946 he was sent home for more treatment and recuperation. But before he was really well enough, he went to work for our sakes. Since he wasn't eating enough and the work was exhausting, his illness grew worse. Finally, his body gave out and he died, leaving me with the four children.

I had no idea what I was going to do. Looking at my children's sleeping faces, I often thought of death. But then I would remember that other people were suffering as much as I was, that I had to be strong to raise our children to the best of my ability. Realizing that crying would not bring food to the table, I vowed never to shed tears in front of the children again. My battle had just begun.

Still I did go on crying, late at night when the children were asleep and I was busily trying to hand-roll cigarettes, a job that some friends found for me. This work proved a failure because my tears spoiled five out of every ten cigarettes.

Next I got a job washing drum cans on an American military base. This was so tiring, however, that at the end of each day I could do nothing but go home and lie down. Mother looked after the children while I was away.

I was still far from secure. Often I would be so exhausted that I thought of poisoning all the children and then committing suicide myself, or throwing them under a train and then following them. I soon came to see, however, that I would have to be strong to survive with four children (two years old, five, nine, and the oldest eleven). Crying would get me nowhere.

At last, I found a regular job, in a cast-metal factory. But the work was exhausting and hot and kept me in a crouching position most of the time. It took me a while to get used to it, and I had personal problems with some of the other workers. Nevertheless, it was for the children's sake: I could not give up.

I made 3,500 yen a month, which was barely enough to keep our whole family alive. As a worker I received a monthly ration of 3.6 liters of rice, which, of course, we had to stretch as far as possible by adding whatever

In the ruins of Japan's cities, people made homes of hastily erected shacks.

other food we could obtain. The place we lived in belonged to the company I worked for.

I never referred to myself as a widow, and while at work steered conversations away from the topic of my husband and where he was. When, as happened on rare occasions, friends from the company called on me, I always asked them not to tell others about my home situation. People tended to treat widows with disapproval or to consider them loose. I wanted no unpleasant rumors to have a bad influence on my children's education. That was why I always tried to be as strong as a man and never to show weakness or tears.

I became a stronger person from having to provide for the children in postwar Japan. Though they were deprived in some ways, I always worked to improve their way of life in any way I could. My oldest daughter, Noriko, who fought with illness all her life, was my mainstay. She looked after her brothers and sisters and was in general so good that, when she finished primary school, the principal awarded her a citation, which I now keep as one of my dearest treasures.

CITATION
Noriko Arayama

You have been handicapped from childhood in spite of the care given you by your parents. You lost your father to illness after he had returned safely from the war to the bosom of your family. His death made it necessary for your mother to assume the duties of both parents by working outside the home as well as caring for her children's needs in the home. Suffering with her, although physically handicapped, you have assisted your mother by cleaning the house and preparing meals when she is late returning home, and by looking after your younger brothers and sisters, while at the same time being a serious, open-hearted, good student in school.

In all these things, you are a model for others. For this reason, we award you this citation.

Hideyoshi Yonemoto, Principal
Kawasaki Municipal Oda Primary School

Noriko was still worrying about the welfare of her brothers and sisters when she died, after a long battle with illness.

Finally the Spring

Yori Ueyama (65)

When my husband left for the battlefield in February 1944, leaving me and our two small children, I was apprehensive about the future but put up the bravest possible front. Later we managed to stay alive by bartering kimonos for rice. But soon the air raids became so frequent that women and children were ordered to evacuate to the safety of the countryside. I took the children and went to my family home in Saitama Prefecture. There we lived with my two elderly parents. From early morning till late at night I helped in the fields with the farm work, something I wasn't used to. My husband was fighting for our country, and I considered it my duty to protect the children in any way I could for his sake.

On September 22 of that very same year—I shall never forget the date—I received word that my husband had been killed in battle. It was only seven months after he had shipped out. He was thirty-four and I was twenty six at the time. I cried constantly after that. But my parents tried to encourage me by saying over and over that his death had been for the country, that other people were suffering just as much as I was, and that I ought to try to be strong so that I could raise the children properly.

I resolved to take their advice and make up for my dead husband's absence. In the daytime I worked in the fields; at night I wove bags for charcoal. To do this, I gathered reeds about two meters tall and soaked them in water to make them pliable. Trembling and weeping in the winter cold as I wove, I could make about one bag an hour; four or five were my limit for a day. Day in, day out, I labored this way for the children. Most of our rice and wheat went to the government, and we had to mix what we had with other things. Still it was better than living in Tokyo and selling clothing to buy food.

In March 1945 I received word that my husband's remains were to be delivered to his family home in Kagoshima Prefecture, in the far southern part of the island of Kyushu. I took the children and set out for Kagoshima. Because of all the air raids along the way, it took a week to get there. But the remains had not arrived. There was nothing to do but help my mother-in-law with the rope-making that she did.

Air raids became more frequent and violent. In the air-raid shelters some people complained that the crying of my children would give us away to the enemy. Finally, my mother-in-law herself ordered me and the children to leave. I will never forget the look on her face as, thinking only of herself, she turned her grandchildren out.

We knew no one in the town at all and had nowhere to go but the mountains. We slept out in the open and ate whatever grasses and berries that looked edible. Rainy days were the worst because we could not move about. I would sit under a tree with the children close to my knees, waiting for the rain to pass. Fortunately, it was summer.

We had brought nothing but the clothes on our backs. Soon we were dirty, exhausted, and emaciated. It gives me chills today just to think about it.

Low-flying enemy aircraft strafed whoever they saw, and there were dead bodies everywhere. Sometimes when we saw the planes flying overhead, we would kneel in full view, bring our hands together in prayer, and wait to be shot. I told the children it would be better to go to join my dead husband than to continue living like this.

One day, after wandering about in a daze, I collapsed and woke later to find myself under the eaves of a farmhouse. After hearing my story, the kind lady of the house told me to stay with her till I was rested. That night, for the first time in a long while, we slept in proper bedding. No words can tell how happy it made me.

After two or three days of her kindness, however, I decided that it would be wrong to stay any longer. I thanked her for the food she gave us and took the children back to the hills. From time to time this good woman brought us a little something to eat. Then, about a month later, she told us that Japan had surrendered.

I was too confused and stunned for a while to say anything. After I had recovered, the old woman said that my husband's younger brother and his family lived not far away. With the kind woman's oldest son carrying my boy on his back, they took us to our relatives' house. I shall never forget this woman's kindness. Although it would now be impossible to locate her, in my heart I am deeply grateful for what she did.

We stayed with my brother-in-law for a while and then, in November, returned to Saitama Prefecture and my parents' home. They were delighted to see us but also surprised. They had thought we were dead and had had wooden Buddhist memorial plaques made in our names. I went back to work in the fields, looking forward to the time when my children would be fully grown.

Just at about the time my son entered primary school, my own younger brother returned from the war safe and sound. We were all overjoyed to see him. The house was suddenly bright and filled with laughter. After a while, however, I began to worry that our presence might hurt my brother's chances of finding a good wife. I rented a small room in the same village, where my children and I lived in poverty but were contented.

I found a job at a textiles mill. The work was unfamiliar but good. When I came home tired from work, my children—one five and one seven—had returned from the mountains with firewood and herbs and had prepared the evening meal. Though I may have shed a few tears, remembering our earlier experiences in the mountains outside Kagoshima, I thought the herb-flavored rice gruel they cooked for me was the most delicious food in Japan.

Then suddenly the textiles mill closed down, leaving me without a job. Day after day I took the children and hunted for a job, but was always coldly turned away. I constantly wished that my husband were alive. If

Work being scarce, women line up with men
for jobs as day laborers.

only he had been there, we would not have had to live in a kind of hell. No matter how hard things got, however, I could not give up. It was for the children's sake. Sometimes I found work weeding fields. But gradually I grew tired and weak from malnutrition and collapsed. As we stood on the verge of family-suicide, members of Soka Gakkai came warmly to our aid. Though poor too, they encouraged me to wait for the spring that inevitably follows winter. They shared things with us and treated us so kindly that, grasping at straws, I too became a member.

I decided then and there to wait for that spring and to do all that I could for my children. When my boy was in the second year of middle school and my girl in the sixth year of primary school, I sent them into service to make certain they always had enough to eat: my son as a farmhand and my daughter as a baby-sitter. I had to steel my heart to do it, but I parted with them because it was for their own good. Many was the time that I leapt from bed and opened the window because I thought I heard one of them calling me in the wind.

After a while I recovered my health and found work in a *tatami* factory. Three years later I was able to bring my daughter home. When I learned that the people she had worked for had broken their promise and had not let her attend school, I was less angry with them than sorry for her.

My son was already at work after having successfully completed a vocational school. At last, the long winter of suffering and bitterness had passed and spring was arriving.

Energy for Peace
Nobu Aoshika (64)

In 1932, four months after our marriage, my husband was drafted into the army. In the following ten years, he was called up four times and spent time here and there, some of it in northern Manchuria. He was with his family only once or twice a year, when he managed to get leave. The longest period he was ever with us was a year and half, when our oldest daughter was two and our second daughter was born.

In the name of the homeland he was taken by the war, forcing us to lead an unnatural married life filled with anxiety. Over the years I gave birth to four daughters, but none of them ever lived with their father long enough to remember his face.

In 1944, when the war had gotten much worse, my two younger brothers were drafted. I was left at home to help my aging father with the work of tenant farming. When time came for us to pay our farm rent in kind, I worked till midnight, and then, with the children pushing from behind, I pulled a wagon loaded with bales of rice to the landlord's house.

The children were very helpful and worked well together. Cutting grass to feed Father's horse was one of their duties. Of course, they were small and wanted to play after school. I tried to encourage them in their work by saying that we only had to do our best till Father was home again.

I had a great deal to keep me busy. The children often hurt themselves, and my mother was ill. Financially, we were in such a pinch that we always had to make do with what we had or make things ourselves. After forcing my tired body through a day of farm work, at night I made over my old clothes into things for my children to wear. Working by the dim electric light of those days, I used whatever could be found to make all their clothes, including footwear. The stiff cloth from *obi* sashes became the bottoms for *tabi* socks; old kimono lining was used to make dresses. Our wooden clogs were also homemade. We sawed a paulownia log into thin round slats, split and trimmed each slat to make the bottoms of the clog, and then twisted bits of old silk into cords to make thongs. What we could not make we could sometimes get by bartering with city people who came to the country in search of food. They gave us clothes and seasonings in return for our vegetables and grain.

On school outings all the other girls wore the skirt and middy blouse that was a kind of student uniform. But we lacked the money to buy such things. One time, however, without the children knowing what I was doing, I borrowed a skirt and blouse from a neighbor to use as a model and remade some of my husband's old navy uniforms. Of course, not having a sewing machine, I did all the work by hand. On the day of the outing, the girls were overjoyed when they woke in the morning to find their new school clothes beside their pillows. As I watched them, I could not help crying when I thought how much happier we all would have been if it had not been for the war.

ENERGY FOR PEACE

The war was over in 1945, and we began waiting for my husband to return. All Japanese soldiers were supposed to have been repatriated by July 1946, but still he did not come back. One day, as my children and I were weeding, they spied a man in uniform coming across a nearby crossing and began shouting that Father had come home. Naturally, they did not even know what their father looked like, and the man turned out to be a neighbor named Mr. Tazaki. I really felt miserable then.

A few days later, the announcement of my husband's death came. We went to a temple in Kuki to pick up a small wooden box containing his remains. There was an inscription on it saying that he had died of illness. We also received 450 yen to spend on the funeral. It turned out that no sooner had we been relieved to learn that the war was over than we lost a husband and father. How was I to go on raising four children alone? The situation seemed so black that I couldn't even cry.

After a while some of my husband's friends came to tell me of his last days. It seems that he had caught amoebic dysentery after the war while working on a food transport ship. He had died on October 23 of that year, surrounded by his friends. Hearing the story, I suppose the thing I felt most strongly was regret. Had I been there, I could have taken good care of him. He had died without ever seeing his children again.

This marked the beginning of my frantic efforts to keep us all alive. Giving the matter a lot of thought, I decided that the only way for me to make a living was as a carrier of black-market rice. Three times a day I made the trip between Kurihashi Station and Shinjuku Station, carrying a bale at a time.

Part of my struggle to survive was riding crowded trains to avoid being spotted by the police. But it was only a matter of time before I was caught. The police confiscated the rice I was carrying and detained me for almost a whole day at the Yodogawa Police Station. This was not to be my last encounter with the law.

At the time I got 2,800 yen for each bale I carried. When I got caught, the police imposed a fine of 4,000 yen a bale. The worst day I ever had was when I made three trips and got caught all three times. In reply to the policeman's reprimand, I said that I was a widow with children to raise and could not give up this work. He only sneered and said that I ought to pin a label on my chest saying "widow."

The war had created a situation that forced me to go on carrying rice for eleven years. Then an acquaintance introduced me to Nichiren Shō-shū Buddhism. In the hope of finding a better way of life, I joined the Soka Gakkai. As if by a miracle, I began to receive protection from many directions. Things started improving. Finally I found work as an insurance saleswoman.

Having triumphed over the years of suffering, today I have my own house and some land. Though they do not remember their father's face, my children too have made homes for themselves. The hardships and grief I knew may have been only what was to be expected during the war and its aftermath. But I do not want my children or grandchildren to experience anything like it. That is why I am now resolved to devote the energy that helped me be a black-market rice carrier for eleven years to the campaign for world peace.

He Stays Young
Mitsuko Hiraki (62)

On September 30, 1943, my husband was drafted into the army, five months after our marriage. Three months pregnant at the time, I was suffering from dreadful morning sickness. Although I was in terrible condition, my parents and other people around me did their best to encourage me.

Two months later my husband was transferred to the navy, and I was granted my first opportunity to visit him at Tateyama in Chiba Prefecture. It was an emotional reunion. The training was so hard, he said, that it gave him backaches. And the military system was so harsh that if one person did something wrong, everybody suffered for it. This made me hate the war. In his company he had been completely devoted to his work, had risen to a managerial position, and was looking forward to the future. But a single sheet of paper had not only dragged him into the military, but was subjecting him to intolerable training.

On January 16, 1944, he shipped out for the South Pacific. A little shy because of my big belly, I went to see him off, my legs unsteady from the exertion. I cried as I handed him the thousand-stitch talisman that wives made for their soldier husbands in those days. He was emaciated and looked entirely different from the way he had when he was inducted. I prayed that he would come home safely.

On March 27, seventy days after his departure, I gave birth to a girl, whom I named "Kazue" (I took the Kazu part from my husband's name). It never dawned on anyone at the time that she would never see her father's face.

In 1945 the air raids became more and more numerous and devastating. I began thinking of evacuating to the countryside. But then I was caught in the hellish confusion of the air raid of March 15 and had to run for my life, a newborn baby in my arms. Somehow we managed to escape and to reach my family home.

To be frank, I was profoundly relieved to hear the emperor's radio broadcast on August 15, 1945, announcing that the war was over.

Railway stations everywhere were filled with servicemen on their way home. I was happy that I had survived and pinned all my hopes on seeing my husband soon. I even saved part of our meager rations for him. Looking back on it now, I see how pathetic this was.

A month went by with no word. My trips to the city hall and prefectural offices produced no information on his whereabouts. Then it was 1946. My child and I spent a sad New Year holiday beside the tray of food I had prepared for my absent husband. He and I had never celebrated New Year's together.

In April the thing happened that I had been dreading most: notification arrived of his death in battle. It was as if I had been struck a terrible blow, and I took to my bed. For six months I lacked the will and strength to go outside, and only wandered about the house, a ghost of what I had been. My younger brother watched over me, never leaving my side. Father was afraid I would commit suicide.

When Kazue was four, a friend told me that it was time I stopped relying on my father for everything. Accepting this advice, I took my child and went to work in a dressmaking shop. I threw myself into the job in the hope of forgetting I was a widow. Gradually I became accustomed to the work. But each time I reached a point where there was a little laughter in my life, I would fall sick again.

When Kazue entered primary school, I decided to leave the shop and do dressmaking at home. For some reason, perhaps because I was not as active as before, I tended to get sick more frequently. Watching my little girl do her best to care for me, I would say how much I wished her father were still with us. And she would ask me, "What kind of a person was Father?" The fact that she had never seen him was hard to become reconciled to.

Occasionally my father and my husband's older brother would take turns being Kazue's father for a day. My younger brother was also very good to her. Because everything was burned in the air raids, I did not have so much as a photograph to show her. I suspect that, in her mind's eye, her father's face is a montage of these three other men's faces. In spite of the loneliness of lacking a father, however, she was a good, reasonable little girl, much praised by her teachers. Perhaps not having a father had a strengthening influence on her personality.

After several years of poor health, I took a cousin's advice and became a member of Soka Gakkai, in the hope of getting better and finding happiness with my child. This was on November 16, 1952. All of a sudden, people—even total strangers—began encouraging me and my daughter. It was a source of great strength to have people to laugh and cry with, besides my own father and brother. I was extremely glad I had accepted the faith.

In 1954 I was strong enough to be interviewed for the position of superintendent of a kindergarten. I was accepted and asked to start work that very day. I hauled my poor possessions to the school in a wagon and started a new life.

Conditions at the new job were excellent. Not only was I to receive a steady salary, but also the kindergarten provided for all our daily needs. It took some time to get accustomed to the work, and I often had blistered hands. But the head teacher and all the other teachers were such splendid people that Kazue and I often gave thanks that our suffering was over. Everyone was especially good to Kazue. She took piano lessons and even went to college. After graduation, she became a teacher at the kindergarten attached to the Tōyō Conservatory of Music.

Now that Kazue was on her own, I decided to follow some friendly advice and give up the work I had been doing for ten years. My retirement pay was so unexpectedly generous that, with the added help of a survivor's pension, Kazue and I were able to live comfortably. Today, the war that robbed me of my beloved husband and took my daughter's father, and the other sorrows and tears of our life, seem like a bad dream.

In 1973 Kazue married and moved to Saitama Prefecture. I followed the newlywed couple there but live in a place of my own. I long to be able to show my three grandchildren to their grandfather. I long to hear him praise me for raising our daughter and sending her to college. I am old now, but in my memory his face is always young. And when I am alone and think of him, I can smile.

Waiting for their husbands to return from the war, women found great comfort in their children.

x

定価3,400円
in Japan